ALCHEMIES OF VIOLENCE

ALCHEMIES OF VIOLENCE

Myths of Identity and the Life of Trade in Western India

Lawrence A. Babb

SAGE Publications
New Delhi/Thousand Oaks/London

First published in 2004 by

Sage Publications India Pvt Ltd
B-42, Panchsheel Enclave
New Delhi 110 017

Sage Publications Inc
2455 Teller Road
Thousand Oaks
California 91320

Sage Publications Ltd
1 Oliver's Yard
55 City Road
London EC1Y 1SP

Published by Tejeshwar Singh for Sage Publications India Pvt Ltd, Phototypeset in 10/12 SouthAsia Roman at C&M Digitals (P) Ltd., Chennai and printed at Chaman Enterprises, New Delhi.

Library of Congress Cataloging-in-Publication Data

Babb, Lawrence A.

Alchemies of violence: myths of identity and the life of trade in western India / Lawrence A. Babb.

p. cm.

Includes bibliographical references and index.

1. Marwaris—India—Rajasthan—Ethnic identity. 2. Marwaris—India—Rajasthan—Folklore. 3. Merchants—India—Rajasthan—Social life and customs. 4. Violence—India—Rajasthan—Folklore. I. Title.

DS432.M28B33 381′.092′2544—dc22 2004 2004008548

ISBN: 0-7619-3223-2 (US-Hb) 81-7829-352-8 (India-Hb)

Sage Production Team: Geetanjali Minhas, Radha Dev Raj and Santosh Rawat

Contents

List of Figures

A Note on Transliteration

I have given most Indic terms in italics with standard diacritical marks. I have not italicised proper names and titles. I have provided diacritical marks for the names of authors of Hindi materials and names appearing in Hindi writings or discourse. I have not used diacritics on place names appearing in standard English-language maps and have used standard English spellings for these. I have, however, given the names of more obscure locations with diacritics. With some exceptions, the criterion on which I have based this judgement is whether or not a given term appears in *The Rajasthan Road Atlas* (Arya and Arya 1997). In keeping with the vernacular character of this study's subject, I have privileged the Hindi as opposed to Sanskrit versions of most terms where there is a choice to be made (thus, Tirthaṅkar as opposed to Tirthaṅkara and *dān* as opposed to *dāna*), but have kept the Sanskrit ending in the case of terms most familiar in that form (such as Śaiva or *karma*).

Acknowledgements

The research on which this book is based took place, sometimes episodically, over a period of several years. The bulk of the research was done in Jaipur from August 1996 to May 1997 and was supported by an American Institute of Indian Studies Senior Research Fellowship. Additional material (appearing in portions of Chapters Two, Three and Five) was gathered during the spring of 1998 while engaged in a collaborative research project on the temple complexes at Goṭh-Mānglod (Dadhimatī) and Osian conducted with John E. Cort and Michael W. Meister and supported by the J. Paul Getty Trust. I would like to thank my Getty colleagues whose fellowship and intellectual stimulation have added to this book in many ways and at many levels. Amherst College Faculty Fellowships supported brief visits to Rajasthan in 2000 and 2002. I would like to thank Dr R. C. Swarankar and the Department of Anthropology, University of Rajasthan, for institutional hospitality in 1996–97 and the Institute for Rajasthan Studies and its then Director, the late Professor Rajendra Joshi, for providing an institutional base for the Getty project.

The individuals who assisted me in the course of this lengthy investigation are far too many for all to be singled out by name, but some deserve special mention. For assistance and kindnesses of various kinds I am grateful to Ashok Bhandari, M. C. Khandelval, Gyan Chandra Khinduka, Jyoti Kothari, Fateh and Indu Singh, Rajendra Shrimal and Ranbir Sinh. Radhe Shyam Dhoot and I explored Khandela and Lohargal together—a happy memory for both of us—and he assisted my investigations in many other important ways. Mukund Lath and Rajendra Joshi were sources of valuable advice and intellectual stimulation throughout the period of research. Vivek Bhandari took the time to give me a valuable critical reading of a portion of the manuscript. John Cort, companion in the field and critical reader of this manuscript, is the very model of what a colleague should be: interested, always willing to lend a hand, and the sharpest of critics. Surendra Bothara is a friend and colleague whose helping hand, warm support, and invaluable advice have long been indispensable to my work in Jaipur, and the Bothara family has been my family away from home. To all of the above I am deeply grateful. To these expressions of gratitude, however, I must append the declaration that all errors of fact and interpretation in this book are my responsibility alone.

I would also like to thank the editors of *Contributions to Indian Sociology* and *International Journal of Hindu Studies* for permission to include reworked materials from two previous articles of mine (Babb 1998 and 1999 respectively).

My wife, Nancy, supports my endeavours in too many ways to describe. For her patience and so much else, my thanks indeed.

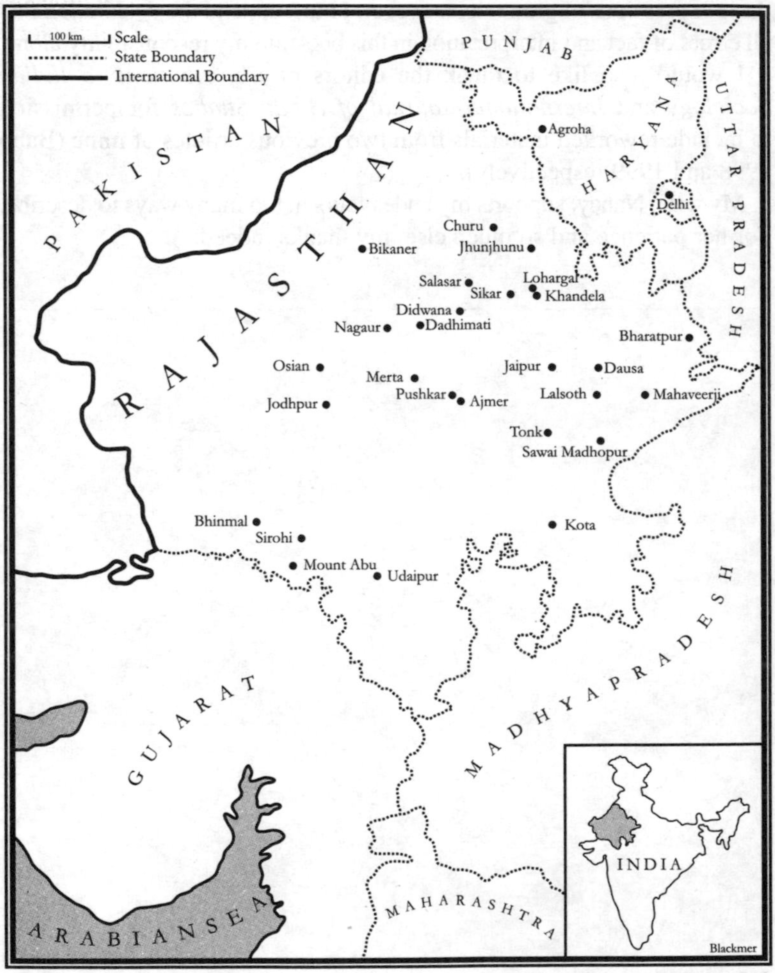

Figure 1
Rajasthan with selected locations.

Chapter One

Introduction

An extraordinary confluence of myth, social identity, violence, and non-violence is our subject. The venue is India, and our focus is a cluster of western Indian communities whose social function and raison d'être are trade and business. At the book's core are origin myths, a type of myth long known to students of culture to be a canvas on which social groups depict their identity. The violence in the equation is the violence of the martial life of warriers and of sacrificial rituals that ratify such a life. Our story is about how the origin myths of non-violent traders employ the theme of martial violence and its rejection as a way of contructing collective identities—identities that are, in their wider regional and civilisational context, culturally intelligible and morally satisfying. Awaiting us is a surprise. As it turns out, violence and non-violence can be two sides of the same coin.

Our traders, known collectively and somewhat loosely as 'Marwaris', are among India's (and the world's) most successful merchants, and although they are not well known to ethnographic literature, they are among the wealthiest, most powerful, and nationally conspicuous groups in modern India. While they are indigenous to the Indian state of Rajasthan, many have migrated and spread the net of their enterprises widely in other parts of India and the world beyond as well. Our focus, however, is primarily on these traders in their homeland—Rajasthan. As will be seen, their mode of life and patterns of interaction with other groups give rise to complex problems of social identity. They also possess a rich body of origin myths—myths telling of how these traders came into existence and acquired their social roles—that can be seen as responses to these problems. Most of this book is devoted to retelling and analysing these myths.

Our encounter with these narratives will require us to deal with three separate but related matters simultaneously. One is the issue of the nature of India's caste system. The myths examined here are about specific *castes*—a term we shall define more carefully shortly—and who and what they are. Analysing what the myths have to say about traders will tell us a lot about the nature of caste in general, as well as the specific place of trading castes among other castes in Indian society. Our second concern is the special character of the trader's position in society, which, though powerful, is fraught with ambiguities and vulnerabilities. We shall examine the life of trade and its social implications in the next chapter. Later chapters will show how myth projects social identities expressive of the problematic features of such a pattern of life. Our third main concern is the role of myth itself as a repository of socially important knowledge. The moral of this part of our story is continuity, for we shall see evidence of the extraordinary degree to which myth can retain and transmit older meanings in a context of profound social change.

The book will show that non-violence is central to mythic constructions of trader identity in Rajasthan. In the South Asian context, non-violence is usually associated with the soteriological strategies of certain religious traditions. But whatever its soteriological significance, non-violence can also be seen as socially and politically adaptive for traders who must live in close social proximity to groups that are (or once were) very violent indeed. Predictably, non-violence is central to the social personae of these groups, and violence and the control of it emerge as the symbolic keys to their social identity as portrayed in myth. We shall see how origin myths engage the issue of violence and its negation by drawing upon images and symbols of great antiquity in the Indic world, especially those having to do with the rite of sacrifice and sacrificial violence.

Rajasthan

Located in a mostly dry zone to the south and west of Delhi, the state of Rajasthan presents a rugged and sere landscape littered with the ruins of fortifications. It is a state with numerous problems—drought-prone, and currently facing severe problems of population pressure, deforestation, and desertification. The state was fashioned out of a cluster of pre-existing indigenous kingdoms (plus the small British province of Ajmer/Merwar) that were absorbed by the Indian republic in the aftermath of independence.

Its name means 'Place of Kings,' which befits its history as a zone of kingly rule. Its capital is Jaipur, a city of approximately two million that was founded in 1727 and built by Maharaja Sawai Jai Singh II (1688–1743). We shall visit various locations in Rajasthan in later chapters, but Jaipur was the site of the greatest part of the research on which this book is based and will thus occupy center stage.

Leaving aside its current status as a constituent state of the Indian republic, the issue of whether Rajasthan is an actual entity of any other kind is highly debatable.[1] Even its physical unity is problematic. Despite the common image of Rajasthan as a desert state, and despite its generally arid or semi-arid character, it is in reality climatically variegated internally and environmentally unbounded. Running from the northeast to the southwest, the Aravalli range bisects the state into two major zones. The northwestern zone is truly arid desert, and belongs to the watershed drained by the Arabian Sea. The southeast is only semi-arid and is significantly more fertile than the northwest. This zone is actually part of the Indian subcontinent's central highlands, and belongs to the watershed of the Bay of Bengal. More importantly, it is clear that Rajasthan is neither culturally nor linguistically unified. Despite the importance of the culture of the Rājpūts to the state's internal and external image—a matter to be discussed in detail later on—the state is in fact a cultural patchwork. And the notion that 'Rajasthani' is a discrete language (as suggested by linguist George A. Grierson early in the twentieth century), an idea that has played a major supporting role in conceptions of Rajasthan as a unitary ethnographic zone, seems to lack linguistic validity (Lodrick 1994: 17–18).

In one respect, however, Rajasthan is indeed a unity—it has constituted what Deryck Lodrick calls a 'political space' since the sixteenth century (ibid.: 6–12). As will be seen, this has had far-reaching implications for its regional cultural character. The political space in question was a product of episodic struggles and accommodations between the region's indigenous kingdoms and the expansionist Muslim powers of North India. There once existed a vast belt of kingdoms, ruled by warrior-kings who called themselves 'Rājpūts', extending from the Arabian Sea to the central Gangetic plain. Muslim victories at the end of the twelfth century erased the western and eastern sections of this belt, leaving the kingdoms of what is now Rajasthan more or less encircled and isolated. Thus arose a political space. Then ensued four centuries of intermittent and inconclusive conflict among these kingdoms themselves and between them and Muslim rulers in Delhi.

The situation froze into place when, using a mixture of diplomacy and warfare, the Mughal ruler Akbar finally succeeded in cementing these Rājpūt kingdoms into his empire in the sixteenth century. The historical continuity of this cluster of kingdoms was such that Akbar brought them into the empire as a separate administrative province, and during the entire Mughal period they were able to maintain some degree of political autonomy, albeit in subordination to the empire. The kingdoms came under British hegemony in the aftermath of the Maratha wars of the early nineteenth century. Instead of imposing direct rule (except in Ajmer/Merwar), the British grouped the kingdoms under the umbrella of the Rajputana Agency, which later became the Rajputana Province. This entity ultimately became the State of Rajasthan in the post-independence period. As Lodrick points out, the most significant features of this history are the durability of the Rājpūt kingdoms and the continuity of the idea that they possessed a special quality of historical unity as a cluster. The present-day state of Rajasthan is a legacy of this idea.

The continuity of the Rājpūt kingdoms, both a cause and consequence of their sequestration within a discrete political space, gave rise to extremely important cultural effects (and contrasts strikingly with the situation in neighbouring Gujarat). The incubation of distinctively Rājpūt traditions, which Lodrick traces to the seventh and eighth centuries, took place in states like these, and the kingdoms of Rajasthan then became venues for the subsequent cultivation and social transmission of these same traditions. In other words, the existence of Rajasthan as a *political space* made possible the continuous preservation and elaboration of a distinctive Rājpūt *culture* within its boundaries. It needs to be stressed that Rājpūt culture is not the same thing as the culture of Rajasthan. The state is culturally variegated, and Rājpūt traditions are only one element in a regional mix of cultures associated with castes and other groupings. Nevertheless, the Rājpūts' traditions have left an impression on regional life crucial to the state and region's contemporary identity. While a true Rajasthani 'regionalism' has yet to emerge (ibid.: 33–34), the people of the state have certainly come to identify with the region and to take pride in its traditions. And there is no question that the Rājpūt heritage is more deeply linked with the contemporary concept of Rajasthan, both within and outside the region, than any other feature of the region's cultural map.

One more point should be made about Rajasthan as a political space. The continuity of the kingdoms during the British period has meant that, even as other parts of India came under the direct influence of the administrative structures of colonial rule, the characteristic political, social and economic institutions of the Rājpūt kingdoms survived more or less intact up to the post-independence period. These continuities are extremely important from the standpoint of the subject of this book. As will be seen, the Rājpūt kingdoms provided the political and social niches in which traders fashioned their way of life here. Moreover, the strong presence of a Rājpūt ethos and the great prestige possessed by Rājpūt values in the region have had a critical role to play in the self-conception and social identity of Rajasthan's trading communities.

Rajasthani Traders

Rajasthan is famed for two great communities. One, mentioned above, is the region's erstwhile ruling aristocracy, a cluster of clans and lineages bearing the label 'Rājpūt'. This term means 'Son(s) of Kings'—a designation that fits well with their social persona and self-image as a ruling and warrior class. They are in fact one of India's most illustrious martial communities, renowned and greatly admired throughout the country for their fighting spirit and military prowess. Even though large numbers of Rājpūts live outside of Rajasthan, the special historical and cultural connection between Rājpūts and the region is strong and abiding. To outsiders as well as the state's residents, no single group is more deeply identified with Rajasthan than the Rājpūts, and images of Rājpūt valour and chivalry have become one of the main ingredients of the region's touristic appeal. But the matter goes deeper than that. Although, as we have said, Rājpūt culture is not to be conflated with Rajasthani culture, the Rājpūts are, or were, regional cultural pacesetters in the sense that their values have historically been widely admired and imitated by other groups. This is a point to which we shall repeatedly return in this book.

The other group for which Rajasthan is famous is the region's traders. Rajasthani traders project an image that is, at least in some areas of India, even more powerful and vivid than that of the Rājpūts, but it is also a much less positive image. The rest of India knows Rajasthani traders primarily as a migrant merchant and moneylending class. They are well known and possibly even grudgingly admired for their business acumen. However, because of the widespread perception that they engage in shady dealing and ruthless economic exploitation, the peoples of other regions frequently regard them with a mixture of resentment and contempt. To report this unpleasant perception is not, of course, to endorse it, but merely to register a significant reality.

The pattern of migration of Rajasthani traders seeking economic opportunities elsewhere in India and beyond is an old one. Semi-permanent enclaves of these traders had arisen in Bengal and elsewhere in Mughal times, but the main migrations occurred from the 1860s onward (Timberg 1978: 41–66). In the areas where they settled, they came to be known by the generic appellation *mārvāṛī* ('Marwari'), apparently on the mistaken premise that they all originated in *Marwar*—a term that technically refers to the old Jodhpur State.[2] The famous abandoned mansions of Shekhawati (a subregion comprising Rajasthan's Churu, Jhunjhunu and Sikar Districts) are dramatic residues of the great trader migrations from Rajasthan to the Ganges valley. These imposing structures, much celebrated for their colourful murals, were built by successful migrant merchant families and then, in many cases, allowed to fall to ruin by their absentee owners. Their decay demonstrates the fact that some migratory trading families allowed their ties to their region of origin to lapse more or less completely.

But the importance of Rajasthan's migratory traders elsewhere in India should not be allowed to eclipse the significance of the role that trading communities have played, and continue to play, in the region itself. Large numbers of Rajasthani traders never left Rajasthan, and continued to occupy traditional roles in the region's villages and cities. Moreover some migratory traders have actually returned from other areas of India and resettled in Rajasthan. Others have kept their feet in both worlds, and it is not uncommon for extended families to consist of interacting branches located in Rajasthan and such distant places as Kolkata and Assam. While it is not possible to discuss Rajasthan's traders without a reference to the migrant community, this book's main focus is the region's trading class in the historical, social, and cultural contexts of Rajasthan itself.

Trading Castes

Among the most important of the many kinds of social groupings to which the people—and thus the traders—of Rajasthan belong are those entities known in English as 'castes'. Caste affiliation regulates marriage and other forms of social interaction in a great variety of contexts, and is a basic feature of the region's social organisation. Indeed, it can be fairly said that, from the standpoint of the traders themselves, caste identity is considerably more salient that their social identity as traders. To outsiders, they are traders as a generic class; but traders themselves tend to think of themselves, and to identify themselves when asked to do so, as members of specific castes. Writings on these traders tend to treat them generically as 'Baniyas' (a term to be discussed in the next chapter) or 'Marwaris' (see, e.g., Hardiman 1996, Timberg 1978), which is perfectly legitimate in some contexts. A major goal of this study, however, is 'de-essentialising' the traders into the groups and subgroups that form their social world.

In this book, I use the term 'caste' to translate the Hindi word *jāti*. This word possesses a wide range of meanings, but for our purposes it can be considered to refer to named, endogamous (that is, in-marrying) groups that are usually associated with a particular traditional means of livelihood. The 'trading castes' are therefore those *jātis* whose members traditionally engage in buying, selling, moneylending, and related activities. Each of these castes, in turn, is subdivided into exogamous (that is, out-marrying) clans, commonly (though not always) called *gotras*.[3] The membership of clans and their lineage segments is based on patrilineal descent. That is, the membership of such a group consists of the descendants of a common male ancestor, with descent traced through males. Among traders, the clans are often, though not always, the basis for family surnames. Normally, caste identity completely eclipses clan affiliation, which tends to come into play only in the context of marriage arrangements.

There are several important trading castes in Rajasthan. Because this book's social and spatial vantage point is Jaipur, it concentrates on trading castes prominent in this city and its hinterland. These are (in alphabetical order) the Agravāls, Khaṇḍelvāl Jains, Khaṇḍelvāl Vaiśyas, Māheśvarīs, Osvāls, Śrīmāls, and Vijayvargīyas. Most of these names are extremely well known, not just in Rajasthan but also throughout India, as the names of important trading castes. We shall meet these groups in more differentiated detail in later chapters, so we need not linger over the fine points now. At this stage, it is enough to note that they are socially quite distinct, each possessing a strong and highly individuated identity vis-à-vis the others. However, they also constitute a socially recognised cluster. Their identity as a cluster is partly based on their common image as a business class. It is also based on the perception, shared by traders and non-traders alike, that these castes are culturally quite similar.[4] This belief is well-founded. Trading castes share many cultural traits, and pre-eminent among them is a cultural emphasis on non-violence as expressed in dietary rules and in other ways. As will be seen anon, this point lies at the heart of this book's argument.

Throughout this book, the terms 'trader' and 'trading' will be used in reference to these castes, but readers should know that this usage is misleading in some respects. In the first place, members of these castes are not the only people who engage in commercial activities in Rajasthan; individuals belonging to most if not all the region's castes can be found in businesses of one kind or another. Furthermore, the term 'trader' does not completely convey the actual range of the commercial and mercantile activities of members of these castes. These activities fall on a spectrum from petty shopkeeping and small-time moneylending to big-time banking and major industrial enterprise. Finally, it should also be stressed that not all members of these castes engage (or previously engaged) in trade. Essential to the analysis presented in this book is the fact that many members of these castes were prominent as managers and officials in the region's indigenous chiefdoms and states—a tradition of bureaucratic service that continues to the present day. We shall address the question of how the trading castes once fitted into the region's economic and political structures in much greater detail in the next chapter.

Within Rajasthan's trading class there is a major religious divide between Hindus and Jains, a distinction partly, though not exclusively, associated with caste. The difference between Jainism and Hinduism is itself an analytically hazy matter, and will be addressed in greater detail later in the book. For the present, it is sufficient to say that the difference reflects a significant cultural and social reality among Rajasthani traders. Four of the castes considered in this book are mostly or entirely Hindu: the Agravāls, Khaṇḍelvāl Vaiśyas, Māheśvarīs, and Vijayvargīyas. In subsequent chapters, these castes will be collectively referred to as the 'Hindu cluster'. Three castes are mostly or entirely Jain: the Osvāls, Khaṇḍelvāl Jains, and Śrīmāls. These will be referred to as the 'Jain cluster'. Among the Agravāls, there is a small but important minority of Jains, and among the Osvāls a significant number of Hindus. Both the Jain and Hindu categories are further crosscut by sectarian distinctions at various levels.

Violence and Myth

The issue of the common social and cultural personae of Rajasthani trading castes brings us to the question of violence. In Rajasthan and elsewhere in India, traders (whether Hindu or Jain) tend to be associated with vegetarianism and non-violent traditions. This being so, in order to explore the culture of trader identity we must first reach some understanding of the place of violence and non-violence in Indic cultures. This is a complex subject that merits a preliminary discussion on its own account.

Let us begin by saying that the relationship between violence and Indian life has been persistently misunderstood by foreigners and, to some degree, by Indians themselves. This is a consequence of the existence of a powerful myth-image of India as a non-violent country, an image nourished by filtered recollections of Mahatma Gandhi, and (for foreigners at least) given additional plausibility by the stereotype of allegedly useless cattle wandering the streets of India's cities. The export of a somewhat limited range of Indian religions to the west—especially Buddhism, but also an assortment of vegetarianised versions of Hinduism—has also contributed to the worldwide propagation of the image of a non-violent India. But although it possesses an important grain of truth, this perception of India is extremely misleading. I know of no empirical evidence showing that Indian national society is any less violent than any other. Indian history presents the usual disheartening picture of strife and carnage, and any fair assessment of the violence quotient of the contemporary Indian scene would have to include reference to such matters as the seemingly endless conflict in Kashmir and intercaste warfare in Bihar and elsewhere.

Given the role of religion in perceptions of India's alleged non-violence, it is particularly important to point out that the widespread notion that Indian religions promote non-violence is at best a partial truth. The religiously sanctioned duty of the *Kṣatriya varṇa*—the ancient social class of rulers and warriors—has always included violence, which is seen as quite legitimate when utilised for the protection of the social order. Because of its links with Rājpūt norms of conduct and social identity, this Kṣatriya ethic will also figure prominently in later chapters. Moreover, animal sacrifice plays a conspicuous role in many Indic ritual cultures. As we shall see later, it is central to Rājpūt traditions, a fact highly relevant to the argument of this book. Warrior figures of both sexes abound in the Hindu pantheon. The goddess Durgā, one of the most important female deities, is a warrioress. And the deity Rāma, a figure central to the Hindu devotional traditions of (especially) northern India, is a warrior-deity, notwithstanding the fact that the cultic milieu over which he presides tends to be largely vegetarian.

But at the same time, it is also true that non-violence does indeed have a special place on the Indian religious landscape, even if it is not the whole story. Famously, non-violence (*ahiṃsā*, meaning 'non-harm') has been emphasised and promoted by some of the subcontinent's most influential religious traditions. Jainism and Buddhism (the latter no longer a factor in India) are probably the best-known examples. Of the two, Jainism is especially renowned for the extent to which it promotes non-violence and fosters non-violent lifestyles. In addition, some of the most important of the strands in that bundle of religious traditions known as 'Hinduism' emphasise non-violent values. This is particularly true of certain Vaiṣṇava traditions of great cultural importance in Rajasthan and Gujarat.[5]

Furthermore, non-violent religious traditions have acquired a privileged position in the social and political structures of contemporary India. This is so because these traditions, both Hindu and Jain, are socially borne and transmitted (though by no means exclusively) by some of modern India's wealthiest and most influential communities, and this includes the trading castes with which this book is concerned. These same groups, in turn, form an important part of the social base of Hindu nationalism, which has acquired unprecedented political influence in recent years. Although Hindu nationalists have sometimes sought to realise their goals violently, the type of Hinduism that Hindu nationalism seeks to place at the center of India's nationhood is a version that has a strong affinity with such anti-violence issues as cow protection and the banning of animal sacrifice.

In sum, India is neither violent nor non-violent; it is both. Whether we find violence or not depends on where we look. What is probably most distinctive about Indian society in this regard is not non-violence as such, as is so often supposed, but the way in which it is distributed among social groups. For violence and non-violence turn out to be strong markers of social identity.

In Rajasthan, social identity connects with violence and non-violence at two levels. First, some groups are actually more or less violent—as these matters are judged by prevailing cultural standards—than others. Second, and equally important, some groups *see themselves* and are *socially recognised by others* as characteristically violent or non-violent. When this is so (and to some degree this matter is separable from the issue of actual violent behaviour), violence or non-violence has become part of the group's social identity. These traits are not equally salient in the social identities of all groups in Rajasthan, but are deeply implicated in the social identities of two communities, the Rājpūts and the traders. As we know, the Rājpūts are renowned for their courage and fighting prowess, and are seen generically as a martial community. The traders are equally well known for their vegetarian and pacific ways, and are definitely seen as non-martial.

These points will be addressed in greater detail in later chapters. For the present it will suffice to say that this book argues that the radical disparateness of Rājpūt and trader values is no mere happenstance, but rather a deep structural feature of Rajasthani culture. It further argues that appearances to the contrary notwithstanding, violence and nonviolence are actually two linked components of a single cultural molecule. Seen from the perspective of indigenous social symbolism, the nonviolence of Rajasthan's traders is actually the inverted twin of Rājpūt violence. But understanding the logic of this connection will require us to journey into the region's mythic past.

Myth and the Role of Sacrifice

More than a mere group label, social identity is best seen as a cultural complex. It consists of a cluster of ideas, values, symbolisms, and modes of behaviour that mould and are moulded by a group's shared conception of who they are. The traders of Rajasthan possess a general culture of identity in this sense, and within it there are at least two major identity subcultures, Hindu and Jain, with still further subdivisions.

This book is based on the idea that myth is a window of unusual transparency into cultures and subcultures of identity, giving a clear view of their basic organising themes and ideas. This is not to suggest that myth is the only valid means of exploring social identity, nor is it to suggest that identity is the only thing that myth (even origin myth) is about. But it is incontestable that one of the most fruitful ideas in anthropology has been the notion that the key to the present is often the past as portrayed in myth, and this is especially true in the realm of social identity. To ask the question 'Who *are* we?' is to ask 'Who *were* we when we came to be?' As this book will show, moreover, myth not only defines and projects social identities but can also be an arena in which problematic aspects of social identity are addressed and resolved. Because of certain ambiguities surrounding the social place of trade itself, trading groups face special problems of identity. These problems emerge as a central preoccupation of their origin mythologies.

The myths to be presented and discussed in later chapters are mostly about how specific castes were created. We shall treat them as repositories of what we shall call 'mythohistorical' knowledge. The use of the term 'historical' in this expression refers to the fact that these myths are accounts of the past that view the past as causally related to the present. The prefix 'mytho' is not employed to insert a pejorative suggestion that these narratives are untrue, but rather to indicate that their authority is not conferred by the kinds of systematic testing against evidence that we expect to see in the work of modern historians. Their authority, rather, stems both from their alleged antiquity and their functional relationship with the social identity of existing groups. Their truth, we can say, is at least partly ratified by the reality of the structures for which they serve, to use Malinowski's old phrasing (1954 [1925]), as a 'charter'.

Our myths were originally told and retold by traditional genealogists of various kinds, although nowadays the printed page has mostly supplanted the genealogists. We cannot actually know how the sensibilities of tellers, auditors, and bystanders—that is, the sensibilities of the genealogists themselves, their patrons, and the wider society—mingled and interacted in the creation of the knowledge they contain, for the process itself is now almost entirely a thing of the distant past. But later chapters will provide ample evidence that these myths do indeed powerfully reflect images that these groups hold of themselves and are held of them by others.

Mythohistorical knowledge is never created in a vacuum. That is, a group's vision of its socially significant past necessarily draws from the worldview and other symbolic resources available within the group's cultural surround. The mythology described in this book draws on many aspects of the surrounding culture. As will be seen, it takes for granted the cosmologies and cosmogonies of major religious traditions of Rajasthan and India. It also takes for granted Rajasthan's sacred geography, which forms the backdrop to many incidents described by these narratives. The deities and other sacred beings of Hindu and Jain traditions, both local and subcontinental, play a key role in most of them. But perhaps most important of all, these narratives utilise a single paradigmatic metaphor drawn from the ancient Indic tradition. The metaphor is that of the Vedic rite of sacrifice.

The symbolism of the sacrifice is nearly ubiquitous in the materials presented in this book. The rite touches on everything, and is the foundation and framework of mythohistorical knowledge of social things. Later chapters will show how it connects the present with the past and the human with the cosmic. We shall see that origin myths portray social groups and the social order as having been created by means of sacrificial rituals. Indeed, they visualise the social order as a sacrificial order.

That is, the myths assume that *social* relationships are best understood as *ritual* relationships, and that social change is essentially a change in the way groups relate to the sacrifice. And of special importance from the standpoint of this book's overall argument, the myths also use a sacrificial metaphor as a means of representing the place of violence in the social order.

In fact, the sacrifice emerges in our materials as an excellent example of what Gananath Obeyesekere has called a 'myth model' (1992: 8–15; also 1981), a concept that will play a major role in chapters to come. As Obeyesekere puts it, a myth model is a 'paradigmatic myth' referring to 'an underlying set of ideas' that can, among other things, serve as a model for other myths. In the wider context of Indic culture, the sacrifice, which is portrayed as the source of the cosmos and everything in it, serves as a model for creative power and social order. This concept is replicated in caste origin myths that portray social groups as having been created, albeit in different and sometimes indirect ways, by means of sacrificial rites. As later chapters will show, the sacrificial myth model is often supplemented by another, that of the protective goddess who plays a role in the creation of the group. But the sacrifice is truly basic.

Myth in Historical Context

To stress that this book is fundamentally about myth is also to say that it is not fundamentally about history as understood by historians. That is, even though our analysis *refers* to a past—or, more precisely to certain conceptions of the past—it is far more about the present than the past. But that does not mean that history is irrelevant to our inquiry, for there is a significant complication that has to be acknowledged and factored into our analysis. It arises from the obvious fact that the origin myths of castes have changing social and historical contexts. Who, we must know, composes and transmits these narratives? And when and under what circumstances did or do they do so? These questions will be addressed in much greater detail in subsequent chapters, and we shall see that there are significant differences between the historical contexts out of which the origin myths of different trading castes have come into our purview. It should be noted now, however, that most of the narrative materials presented in this book were collected from traditional sources and published in the late nineteenth and early twentieth centuries. This has an important bearing on both their content and format because this was a period in which caste was rapidly changing and the collection of origin mythology was itself an aspect of the process of change.

Caste has never been a static institution. And while it has always been in a state of change, it now seems clear that caste, including the trading castes of Rajasthan, acquired many of the traits that twentieth-century observers came to see as essential features of the so-called 'caste system' in relatively recent times. Although the details of chronology and causality are contested, it also seems clear that by the mid-nineteenth century many of these characteristics were in place (S. Bayly 1999: esp. Ch. 2). At this point caste boundaries among service and trading groups had become more crystallised structurally and more focused on 'purity' and 'pollution' concerns than ever before, and by this time, too, the 'Vaiśya-type merchant' had emerged into historical visibility (ibid.: 70–72). The significance of this latter concept will become clearer in the next chapter. But from the standpoint of the concerns of this book, one of the most important facts about the mid-nineteenth century was that this was the period of the first stirrings of the movement that would ultimately give rise to modern caste associations.

A caste association is a caste-based organisation, typically established on an all-India basis (actually or fictively), that attempts to promote the social, cultural, legal and political interests of the caste it represents. It also frequently attempts to rationalise the caste's internal structure. These organisations usually publish journals containing articles of special interest to members of the caste in question as well as matrimonial advertisements. The process by which these associations initially formed was directly related to what Susan Bayly calls '… the increasing self-confidence of the large and growing Indian intelligentsia which had been expanding rapidly since the 1850s' (ibid.: 148).[6] They were the creations, in other words, of an emergent intellectual elite. The early associations were often short-lived, and frequently competed with each other fatally; but the trend was durable, and by the early twentieth century such organisations were extremely common.

An important matter with which these associations were concerned was the maintenance of proper marriage restrictions. This issue, which is very conspicuous in some of the materials presented in later chapters, probably arose in direct response to a dramatic widening of local social horizons in the nineteenth century, a process that inevitably generated new questions about who were and were not eligible marriage partners.

Caste associations also typically tried to address issues of social reform that became especially insistent in the cultural shatter zone in which the educated middle class found itself during this period. Among traders in particular, such matters as dowry reform, age-of-marriage, and excessive ceremonial expenditures tended to loom large in the deliberations of caste associations.

Caste associations have left highly significant marks on most of the materials to be presented in later chapters, mythic materials in particular. Caste origin myths were once the monopoly of caste genealogists and other traditional specialists, and were usually presented orally (although preserved in handwritten books). In the early twentieth century, however, caste associations were beginning to replace traditional genealogists as the principal transmitters of mythohistorical knowledge in many castes. This was partly because the increasing physical dispersal of these castes was making it very difficult for genealogists to maintain their traditional relationships with patron families, a trend that was particularly pronounced among migrating traders. As a result, oral performances that had been the principal traditional means for the transmission of origin myths and other genealogical information were becoming a thing of the past (and indeed occur only rarely today).

In the meantime, caste associations and caste-oriented intellectuals had been taking an increasing interest in caste origin myths as material to be utilised in providing their castes with modern-style 'histories'. As a result, narrative material that originated with traditional specialists and was once transmitted in oral performances began to find its way into print, usually in standard Hindi (as opposed to local vernaculars) in caste journals or in booklets published by caste associations. These new printed versions of old myths tended to reflect the social and political agendas of the organisations that sponsored or produced them. Above all, these organisations needed to define the castes they represented as social and historical entities. Origin myths, picked out of traditional sources and standardised, became a means of constructing caste identity as a symbolic foundation for the constituencies of caste associations. We shall see this process at work in later chapters.

Because this book is based on research that took place in the late twentieth and early twenty-first centuries, it relies heavily on these printed versions of myths, though it does reproduce and use some orally presented narratives too. We should be thankful indeed that the printed versions exist, for otherwise a great body of mythohistorical knowledge would be lost forever. In this sense, it can be said that those who collected and recast these materials were engaged, if unwittingly, in a project of salvage ethnography. But in utilising these narratives, we need to maintain constant awareness of the changing historical and institutional contexts from which they were drawn. This we shall endeavour to do, and the process will provide us with an instructive glimpse of how caste identities have evolved in modern times.

Caste and Continuity

The nature of caste and caste identities has been the focus of much recent scholarly debate. In question is the extent to which such identities are legacies of pre-colonial times as opposed to constructions of the colonial era.[7] Among the most important recent contributions to this debate is that of anthropologist Nicholas Dirks (2001), who has argued that caste, as we have come to know it in the literature of social science, is largely a product of the British colonial state's engagement with the subject peoples of South Asia. Susan Bayly's equally important but somewhat differently argued interpretation (1999) pushes the formative period of caste, again as we see it today, further back to the era of state-formation in the aftermath of the Mughal collapse. The difference between these views is, I believe, more of emphasis rather than of true fundamentals. And however these issues are finally resolved (assuming they can be), it is now obvious that caste can no longer be regarded, if it ever truly was, as a timeless social formation. Clearly, the caste system has undergone profound changes over the course of India's history. Clearly, too, caste assumed its ethnographically familiar contours in a historical process that began in the eighteenth century and continued, with changing inputs, during the colonial and post-colonial periods. Our current appreciation of these basics represents real progress in our understanding of South Asian society.

Where, then, does this book fall in the give and take of these discussions? Let me say at once that it has not been written to contribute to the debate about when caste became what we see today, and the materials presented here have not been selected to settle this important issue. Still, this book's argument does have implications for our general understanding of caste. Its overall view could be described as syncretic, uniting the recent scholarly emphasis on the historical contingency of caste with a search for elements of civilisational continuity. To borrow Dipankar Gupta's felicitous contrast (2000: 180–81), the book incorporates both sociological and culturological viewpoints, albeit with an emphasis on the latter, and assumes that such a position is not, as some would say, self-contradictory.

Thus, subsequent chapters will endeavour to show that although the current situation of trading castes has been profoundly shaped by historically recent social changes, the symbolic ingredients of their contemporary social identities echo ancient themes in Indian civilisation. The book certainly does not take the position that trading castes are transhistorical essences, and in fact contains much evidence to the contrary. Rather, it takes the general view that such institutions as caste have assumed their current form as a result of historical interactions of all kinds, and that among these the colonial experience looms large. But it also assumes that, even when induced by exogenous factors, the formation or alteration of social groups inevitably utilises cultural materials lying at hand. The formation of caste identities is clearly a dialectical process in which historical circumstance and cultural legacies continually interact in extremely complex ways, but amidst these interactions some cultural elements demonstrate surprising durability. We shall see that truly ancient images of the sacrifice, of sacrificial relationships, of sacrificial violence, and of sacrificial legitimisation of political authority continue to inform the identities of trading castes to this very day. Moreover, we shall see that these same ancient images have even become a factor in trader involvement in contemporary politics.

Our exploration of the social mythology of Rajasthani traders is necessarily a journey with many ports of call. Chapters Two and Three deal with preliminaries. The role traders play and have played in the past in the social and political systems of the region is the subject of Chapter Two. The chapter stresses elements of vulnerabilty and marginality in the traders' social and political position. Chapter Three explains how the ancient rite of sacrifice functions as a metaphor for social relationships. We look closely at the rite itself, and explore how the sacrificial metaphor engages with the social identities of Rajasthani Brāhmaṇs and Rājpūts.

The book then turns to the social mythology of the traders. We shall endeavour to present these myths and the images they project in the context of other relevant ethnographic detail, with special attention given to each caste's clan and lineage structure. As will be seen, the organisation of a given caste's constituent descent groups is connected in the most intimate way with issues of caste origin and identity. Chapter Four deals with three 'Hindu cluster' castes—the Khaṇḍelvāl Vaiśyas, Māheśvarīs, and Vijayvargīyas—and shows how myth tends to depict them as descended from groups (in some cases Rājpūt groups) who were once alienated from sacrificial violence, but who then rejoined the sacrificial order on a new, non-violent basis, thus changing their social essence. Chapter Five deals with the 'Jain cluster' of castes—the Khaṇḍelvāl Jains, Osvāls, and Śrīmāls—and shows how myth portrays them as groups who were once Rājpūts, but whose alienation from sacrificial violence led to their symbolic alienation from the social order itself. From the standpoint of social (as opposed to soteriological) symbolism, this is what it means to be a Jain as opposed to a Hindu. The Agravāl caste is treated separately in Chapter Six. In this chapter, we see how Agravāl caste elites have brought the sacrificial symbolism of caste identity into the realm of modern public culture.

The last chapter summarises the book's overall argument and then turns to a brief overview of the traders' current situation in Rajasthan. The chapter suggests that traders as a class have acquired a new kind of political and social clout in post-independence Rajasthan, and that this has allowed them to create what might be described as a political sub-culture out of the shared symbolisms of their caste identities. The banning of animal sacrifice, an important element in the ritualisation of political authority in pre-independence Rajasthani states and estates, can be seen as a marker of a general political ascendancy of trader values at both regional and national levels.

Notes

1. For a very useful analysis of relevant points in this debate, see Lodrick 1994. In what follows, I have drawn extensively from his discussion.
2. For example, most of the so-called 'Marwaris' of Kolkatta originate, not from Marwar, but from Jhunjhunu and elsewhere in the Shekhawati region. Nonetheless, the term *mārvāṛī* has become a category of self-description and self-understanding among these migrant Rajasthani traders (Hardgrove 2002).
3. While *gotras* are very important in Rajasthan, they are absent in Gujarat. See Cort, forthcoming.

4. See Hardiman 1996: 62–91 for an excellent discussion of how traders are perceived as a general category in western India.
5. The term Vaiṣṇava refers to the worship of the deity Viṣṇu and his various forms.
6. For an excellent account of the passage of a particular caste through the eighteenth and nineteenth centuries and its institutional responses to change, readers could do no better than Frank Conlon's study of the Chitrapur Saraswat Brāhmaṇs (1977).
7. The locus classicus of the essentialist view of caste is Louis Dumont's *Homo Hierarchicus* (1970 [orig. 1966]). For a lucid summary of a range of views relating to caste and colonialism, see Datta 1999: 1–6. With regard to the Jats, the subject of her book, she takes the sensible view that their identity crystallised under the British, but that it utilised precolonial 'cultural resources' (ibid.: 8–9). This is very close to the position taken by this book.

Chapter Two

Violence and the Ways of Trade

How can the vulnerability of wealth be reconciled to the irresistibility of power? It is sometimes said, of course, that wealth *is* power. And it is true that wealth and power are similar in that each is, in its essence, a capacity to command the efforts of other persons. But if by power we mean political power, then wealth and power are, though related, not quite the same thing. Our sense that this is so is registered by the fact that we also say that wealth can purchase power and power can seize wealth—usages that draw upon a realisation that they are, in fact, different, and that their relationship is partly antagonistic. We know, too, that their relationship is also partly complementary. The state depends on wealth, without which political power dwindles. Wealth, in turn, seeks shelter within the state, on which it relies for protection from predation. But the complementation is asymmetrical. In the end, political power trumps wealth, for power, whether exercised through the structures of states or deployed on the field of battle, has direct recourse to violence; indeed, it *is* a form of socially crystallised violence. How, then, is wealth to protect itself? How are groups that bear wealth to engage, *in a single social system*, with groups that wield power? Such questions are probably relevant to all complex societies, certainly to Rajasthan.

The complementation between wealth and power also has a cultural dimension. Common experience and the record of history and ethnography suggest that the social personalities best suited to controlling wealth and controlling persons are usually very different. Getting and staying rich require witholding wealth from others, but legitimate rulership requires the ratification of chiefly generosity. Around these two basic requirements can grow very different value systems focussed on totally different orientations toward exchange in relation to social relationships. We shall see dramatic evidence of this difference in Rajasthan.

This chapter is about how wealth has dealt with power in Rajasthan and how this has come to be reflected in symbolisms of social identity. As the chapter will show, the issue of violence and its control provides a bridge between the problems faced by Rajasthan's principal wealth-bearers, the traders, and their culture of identity. As suggested in the previous chapter, non-violence is a component of trader social identity. This chapter shows how trader non-violence can be seen as a strategy in wealth's ineluctable struggle with power. It also reveals the costs of such a strategy.

Traders and Wealth

Traders as Vaiśyas

We begin with a deceptively simple question: Who are the traders? As it turns out, this question can be answered at more than one level. One answer, a textbook truism, is that Rajasthan's traders (or indeed the traders of any region of India) are modern-day members of an ancient social class known as *Vaiśyas*. This notion is both classical and conventional—classical in the sense that important texts, including the great Hindu lawbooks, sanction the idea, and conventional in the sense that, for the most part, the man or the woman on the street in India takes it for granted that, whatever else traders might be, they 'are Vaiśyas'. Indeed, this is how traders often identify themselves, and the assertion will appear in some of the mythology to be presented in later chapters.

The term *Vaiśya* refers to the *varṇa* system, a well-known idealisation of the Indic social order that divides society into four interdependent classes: Brāhmaṇs, Kṣatriyas, Vaiśyas, and Śūdras. This scheme is very ancient, going back to Vedic times. It is not to be confused with the system of castes; the *varṇas* are ideal categories into each of which many actual castes (i.e., *jātis*) can be classified. Brāhmaṇs, holding the topmost position, are priests and teachers. The Kṣatriyas, second in rank, are rulers and warriors. In Rajasthan, the Kṣatriya *varṇa* is represented by the Rājpūts. Nowadays, the Vaiśyas, third in rank, are usually considered to be traders and merchants. The Śūdras, at the bottom of the system, are (at least within the classical definition of this scheme) those who serve members of the three higher classes. The top three classes form an elite called 'twice-born', so named because males of these classes are supposed to undergo an initiation rite seen as a second birth. Despite the antiquity of this scheme, the names of the four classes are very much a part of current social discourse, and the basic nature of the system is well understood in contemporary Indian society. To say that traders are 'Vaiśyas' is to claim that their social identity is best understood in terms of this system.

This is, however, misleading in several respects. In order to understand the nature of the difficulty, we must begin by pointing out that the definition of the Vaiśya class has in fact changed quite a bit over the centuries. The Vaiśyas (or Viś) originally were ordinary tribesmen, that is, those who were not Brāhmaṇs, Kṣatriyas, or lowly Śūdras. Reflecting the structure of social systems that existed in northwest India in the early centuries of the first millennium B.C.E., the Vedic texts define the Vaiśya *varṇa* primarily as a class to be 'eaten', i.e., taxed, by those of superior rank. According to P. V. Kane, these texts present the Vaiśyas as cattle-rearers who were entitled to participate in sacrificial rites and were more numerous than the Brāhmaṇs and Kṣatriyas to whom they owed obedience and from whom they had to live apart (1974: 42). Nothing at all is said of trade, which only became attached to the Vaiśya class later, after the emergence of a more urbanised social order.

Reacting to the appearance of trade in the equation, *Manusmṛti* (the so-called *Laws of Manu*), probably dating from the first two centuries of the Common Era and the most influential of Hindu legal texts, defines the social duties of the four *varṇas* in the following terms:

> But to protect this whole creation, the lustrous one made separate innate activities for those born of his mouth, arms, thighs, and feet. For priests [Brāhmaṇs], he ordained teaching and learning, sacrificing for themselves and sacrificing for others, giving and receiving. Protecting his subjects, giving, having sacrifices performed, studying, and remaining unaddicted to the sensory objects are, in summary, for a ruler [Kṣatriya]. Protecting his livestock, giving, having sacrifices performed, studying, trading, lending money, and farming of land are [mandated] for a commoner [Vaiśya]. The Lord assigned only one activity to a servant [Śūdra]: serving these (other) classes without resentment (1. 87–91).

These lines embody a view much closer to the modern understanding of the Vaiśya class, but it should be noted that even though *Manusmṛti* has added trade and moneylending to the social duties of the Vaiśyas, the text does not draw a one-to-one correspondence between the Vaiśya category and traders. As we see, it emphasises the rural pursuits of herding and farming at least as much. This heterogeneity obviously reflects the accretion of different denotations of the term Vaiśya as North Indian social systems evolved over time. In all likelihood, when urban society developed, trading groups emerged from the ranks of the Vaiśya commoners whose sources of wealth were cattle rearing and agriculture (Thapar 1984: 92). The common thread uniting the category over time is obviously wealth; cattle-keepers, farmers, and merchants all create wealth for the 'eating' of those who can take it.

Given this background, it can surely be said—as it indeed is, in Rajasthan and elsewhere—that traders belong to the Vaiśya *varṇa*. If trade is not the only social duty of Vaiśyas as defined in *Manusmṛti*, it is one of their listed duties, and traders are obviously linked both conceptually and empirically with wealth. But the fact remains that the identity of Rajasthani traders is only partly, and to some extent misleadingly, captured by the Vaiśya label. That this is so is indicated by three important considerations.

The first of these is the fact the even if Rajasthanis assign Vaiśya status to traders in considered or formal discourse, the term 'Vaiśya' is actually rarely heard in ordinary speech in the region. Rather, in Rajasthan (and elsewhere in northern India), the most commonly used generic term for traders is 'Baniyā'. This term comes from the Sanskrit *vaṇij* (or *vāṇij*), meaning 'merchant' or 'trader', registering the fact that there is a deep association between these groups and the life of commerce. Although many traders use this term in self-reference, many also dislike it because it bears strong negative connotations of tight-fistedness and rapacity in business. However, the term they usually advocate in its place is not Vaiśya, but 'Mahājan', meaning 'great person'.[1] It is true that one of the region's trading castes, the Khaṇḍelvāl Vaiśya caste, actually incorporates the term Vaiśya into its name. I suspect, however, that this is a relatively recent innovation designed to demarcate this group clearly from another trading caste with a similar name, the Khaṇḍelvāl Jains.[2] Yes, the term Vaiśya is certainly used in Rajasthan, but there is apparently something about it that simply does not quite 'come naturally'.

The second consideration is that, in Rajasthani culture, Vaiśya status is clearly not a *varṇa* status in the same sense as Brāhmaṇ or Kṣatriya (i.e., Rājpūt) status. Contemporary Brāhmaṇs and Kṣatriyas are putative descendants of Brāhmaṇ and Kṣatriya ancestors, and Brāhmaṇ and

Kṣatriya ancestors are not something anyone wishes to repudiate. But as we shall see in later chapters, most of the trading castes of Rajasthan deny Vaiśya ancestry, even if they consider themselves to be Vaiśyas. Instead, they unusually claim that their ancestors were Rājpūts. To the extent that Vaiśya is a group identity, therefore, it tends to be something that the group *became*, not something that it always was.

Third and finally, there is yet another and even more basic difficulty with the idea that traders are best understood as present-day Vaiśyas, a difficulty that takes us directly to the heart of the arguments of this book. As this chapter will show, *two* characteristics are definitive of traders as a socially recognised category in Rajasthan. One is wealth, which, as we have noted, does indeed fit with the *varṇa* scheme. The other is non-violence. The description of the Vaiśya *varṇa* in *Manusmṛti* certainly captures the element of wealth, but it says nothing whatsoever about non-violence.[3]

The Story of Sālāsar Bālājī

How, then, are we to get a handle on the indigenous Rajasthani understanding of the status of traders, as opposed to the high textual view? I propose that we do so by examining a myth. This is a myth that defines some of the principal social categories of Rajasthan in a *Rajasthani* way, not in the borrowed terms of Sanskrit lawbooks. It not only characterises the social nature of the traders, but also does so in a way that emphasises the contrast between traders and the region's other principal social groups. The myth is not actually about caste at all; rather, it is the origin myth of a regionally important temple located at Sālāsar, a dusty little desert village about 45 km to the west of Sikar in the Shekhawati region. The temple's fame rests upon the many miracles the deity it houses is alleged to have performed. This deity, named Bālājī, is a protective local godling who has come to be regarded as a form of Hanumān, Rāma's loyal ally and devotee in the *Rāmāyaṇa*.[4]

The temple's origin myth, summarised here from a temple-published booklet (Śankar Pujārī 1991: 2–10), takes us back in time to a very bucolic setting:

> Two and a half centuries ago, a young man named Mohandās lived in Sālāsar village. The youngest of six sons of a village priest, he belonged to the Dāhimā Brāhmaṇ caste (a regionally prominent Brāhmaṇ caste also

known as the Dādhīc Brāhmaṇs). His sister, *Kānhī Bāī*, had married into a family of priests in Sālāsar, and there she bore a son named Udayrām. When the boy was five years old, she was widowed. At first she took her son to her natal village, but after a time, feeling that it was inappropriate for her to live with her natal family for too long, she wanted to return to Sālāsar. Mohandās, unmarried and childless, agreed to accompany her. So they came to Sālāsar, where Mohandās assisted his sister and nephew with the agricultural work. But he was also absorbed in devotion to the deity Bālājī.

Time passed in this way, until one day a most unusual thing occurred. It was in the lunar month of Śrāvaṇ.[5] Udayrām was plowing a field while Mohandās was preparing fallow land for farming. Quite suddenly, Bālājī appeared before Mohandās. Snatching away Mohandās's chopper and throwing it aside, the god commanded him to stop farming. When Mohandās resumed work, the god once more pulled the chopper away and ordered him to turn his life to spiritual pursuits. This occurred several times, and was witnessed by a surprised Udayrām. That evening, he told his mother what he had seen. She was dismayed because she feared that her brother was about to become a celibate ascetic, and so she immediately started the search for a suitable bride. But Mohandās never got married; instead he became a celibate world renouncer, vowed to silence.

There were many further wonders and uncanny events after this. One day, Bālājī came to the house in the guise of a wandering ascetic. At the time, Kānhī Bāī was busy feeding her son and brother and had to delay her offering of alms a little bit, with the result that the ascetic became annoyed and vanished. Mohandās, however, knew that it was Bālājī. Two months later, Bālājī again appeared at the house, once more in the guise of an ascetic. When Mohandās came to the door, he saw to his dismay that the ascetic was walking away. He pursued the disguised deity, who tested his devotion by issuing threats. Mohandās passed the test by clinging to the ascetic's feet, and the deity then revealed himself in his true form and offered a boon. At Mohandās's request, Bālājī returned to the house where Kānhī Bāī fed him a type of sweet known as *cūrmā*. When the deity again offered a boon, Mohandās asked him to become the protector of Kānhī Bāī's descendants. Bālājī agreed, and said that he would stay permanently in Sālāsar, would never harm any of Kānhī's descendants, and would assist anyone who meditated on him with full faith. He then vanished. After this, Mohandās began to live as a full-time devotee of Bālājī in a small hut outside the village; there he and the god played together like children, and Mohandās personally became the focus of many miraculous events.

The scene now shifts to the village of Āsorā (near Ladnun in Nagaur District). There, while plowing in the early morning in the month of Śrāvaṇ in the year 1754, a Jāṭ farmer struck and unearthed a stone image lying under the surface of the ground.[6] He was negligent and paid no attention, with the result that he suddenly developed a severe pain in his stomach. He then lay under a tree and slept. When his wife arrived with food in the afternoon and learned what had happened, she realised that the stone was significant in some way. She cleaned it, and as she did so an image of Māruti Nandan (Hanumān, i.e. Bālājī) became visible. She then placed the image under a tree and presented it with an offering of *cūrmā*, with the result that her husband immediately became well. When the village lord heard about this, he had the image brought to his mansion. That night, Bālājī appeared to him in a dream and commanded him to have the image taken to Sālāsar immediately. That same night, Bālājī also appeared to Mohandās in a dream and told him that he was coming to Sālāsar. When the cart carrying the image arrived at Sālāsar, Mohandās said that it should be placed wherever the bullocks spontaneously stopped, and the spot where they halted is exactly where the image of Sālāsar Bālājī stands in the temple today.

At the time of the image's consecration (in 1754 C.E.), a certain Jorāvar Singh, the lord of a village called Juliyāsar, came to Sālāsar hoping to be relieved of a painful boil on his back. He worshipped the image, returned to his village, and the following morning the boil was gone. The grateful chieftain immediately returned to Sālāsar, where he worshiped the image, made an offering, and also arranged for the construction of a small shrine, which was begun in 1758. Mohandās called an artisan named Nūr Mohammad from Fatehpur for the work.

Once (exactly when is unclear), the accountant (*rokaṛiyā*) of King Devī Singh of Sikar was carrying a large amount of money (100,000 silver *mudrās*) to Ramgarh (in Shekhawati). While passing through a dense jungle, he encountered two famous bandits, Ḍungarjī and Javāharjī, whose custom it was to steal from the rich to help the poor. The accountant was easy prey for the bandits, but they left him and the money untouched. This was because he meditated on Bālājī and resolved to build a temple for him. Afterwards he fulfilled his promise and built the temple. (How this fits with Jorāvar Singh's shrine is not clear.)

After this, the sonless King of Sikar, the same Devī Singh, came to Sālāsar and asked for the boon of a son. Mohandās offered a coconut to Bālājī on the king's behalf, and instructed the king to tie it on a nearby Śamī tree. Ten months later, a son was born. The king then came to Sālāsar with his family and built a mansion near the temple. (This was the origin of the temple's tradition in which worshipers tie up votive coconuts for the fulfillment of wishes.)

Because Mohandās was totally immersed in meditation and ascetic practices, it was not he but his sister's son, Udayrām, who became the new temple's first priest (*pujārī*). Later on, Mohandās decided to take jīvit *samādhi* (burial alive while meditating). This occurred in 1793, and on the spot where it happened, a memorial was built with images of his feet. Later a similar memorial was built at the same spot for his sister after her death. To this day, there is an annual memorial ceremony (*śrāddh*) for Mohandās held here during the lunar month of Āśvin.

Bālājī and Social Identities

This tale illustrates well the limited relevance of *varṇa* for understanding the social order of Rajasthan. I do not say irrelevance, because the Brāhmaṇs play a prominent role in the story, as do Kṣatriyas, who appear in the story as Rājpūts. Outside of this dyad, however, we find ourselves in a world significantly different from that of *varṇa*.

But let us begin with the Brāhmaṇs. They are portrayed in a way that very closely matches their ancient role as priestly mediators between the divine and human worlds. This mediation has two modes, as we see in the story. On the one hand, we have the renouncer, Mohandās, who seems to be the story's exemplification of the ancient ideal of the celibate sage whose connection with sacred power is direct and intimate. He is Bālājī's foremost devotee (*bhakt pravar*, in the words of the narrative), and he is the one most directly responsible for actually establishing a link between the deity and the human world. On the other hand, we have a lineage of priests who can serve others as a fully routinised means of access to the deity. These are two different dimensions of Brāhmaṇhood, and one of the myth's central problems is uniting them. How can a celibate holy man's charisma become heritable? The solution is its transfer to his sister's son, who then becomes the apical ancestor of a lineage of priests who own and operate the temple.[7] The recollection of this transfer is perpetuated by means of memorial shrines for Mohandās and his sister laid side-by-side.

However, in order for a temple to exist, two other figures must enter the picture. One is the finder of the image, the Jāṭ plowman. There is a strong dose of locational symbolism in this part of the story. As a charter myth for a pilgrimage center, the tale is fundamentally an account of how a sacred power, a deity, came to have a fixed position on the earth's surface. Mohandās engages and connects with the deity, but the plowman makes terrestrial location possible by bringing a physical image out of the ground (although the image is ultimately taken to another spot).[8] It is fitting that Jāṭs should discover the image, for this caste's social persona fits well with terrestrial imagery; they are tillers of the soil, renowned as skilled farmers.

But a lineage of priests and a sacred image are not enough, for in order for a temple to exist, it must also have the support of someone who can exercise power over people and territory. A temple, it must never be forgotten, is a crystallisation of social energies, and in order for such energies to be mobilised and focussed, someone must exercise political authority. This is the role of the Rājpūt. In acting in this role, he exemplifies an ancient paradigm. The ideology of the *varṇa* system portrays the Kṣatriya as the sponsor of sacrificial rites that are officiated by Brāhmaṇ priests. In this narrative, the temple occupies the functional niche of the rite of sacrifice.

In our story, the first Rājpūt we see is the lord of Āsorā village. His appearance is brief, but as a Rājpūt (not stated, but implied), his contribution arises directly from his political authority, which enables him to bring about the move of the image to its proper location in Sālāsar. With the image in place, King Devī Singh of Sikar steps into the classic role of royal patron, and in so doing becomes the archetypal non-Brāhmaṇ devotee of Bālājī at Sālāsar. The text tells us that he was the first to offer a coconut in conjunction with the request for a boon, which is the normative ritual act at this temple. Thousands of votive coconuts festooning the temple today reiterate that first ritual offering.

We are told next to nothing about the artisan who builds the temple. From his name, however, we know that he was a Muslim. The fact that he had to be brought from Fatehpur suggests that such skills were then rare in the countryside and were associated with urban or town-dwelling Muslims.[9]

And then we come to the trader. In the story, the King of Sīkar's accountant embodies the trading class. Although his caste is not named (nor is he), no Rajasthani reader or auditor of the story would fail to conclude that he is a 'Baniyā'. The story makes three basic points about him. First, he serves a Rājpūt lord, and does so in a way directly related to the custody and care of wealth. Second, he is rich, which we know because he pledges to build a temple (though a local auditor of the story would have no doubt about his wealth in any case). Third, he is nonviolent, which is indicated by the fact that he is completely unable to defend himself when confronted by the bandits. Here the unstated contrast is with the Rājpūts, who are regarded as capable of defending themselves and indeed eager to do so. By contrast, regional stereotype represents traders not only as non-violent, but as lacking fighting spirit. An additional implication is that he is shrewd, which is suggested by the clever way he is able to circumvent his physical helplessness.

Characteristically, however, it is the trader's wealth that saves him from the vulnerabilities of his non-violence in the end, thus emphasising the pre-eminence of the traits of wealth and non-violence as a linked pair. His well-timed meditation on Bālājī leads to his pledge to use his wealth to build a temple, and this brings about his salvation (earthly salvation in the narrative, but with wider if unstated implications). Obviously this part of the story is, among other things, a charter myth for large donations from wealthy businessmen, who these days are the Sālāsar temple's main source of financial support.

Taking all of these points together, the myth shows us the precise limits of the classical *varṇa* model as it applies or does not to the principal social categories that emerge in relation to Sālāsar Bālājī. The Brāhmaṇs are present to be sure, and so are the Kṣatriyas in their local manifestation as Rājpūts. And although the devotional and image-worshipping context is different, the relationship between the Brāhmaṇs and the Rājpūts replicates the ancient Brāhmaṇ–Kṣatriya complementarity; Brāhmaṇs establish and maintain links with the sacred with the aid of sponsorship from the Kṣatriyas. Outside of this basic dyad, however, we find ourselves in a largely non-*varṇa* world, for the story says nothing at all of Vaiśyas and Śūdras. Instead of Śūdras, we have Jāṭs. They are portrayed as tillers of the soil and a locally dominant agricultural caste, not as servants of the other *varṇas* (the social duty of Śūdras as defined by the *varṇa* scheme). And while the trader in the story could certainly be called a Vaiśya (and would be so called by many), the fit with *varṇa* is imperfect at best. Our trader is not even said to be a merchant. Rather, his most important characteristics are his association with wealth and his non-violence, traits that emerge in the context of his relationship with a king. In this narrative, in sum, the Brāhmaṇ and Kṣatriya categories are the only *varṇa* categories seriously at work.

A system of categories somewhat more closely fitting the social landscape of our myth than the *varṇa* system is a triadic taxonomy suggested by Susan Bayly (1999: 49). Bayly's scheme focusses on three distinct ways of life that served as 'idealised reference points', as she puts it, for the diffusion of caste values during post-Mughal times, which she believes to have been the era in which the modern caste order was beginning to take shape. The three ways of life are those of the 'kingly warrior or man of prowess', the literate 'service provider' (in which category she includes both priests and record-keepers), and the 'settled man of worth, meaning both the productive and virtuous tiller and the man of commerce'. In our narrative, the Rājpūts are the kingly warriors, although the story does not focus on their martial virtues. The Dāhimā Brāhmaṇs are the priests, although it is clear from the tale that this caste's relationship with priesthood is culturally very complex. The Jāṭ farmer certainly looks like Bayly's 'settled man of worth'.

Bayly's scheme, however, ceases to engage the world of the myth of Bālājī when we come to the trader. The narrative does not, as Bayly does, lump the tiller of the soil together with the trader, the narrative's equivalent of Bayly's man of commerce. Rather, the tale's trader-figure is a king's accountant, which seems to put him in an entirely unique category, one that combines wealth, literacy, numeracy and administrative service. Certainly the trader shares little common ground with farmers. Bayly's scheme has the virtue of moving us away from attempting to impose *varna* on a social reality to which its fit is imperfect, and her groupings do capture important aspects of on-the-ground reality in Rajasthan. But her scheme seems to miss the distinctive amalgam of elements that constitute the trader's social persona. As we shall see, the presence of administrative service in the mix is crucial to the social niche occupied by traders as a class in Rajasthan.

So who are the traders of Rajasthan? Yes, they are Vaiśyas, but this is an infrequently used label, one poorly rooted in Rajasthani social perception. They are certainly not Kṣatriyas, but it has to be significant that the story places the trader very close to the Rājpūts in social space. The story emphasises that the trader serves the Rājpūt, and they are both supporters of the temple. In fact, the nature of their mutual positioning in social space will be the focus of much that follows in this book. But what clearly emerges is that wealth and non-violence are the true keys to how traders fit in the social order of Rajasthan. The trader both possesses wealth and manages it for others—wealth that he is unable to defend through violence. This is the nub of what the story of Bālājī has to tell us about traders.

We must now examine these traits in more detail. We begin with wealth.

Money and the Social Order

Filthy Lucre

In his well known analysis of devil symbolism and commodity fetishism in southwestern Colombia (1980), anthropologist Michael Taussig describes how peasants of the Cauca Valley believe that some plantation wage-workers enter into secret pacts with the devil in order to increase their production and hence their wages. The peasants also believe that occasionally a godparent-to-be will secretly hold a currency note while his or her godchild is being baptised. As a result, the note is baptised instead of the child, becoming invested with a power that will cause it always to return to its owner—who has become its godparent—with interest. Taussig interprets these beliefs as a reaction by the peasants to exploitative, dehumanising and socially corrosive capitalist relations of production. That is, they are the peasants' way of expressing, using an idiom drawn from their culture, their sense of the basically evil nature of money when, as in a capitalist economic order, it has the mysterious capacity to reproduce and multiply itself.

Although the context is totally different, Taussig's materials suggest one possible approach to the question of the cultural construction of trader identity in India. Is it possible, we must ask, that the Rajasthani trader is the South Asian equivalent of the devil-allied rate-buster or the treacherous godparent in Colombia? Such a hypothesis would at least be consistent with the general unpopularity of traders. Nonetheless, there is little evidence that traders are widely seen as radically evil (as opposed to shrewd, greedy or shady) in India.[10] As Jonathan Parry points out, trade was never considered evil in India, nor has moneylending ever been condemned with the severity it was in Europe (1989: 77–82).[11] Nor, as Parry also suggests, is wealth itself seen as polluted or evil in India. Wealth is one of the four classical 'ends of life' (*puruṣārthas*) that the Hindu law books say must be pursued by every householder. And although prosperity is often seen as a soteriological danger, it has an honoured position in the Indic scheme of things (Madan 1987). Indeed, far from being seen as inherently evil, wealth is identified with Lakṣmī, the Hindu goddess of prosperity and one of the most auspicious of deities. The medieval European image of money as excrement (Little 1971: 38; see also p. 44, Figures 10 and 11) contrasts in the most dramatic way with a common pictorial image of Lakṣmī in which golden coins cascade as a blessing from her hand.

On another point, however, Taussig's analysis may have something of importance to teach us about India and Rajasthan. He argues that his peasant informants possess highly accurate insight into their economic situation, albeit expressed in their own cultural idiom. This is a direct result of their location on the frontiers of the capitalist world. Because they are not yet fully in the thrall of a commodity-based economic order, they can see through its mystifications in a way that those who live in fully capitalist societies cannot. Is something of the same sort true of rural India? Could it be that the status of those who traffic in wealth is in some way related to their position in a society in which money and non-monetary forms of exchange operate in close juxtaposition? It seems possible.

As Chris Fuller (1989) has pointed out, the *jajmānī* system—a non-monetary system of exchange long thought to be the heart and soul of India's village economies—is in fact only part of the story, for systems of market exchange are also integral to economic relations in Indian villages. That is, these communities are and were zones of interface between two fundamentally different kinds of economic relationships. To the degree that traders operate on or near this interface, their social persona may participate in its contradictory character. And if this is so, then marginality may be the key to the trader's position, a matter of slippery lucre, not filthy lucre.

Slippery Lucre

In his celebrated treatise on money, Georg Simmel (1978) argues that, historically, money has been a potent source of social and cultural change in practically every department of life.[12] Money is the abstraction of all value and the generalisation of all means. Where money exists, the fulfillment of an obligation need not involve in any way the social position or personality of the fulfiller, for it is a socially frictionless medium of exchange, unfettered by the conditions of its acquisition and possession. Money is therefore corrosive to social orders in which persons are bound to particular ways of fulfilling obligations according to their social position. It is thus the enemy of familial, personal, and local ties. But if money destroys some social ties, it also creates a new kind of bond based on the abstraction of trust. Barter requires trust only of those directly involved in an exchange, but money situates the individual in a vast and ever-expanding universe of social trust, connecting the person to countless unknown others. Persons so bound engage with one another through the narrow aperture of economic function, leaving the remainder of their personhood and individuality untouched. In this way, money liberates the individual from particularistic social and economic bonds.

Into this picture comes the trader. Because of the nature of the money in which he traffics, according to Simmel, the trader's relationship to the social order is different from that of any other social type. Because money is socially frictionless, anyone can accept it from anyone. It therefore becomes a focal interest of persons and classes who, because of low social status, are excluded from opportunities open to others.[13] Also, and more important, its character as a medium of exchange harmonises with the way of life of the social outsider, which is not quite the same thing as low social status. Money belongs to a world of universal values; when it comes into contact with a world of particularistic values, the outsider—that is, someone not entangled in the particularistic social order—is in the best position to preside over its flow. Because he has no local roots, this is the only niche open to him; but also his lack of local social ties frees him from the complications of local social obligations. The price of this freedom, however, is the enmity of others. As Simmel puts it, those who are locally rooted feel 'overpowered by an indifferent and characterless force whose essence seems to be personified by strangers' (ibid.: 226–27).

Do these points have any relevance to India? They certainly have to be qualified. Indian traders are obviously not low in social status. Moreover, there is reason to doubt whether money is ever a totally frictionless exchange medium, even in highly industrialised societies. Viviana Zelizer (1994) has shown that in the United States people habitually think qualitatively as well as quantitatively about money, which can be 'earmarked' for particular purposes, evaluated on the basis of how it was acquired, and so on. Maurice Bloch (1989) has argued that it is precisely in industrial societies that money has special moral meaning, which he contrasts with the 'moral neutrality' of money among the Merina of central Madagascar. A true ethnography of such matters has yet to be written for India. Still, the fact that, as Parry tells us (1989: 67), money can transport the sins of a donor when given in the form of a type of charitable gift known as *dān* (or *dāna*) shows that money can act as a medium for the movement of non-monetary values.[14] And the common use of currency notes and coins as symbols of auspiciousness on ceremonial occasions also suggests that there is more to money than mere cash value.

Nonetheless, a case can be made that in India money is in some fundamental way different from other exchange media. For one thing, cash transactions do not have the hierarchical implications of exchanges in certain other media. Cooked food, for example, carries powerful implications of status difference when exchanged asymmetrically.[15] This is not true of cash transfers. Furthermore, although it appears to be true that money in the form of *dān* can carry a donor's sins, Parry also reports that, when given as *dān*, money is usually a substitute for some actual item. 'Specially affluent and fastidious pilgrims and mourners,' he writes, 'tend to regard it as more seemly and appropriate to donate the specific items rather than their cash equivalent' (ibid.). The same principle informs the Jain practice of auctioning key roles in important ceremonies. Although the actual payment is in cash, the bidding is conducted in units of *ghī* (clarified butter), a substance bearing high cultural as well as cash value, suggesting that money itself somehow falls short, if only in the slightest degree, as a medium for merit-generating donations.[16]

But (if we are to follow another implication of Simmel's analysis) are Indian traders in any sense social outsiders? Parry argues that they are not. Unlike the Jew in the Christian world, he says in response to this issue, the Indian merchant was 'a paragon of religious orthopraxy' (1989: 78). But here, I think, Parry is leading us slightly astray. What exactly is 'religious orthopraxy'? Many Indian traders are Jains. Can a Jain, however observant, be orthoprax by Hindu standards? Indeed, by what standards are Hindu traders, who are adherents of various sectarian traditions, to be judged as orthoprax or not? In any case, the issue is surely not where traders are to be found on the religious landscape, but how they fit into the surrounding social order.

Rajasthani traders living outside Rajasthan can certainly be said to be social outsiders in the locales to which they have migrated. It is true that some of these migrant merchants have become, in varying degrees, linguistically and in other ways acculturated to their diaspora regions. And it is also true that in some cases the passage of time has greatly attenuated their connections with their places of origin in Rajasthan. Even so, so-called 'Marwari' traders have generally remained apart from indigenous communities, although the degree to which this is so has varied. In these situations they are indeed social outsiders, aloof from local populations, who typically regard the former as rapacious exploiters (Timberg 1978: 102–3).[17]

But what of their position in Rajasthan itself? What happens when—to use Chris A. Gregory's apt phrasing (1997: 166)—'homeland' and 'tradeland' are the same land? This is a more complex and interesting issue. To address it, however, we shall have to turn to history. The position of traders in post-Independence Rajasthan is very different from what it was during the era in which contemporary caste identities crystallised, and in order fully to understand their position in regional social systems, we must know something of their role in the now-defunct indigenous states of the region. Fortunately, an excellent historical analysis that bears directly on these concerns is at hand, one that gives us a coherent picture—probably typical in broad outline—of that vanished world. Although it is not about traders as such, Vidal's important recent (1997b; see also 1997a) study of modes of protest in Sirohi sheds considerable light on the former condition of traders in one of the region's smaller Rājpūt kingdoms. We shall use it as a case study of traders' relationships with other key communities in this region.

Sirohi Traders

Traders and Sirohi's Social Landscape

From Vidal we learn that the elite of the old Sirohi kingdom fell into the same basic three categories that we have met already in the origin myth of Sālāsar Bālājī. Foremost were the Rājpūts, the kingdom's aristocracy and rulers at every level. The Brāhmaṇs were closely associated with the Rājpūts, whom they served as family priests. They bore a clear identity as ritual specialists and interpreters of *dharma*,[18] and were deeply respected because of this. The middle-status Bhāṭs and Cāraṇs, genealogists and bards respectively, were symbolic specialists like the Brāhmaṇs. The Bhāṭs self-identified themselves culturally with the Brāhmaṇs, whereas the Cāraṇs' traditions pulled them into the cultural ambit of the Rājpūts. The third elite group in the kingdom consisted of the traders. Most of the traders were Jain and belonged to the Śvetāmbar sect and to the Bisā Osvāl, Dasā Osvāl and Porvāl castes.[19] Although members of other castes (as well as Bohra Muslims) were involved in commercial activities in the kingdom, the Jain traders were overwhelmingly the main players.

The traders lived by their wits and were highly versatile. They were skilled in business, and they alone possessed knowledge of accounting. Literate and far more cosmopolitan than other groups, they formed 'practically the entire intellectual and economic elite of the kingdom'(1997b: 165). They conducted business of every description at every level of the economy, and were vital to the prosperity of the kingdom. They also served the petty chieftains as estate managers. In addition, they served as bureaucrats and advisors for the Rājpūt rulers and occupied almost every administrative post in the state, including that of Chief Minister.

Moving back from Sirohi temporarily, we should note that the pattern of traders serving as managers and state officials, often at the highest level, was widespread in Rajasthan (also see e.g., Kapur 2002: 117–24, Mehta 1999: 49, Qanungo 1960: 50–59).[20] Members of other castes (such as Kāyasths) sometimes served Rajasthani rulers in this capacity, but the trading castes seem to have predominated. One reason for this was clearly the wealth connection. Speaking specifically of the role played by Jains in the Mewar state between the thirteenth and fifteenth centuries, Nandini Kapur (2002: 118–19) points out that the state depended on the Jain community because of the resources they could put at the state's disposal, especially during periods of incessant warfare. The Jains, in turn, sought links with the state out of a desire to gain state support for their business activities, which in fact they received. Another reason for the prominence of traders in the political structures of these states was that, not being Rājpūts, they could never pose a viable challenge to the ruling nobility (Qanungo 1960: 50). Vidal suggests, I believe rightly, that Rājpūt, Brāhmaṇ and trader formed a triad—the 'authority figure, his chaplain, and the steward of his domain'—that was one of the basic structures 'through which authority was exercised in the ancient political traditions of North India' (1997b: 12).

At first glance, the connection between the petty shopkeeper and the high state official might seem incongruous, but culturally it is far more logical than appearance suggests. Rājpūt rulers and chieftains were men who controlled other men, and therefore territory. By contrast, traders were (and remain) men who controlled and knew how to handle money. The kind of rational calculation required to manage money encourages habits of thought well suited to the requirements of rendering administrative service to those who control men and territory. It is the foundation of bookkeeping and is invaluable for the rational supervision of bureaucracies and armies. Village moneylending, estate management, and affairs of state thus form a connected series.

To return to the specifics of Sirohi, beyond the ambit of affairs of state and estate the traders were businessmen, mostly small, who were part of the local scene everywhere in the kingdom. Their relationship with the rural populations was mostly of the 'lender–borrower' type. They lent to the farmers in times of material need and also to meet ceremonial expenses, especially those of marriage, on which a family's standing and social reproduction depended.[21] The bulk of the population was typically indebted to them. They, in turn, recovered their loans directly from the harvest, which they marketed along with the surpluses of other groups who had a right to a portion of the harvest. Crucially, they had connections to non-local markets that were essential for the selling of crops. The traders also had the duty of collecting land revenues in kind; this they marketed, handing on the proceeds to the state. The presence of the traders was therefore at the very foundation of an economic system to which credit was central. This was an economy, moreover, that was largely based on money, despite the relatively small amount of cash in circulation.

The Sirohi traders were clearly a local example of a more general type described for western India by David Hardiman. Inspired by Pierre Bourdieu, he characterises the primordial exchange mode of the region's rural population as having been that of a 'good-faith' economy of gifting, an economic world in which buying from and selling to fellow villagers was seen as dishonorable, and in which economic and social capital were easily interconvertable (1996: 100–101). In the good-faith economy, borrowing occurred, but in a non-commercial mode. Normatively, the well-off were expected to assist their less fortunate fellowmen in times of need, and loans were unrecorded and interest free. The recipient would be expected to reciprocate with a gift of produce or labour. The system's Achilles heel, however, was the direct connection between social honour, which was the system's central measure of all value, and wealth. Because of this linkage, seeking help from others with locally established status was a manifestation of social inferiority, which tended to push borrowers into the hands of the well-capitalised 'professional usurer' (ibid.: 105). This became the moneylender/trader's point of entry into otherwise solidary peasant communities. The trader brought a totally different ethos into the picture, a 'calculating, merchantile mentality' in which the 'chief yardstick of value was money' (ibid.: 117).[22]

In Sirohi, the traders were indispensable, and others, including the Rājpūts, depended on good relations with them for their own welfare. But despite their indispensability, the position of the traders of Sirohi was extremely precarious in comparison to other groups.[23] Vidal argues that others—rulers, chieftains, and farmers—generally did not resent the fact that they were indebted to the traders so long as this relationship enabled them to maintain or improve their status. A condition of this tolerance, however, was that traders should not try to use their wealth for 'ostentatious display or to gain social or political power' (1997b: 170). They were subjected to irksome sumptuary restrictions in such matters as the size of their houses. Unlike the traders in British India, those of Sirohi were not allowed to 'own land' (ibid.: 161).[24] This meant that they could never be directly involved in agricultural production or, more crucially for us, occupy the same social and political position as the Rājpūts. Furthermore, in times of trouble they became natural targets for the frustrations of others, and were blamed for calamities, such as drought, affecting the kingdom's general population. This often led to physical attacks on Jain shopkeepers and mendicants. As a consequence, they were highly dependent on the Rājpūts for protection, since they were unable to use violence in their own defence, a matter to which we return shortly.[25]

However, ties that spread beyond the locality and even the region counterbalanced the traders' rather problematic status at the local level. Although they were scattered and isolated locally, this was untrue at a higher structural level, where they were probably less isolated than any other group. They were plugged into regional and supraregional economic networks. These networks were anchored in kinship and business relationships that enabled them to invest with fellow traders outside the kingdom and afforded them a hedge against the shifting fortunes of local political and economic life. This pattern was accentuated in the case of the Jains because of their strong connections with their co-religionists elsewhere. For the Jain merchants of Sirohi, Gujarat was always an alternative base, and in fact many of them ultimately migrated and settled there, just as traders to the north and east migrated in the direction of Agra, Delhi, and beyond. Migration itself buttressed the familial and business networks that were so centrally a part of the trading mode of life.

Overall, Vidal's work shows us that the trader community of Sirohi occupied a social and economic position on the interface between two different economic realms. Economically, they operated at the point of connection between the non-monetised sector of the village economy and a world of money and credit that extended far beyond local boundaries.

It was their function to transmute kind into cash as lenders, marketers and agents of taxation. There was also a political dimension to their role, for they were the links between villagers and political structures at every structural level of the kingdom. But their position was ambiguous. Their economic indispensability placed them at the center of things, and yet to a significant extent they operated at the margins of local social systems.

Wealth and Vulnerability

Perhaps the most notable feature of the traders' role in Sirohi was their ambiguous relationship with power. Because of their wealth and economic and political connections, they were clearly powers in the land. Theirs, however, was a problematic sort of power that lacked the physical insistency of military force as well as the cultural legitimacy that is the most crucial ingredient in true political authority.[26] These belonged to the Rājpūts. Their economic position was itself largely contingent on Rājpūt protection and forbearance. They did indeed possess political power, but it could only be exercised through the medium of state structures ultimately controlled by Rājpūts and to which Rājpūts alone had legitimate claim. Moreover, the traders were also denied the socially elevating effects of conspicuous expenditure or sponsorship of great public ceremonials. Vidal notes that, in cultural terms, the traders had no 'rights' at all to the surpluses that came into their hands, and the rest of society 'accorded them no formal privileges, status or legitimacy' (1997b: 167).

It is hardly surprising, therefore, that despite the great antiquity of their presence in the region, others saw them as outsiders. Some believed that they originated in Sri Lanka, and their relationship with other groups was, as Vidal puts it, 'always marked by a greater or lesser degree of "otherness"' (ibid.: 161).[27] Here is Simmel's outsiderhood. For in truth, the Sirohi traders *were* outsiders, though often locally situated. The traders' economic and political networks made up a kind of alternate social universe to which they belonged and to which locals had little direct access. Socially slippery money moved across the boundaries of local communities and kingdoms with ease.

Furthermore, and this point should never be minimised, the traders were also denizens of a very special world of information and thought.

As human activities, business and trade impose intellectual demands that are both substantial and, in a social milieu such as that of rural Rajasthan, distinctive. Leaving aside the fact of literacy, fundamentally important in itself, the conduct of trade requires quantification, abstraction, and the creation of what Arjun Appadurai (1986: 42) calls 'logistical and price bridges between worlds of knowledge' that are otherwise hardly in contact.[28] It is precisely moncy that makes these bridges possible, thus bringing into being an intellectual cosmos that was probably mostly quite beyond the experience or understanding of other groups. Gregory (1997: 163–209) uses the term 'territoriality' to refer to the worlds-beyond-local-worlds to which traders belong. I think this term is useful but somewhat misleading because it fails to register the intellectual and moral (as well as spatial) character of these domains.

The traders' ability to transmute grain into cash and cash into credit must have seemed deeply mysterious and even magical to others. Indirect evidence of this is the fact that droughts were often attributed to the magical powers of Jain mendicants who, at the behest of their trader sponsors, supposedly blocked rain in order to raise the price of grain.[29] In this respect, their position was comparable to that of the Brāhmaṇs, for Brāhmaṇs were also intellectual cosmopolitans (relatively speaking) who mediated what were believed to be powerful forces. But there was a big difference. The intellectual cosmopolitanism of the trader lacked the deep cultural legitimacy of the ideas and symbols that were the Brāhmaṇs' stock in trade. By this I mean that the Brāhmaṇs operated in the highly respected realm of *dharma*; they were specialists in matters pertaining to the sacred world and the normative order, and the powers they mediated were connected to this domain. Mere tolerance best describes the prevailing attitude toward traders, and the fact that others often blamed the traders for general calamities suggests that they viewed the traders' powers as potentially inimical to the proper order of things.

Traders and Rulers

The foregoing strongly suggests that, in pre-Independence Rajasthan, the destiny and identity of traders were more closely linked to the Rājpūts than to any other group. It also suggests that the general tendency on the part of analysts of the Indian scene to focus on the

Brāhmaṇ–Kṣatriya relationship as basic to the Hindu social order may miss crucial features of on-the-ground social systems. In Rajasthan, it seems, the key pairing may well be Kṣatriyas (i.e. Rājpūts) and traders, with Brāhmaṇs playing an important but less central role. At this point, we have indeed come a long way from the classical *varṇa* system.

But our materials also show that the relationship between Rājpūts and traders was highly ambiguous. From one point of view, they were much alike. We have seen that the traders possessed, as did the Rājpūts, considerable power, though of a different sort. Indeed, Rājpūt rulers found trader financial power to be indispensable to the proper running of their own states and fiefdoms. This fact set these two groups off as a linked pair, from other groups. But at the same time, there was a major difference. Consistent with its monetary and cosmopolitan foundations, trader power was fungible in almost every way but one: in the absence of culturally conferred legitimacy, it could not be converted easily into political authority.

Exchange Strategies

The Rājpūts' political authority was manifested in exchange networks of a distinctive type. Writing of the Rājpūts as a class, Norman Ziegler tells us that a great Rājpūt warrior was known as *dātār* (the giver). The ruler gave grain and sustenance to those who served him, and he was a 'giver of protection to all' (Ziegler 1973: 69). The recipients of this largess owed him devoted and loyal service, seen as an obligation imposed by eating the master's grain. This, in turn, put in the ruler's hands 'a coercive force which he could use to maintain and strengthen the [political] order and the hierarchy' (ibid.: 97). The picture that emerges is that of the Rājpūt ruler as the focal point of complex networks of gifting and reciprocal obligations. In this context, conspicuous expenditure is in no way frivolous, but a vital political investment.

The trader's position was very different. The Rājpūt's redistributional strategy, probably the foundation of rulership in most preindustrial societies, was unavailable—as a practical matter and perhaps in principle—to traders. The medium of exchange lying at the heart of the trader's engagement with economic structures, namely money, is an exchange medium that lacks the social stickiness that is a prerequisite for the creation of long-term political loyalties. But more important, we know that, in Sirohi, at least, some of the kinds of conspicuous expenditures central to political authority were prohibited to the traders. Whether this was true in other states of the region will require further research to determine, but royal largess is not the trader's style in any case. Exuberant conspicuous consumption is the deadly enemy of accumulation and a sure solvent of the reputation for business acumen so vital in maintaining creditworthiness.

In his study of the middle-Ganges region, C. A. Bayly (1983) has provided an illuminating description of the contrast between the transactional styles of Indian kings and traders. In Bayly's work, the king emerges as 'chief gift-giver and receiver', which reflects the king's ancient status as 'sacrificer-in-chief' whose lavish expenditure 'was an expression of legitimate rule' (ibid.: 58–59). In contrast, the merchant's behaviour 'stressed the husbanding of resources' (ibid.: 61). A middle ground between these poles was indeed difficult to occupy, and in the early nineteenth century, merchant families of Bayly's region could find themselves 'trapped in the limbo between these two styles of life, unable to command the power and respect of the ruler yet "expensive" enough to forfeit credit in the mercantile sphere [for which a reputation of frugality was necessary]' (ibid.: 387).

The contrast that Bayly draws between the political munificence of rulers and the apolitical parsimony of traders is also applicable to the Rajasthani scene. An old stereotype, one that continues in circulation in the region today, holds that Rājpūts, in contrast to traders, simply cannot hang on to their wealth. The Rājpūts themselves promote this image and see it as illustrative of Rājpūt virtues. To them it is a matter of generosity, not of spendthrift ways, and an expression of the principle that a Rājpūt's purse is as open as his heart. But whether one sees it as a virtue or a flaw of character (the trader view), the alleged inability of Rājpūts to retain their wealth fits well with the overarching social and economic context we have been exploring. As a ruler—at whatever level—the Rājpūt is necessarily a man of many 'friends' whose connections to others are established and maintained through generous giving. In contrast, the trader must follow Simmel's dictum, as true as it is dispiriting, that friends (as well as foes) are the enemy of business success (1978: 227).

Bayly also suggests (1983: 388–89) that, in the region he studied, the traders' notoriously lavish expenditures on rituals and temples represented a safe medium for socially conspicuous gifting—an insight highly relevant to Rajasthan where such expenditures were, and are to this day, one of the most notable features of trader culture, Hindu or Jain (see Hardiman 1996: 76–79). If, however, traders of the middle Ganges region wanted to acquire political clout, then it was necessary for them to assimilate the courtly cultures of the region. However, to do so was to place one's business reputation at risk. In Rajasthan, too, some of the most politically prominent trading-caste families assumed the manners and customs of their Rājpūt patrons (the consequences of which for business reputations I do not know). This phenomenon appears to have been most pronounced among Osvāls, to the extent that some Osvāl families dropped Jainism and became Hindus in imitation of the Rājpūt rulers with whom they were closely associated.

But here we encounter a most interesting and significant fact. Whatever else it might have involved, trader emulation of Rājpūt ways did not generally extend to the eating of meat.[30] In this context, I once had an illuminating conversation with the senior male member of an Osvāl family that for generations had been closely linked with Jodhpur's royal family. He was the last of his family to have experienced life at court. He reminisced about their former high living and hard drinking, traits more normally associated with Rājpūts than Osvāls. In those days, he said, he drank a lot and it was 'all imported'. And he and his family were 'hospitable' (English) like Rājpūts—a reference to the stereotype of Rājpūts as generous and traders as stingy. But his response to my inevitable query about diet was vehement. No, he never touched meat. Not ever. 'Why eat meat, when there are so many tasty vegetarian dishes?', he asked. This points to a truly fundamental matter, which is the general association between trading castes and non-violence. However much my elderly Osvāl interlocutor might have admired the non-vegetarian Rājpūts, and however much he imitated their style of life, his vegetarianism marked him as a fundamentally different social and cultural type.

Violence and Social Identity

It must not be supposed that the link between traders and non-violence permits any easy generalisations. Let us begin by saying that it is not our claim that traders are non-violent, even though regional stereotype certainly tends to represent them as non-martial (as we have seen in the myth of Sālāsar Bālājī). Individual members of the trading castes can of course be violent. However, it is unlikely that the sorts of violent crimes born out of poverty are common in these castes, true poverty itself being rare. There is no question, however, that domestic violence related to such issues as dowry does indeed occur. Moreover, it is not the case that there is a uniform or complete intolerance of soldiering in these castes. Although the military profession is not considered ideal for traders, state officials belonging to trading castes often had distinguished military careers in the region's former kingdoms. Perhaps the most famous is Muhaṇot Naiṇsī, an Osvāl Jain who, in the seventeenth century, took part in several military campaigns in the service of Jodhpur (Qanungo 1960: 80–95).[31] Members of trading castes, including Jains, have also served in modern India's armed forces. Also, there are subcultural differences between trading groups with respect to non-violence. Some, the Jains in particular, are significantly more committed to non-violence than others.

Nonetheless, there certainly exists a general association between non-violence and the lifestyles and social identity of trading castes.[32] Diet is culturally emblematic of this association. Vegetarianism, strictest in the case of the Jains, but adhered to by all trading castes, is the sine qua non of the trader group subculture (see esp. Carstairs 1961: 119–23; Cottam Ellis 1991: 88–94). This does not mean, of course, that all traders are actually vegetarian. I know of many exceptions. But the issue is at least as symbolic as it is behavioural; what matters is the fact that traders see themselves and are seen by others as vegetarians. Traders, of course, are not the only vegetarians in Rajasthan; Brāhmaṇs are normatively vegetarian, as are other groups, too. But in the case of traders, vegetarianism is part of an internally consistent package of behaviours and attitudes recognised as characteristic of trading castes. This is a general social demeanour that rejects activities that regional culture associates with martial lifestyles. In addition to meat-eating, blood sports and alcohol consumption (culturally linked with loss of self control and anger) are prime examples of such activities.

But from the standpoint of this book, the most important domain in which trader social identity is linked with non-violence is their origin myths. This is a matter that will have to await documentation in later chapters. For the present, let it suffice to say that a deep theme in trader origin myths is the idea that trading castes became the castes they are in symbolic opposition to ritual violence. The theme is most strongly emphasised by the Jains, but is present in the case of Hindu trading castes as well.

The Rājpūts present an opposing picture. Again, it is important to be clear about what this does and does not mean. It certainly does not mean that all Rājpūts have a propensity for violence. What it does mean is that in the same manner that trader non-violence is expressed in a broad range of cultural preferences and tendencies, the Rājpūts' general cultural orientation idealises martial virtues and fosters certain behaviours that express or dramatise (as does vegetarianism among traders) this orientation. Nor are all Rājpūts soldiers by any means. However, military careers are common and much admired among the Rājpūts. All Rājpūts do not have a hair-trigger sense of social honour and disgrace, but the willingness to defend one's honour violently is considered a major virtue among unreconstructed Rājpūts.[33]

These tendencies, of course, were directly related to the necessities of Rājpūt life. Violence was the means by which Rājpūts won their kingdoms, and was crucial to their exercise of political authority in their former kingdoms and chiefdoms. The transmutation of violence-based power into the right to be obeyed (political authority in its essence) was made possible by a culturally elaborated ideology of protection. In Norman Ziegler's words, the Rājpūt ruler's code for conduct 'was bearing arms, and fighting to preserve his kingdom ... giving protection and sustenance to all of his subjects ..., and maintaining the proper order of society' (1973: 29). A ruler's right and obligation to serve in this role were conferred by the martial valour of his ancestors and also by his own courage and military prowess. In consistence with this idea, martial imagery was, and is today, a deeply entrenched feature of Rājpūt culture.

These martial values were, in turn, merely one aspect, albeit central, of a total Rājpūt style of life that contrasts radically with that of the traders. Eating meat, alcohol consumption, and blood sports are some of the activities seen as most characteristic of the Rājpūt way of life. As we noted earlier, these are specific behaviours that traders avoid (or are supposed to avoid) and criticise. The value orientation of traders stresses care, prudence, and forethought. To the Rājpūts, these trader virtues seem like mere cunningness or wiliness. Impetuosity, not forethought, expresses the Rājpūt sense of the good. Lloyd and Susanne Rudolph have worded this succintly: 'The dominant ethic of the Rajput warrior–ruler caste and class stressed feudal honour and valour without regard to consequences. Heroism was valued over prudence, action over thought. Intellect and calculations of utility and advantage were disparaged' (1984: 41).

Violence and Ritual Symbolism

The Rājpūt outlook as a conquering and ruling class found vivid ritual expression in the sacrifice of buffaloes (see Figure 2.1). This rite, now under wraps (as we shall see in the final chapter), was once a key ingredient of Rājpūt ritual culture. Rulers and chieftains sponsored the rite during the twice-yearly *navrātrī* festivals[34] in honour of their clan and lineage goddesses (*kul devīs*), who were usually variant forms of the martial goddess Durgā (see Harlan 1992). The phenomenon of clan goddesses is by no means confined to the Rājpūts; the veneration of such goddesses in both vegetarian and non-vegetarian modes is a widespread pattern, and is common, as we shall see, among traders as well as many other communities in Rajasthan. The buffalo sacrifice, however, was something special. It was a state ritual as well as a lineage ceremony. The goddesses to whom the buffalo was offered presided over the welfare of ruling lineages or lineage segments, and the origin myths of these groups frequently linked them to the military victories that established their local suzerainty. The blood spilt by the rite symbolised the blood of the sacrificing lineage, offered in a sanguinary exchange for the goddess's continuing protection. The rite affirmed the valour and military prowess of the sponsoring lineage, and connected these qualities to the right to exercise dominion over a state or chiefdom.

As later chapters will show in detail, animal sacrifice is also at the very heart of trading caste identity, but in a negative and not a positive sense. For the present, it needs only to be noted that, in the era of the erstwhile Rājpūt kingdoms, trader commitment to non-violence meant—among many other things to be sure—that they would never sponsor such rites as the buffalo sacrifice. To the extent that this rite conferred political authority on those who sponsored it, such authority was necessarily unavailable—except by delegation—to traders.

Identities Opposed

The associations between traders and non-violence cannot be reduced to a single essence. Their multiple strands, moreover, have a rich history of which the Rajasthani traders' historically recent juxtaposition to Rājpūt martial ways is but a late chapter. Exploring this history is beyond the

Figure 2.1
An eighteenth century depiction of a royal buffalo sacrifice on *navrātrī* at the Ambā Mātā temple, Udaipur.

scope of this study. But for our purposes the important point to note is that, in the Rajasthani context, trader non-violence forms part of a cultural system of which violence is also a crucial part. As we have said, violence and non-violence alike are the foci of value systems that—for the Rājpūts and traders respectively—support and inform contrasting (and in some ways radically contrasting) symbolisms of identity. In Rajasthan, our materials suggest, trader non-violence is not culturally freestanding, but derives a significant part of its meaning from its opposition of Rājpūt ways, an opposition that is manifested in highly visible and symbolically important behaviours and behavioural avoidances. The reverse is also true. Such activities as meat-eating, hunting, animal sacrifice, and alcohol consumption therefore place Rājpūts and traders in polar opposition.

One cannot avoid being struck by the fact that the traditional relationship between traders and Rājpūts (i.e., in states like Sirohi prior to independence) presents us with that holy grail of structuralist anthropology, a polar opposition within a unifying context.[35] As a pair, traders and Rājpūts opposed all other groups as powerful, although the power they bore was of two very different sorts. In relation to each other, they were culturally opposed as violence is to non-violence. This opposition supported social complementation: trader and ruler could be socially close by virtue of cultural distance.[36] The non-violent and in many ways socially and politically marginal trader gained protection (or at least tolerance) guaranteed by the political authority of warlike Rājpūts. His non-violence not only rendered him incapable of challenging this authority, but also (and perhaps more important) precluded true participation in it, for martial prowess, in the broadest sense, was the key to political authority as well as the means of attaining political power as such. And his marginality, a product of the nature of his exchange networks, was hardly favourable to the generation of his own political alliances. It is true, as we have noted, that there were martial traders. But these were special and notable cases, for as far as I am aware, traders were only martial by deputation, as it were, in the service of the region's true ruling elite.

But in compensation for his exclusion from the true political center, the trader remained pre-eminent in the world of socially slippery economic exchange. Thus, he lived, and often lived well, albeit with his head in the mouth of a lion. The Rājpūt, in his turn, gained from the trader the means—economic and intellectual—of winning and maintaining true political authority, which could not be realised by martial means alone. The trader's ability to serve in this role was made possible by a parsimony that, for the Rājpūt, was precluded by the practical requirements of political life. The clarity of these extremes was a product of their sustained opposition in the social and political life of the region.

But this opposition was never symmetrical. Rājpūts, not traders, lived the martial life which was, in the final analysis, the true source and ultimate guarantee of all forms of power, and Rājpūt values always bore the greatest prestige in this region, at least in the past.[37] If some traders emulated Rājpūts culturally, I am not aware the reverse ever occurred, and Vidal reports that, in Sirohi, Rājpūts and others saw the trader's non-violence as a 'sign of cowardice' (1997b: 166). For their part, of course, the traders looked down upon the Rājpūts for their carnivorous diet, profligate ways and supposed lack of intelligence. But these views to the contrary notwithstanding, the social and cultural niche occupied by the traders was defined by values that were, at least in pre-independence India, eclipsed in social honour by those exemplified by the Rājpūts.

This was and to some extent still is the basic framework defining the socially possible and impossible for the traders of Rajasthan, and later chapters will explore the ways in which myth has constructed social identities within it. But before moving to that stage of our analysis, we need to learn something about indigenous concepts of creative power and social order. This takes us directly to the sacrifice, which is the subject of the next chapter.

Notes

1. This term has been in use for centuries; in Gujarat it is often refers to a traders' guild of a particular place. See Hopkins 1902: 169–205. Cottam Ellis (1991) reports a trader preference for the term in a market town near Jaipur, and she uses it as a blanket designation for the trading castes of this town.
2. Cottam Ellis refers to this caste as 'Khandelval Vaishnava' (1991: 82), which suggests that the concept of Khaṇḍelvāl Vaiśya has not yet become very deeply implanted in the town she studied.
3. Mary McGee (personal communication) has pointed out to me that the *Dharmasutra* of Vasistha (3.24) forbids Vaiśyas from taking up arms unless in self-defense or to prevent *varṇa* mixture. This strikes me as less about the issue of violence than about the lower status of Vaiśyas vis-á-vis the warrior class.
4. An epic poem, composed in Sanskrit and later recast into various regional languages (including Hindi), that celebrates the deed of Rāma, considered a form of Viṣṇu. Hanumān is a monkey-chietain who aids Rāma in the recovery of his wife, Sītā, from the clutches of the demon-king of Sri Lanka.
5. The fifth month of the Hindu lunar calendar (roughly July–August).

6. The Jāṭs are a caste consisting mostly of farmers. They are stereotyped as skilled agriculturalists, hard workers, and tough.
7. The temple is owned by a single lineage (divided into two sublineages), consisting of over 100 families; it belongs to the Sūṭvāl clan of the Dāhimā Brāhmaṇ caste (Mohandās belonged to the Pāṭodya clan). The priests of the temple come exclusively from this lineage. Bālājī is the ancestral protector deity of the lineage. This exemplifies a myth model more commonly associated with ancestral goddesses, as we shall see in later chapters.
8. The discovery of a subterranean image that subsequently becomes an object of worship and source of miracles is a common trope in the region's temple origin mythology.
9. Here is an instance in which on-the-ground reality and cultural expectation (ethnographic/historical fact and mythofact) clearly overlap; Muslims were often employed in precisely this kind of work. Another example of such an overlap is Mohandās's first appearance in the tale as a farmer; it is likely indeed that most Dāhimā Brāhmaṇs were farmers in those days. As a myth with at least some grounding in fact, this story interposes a somewhat hazy boundary between cultural expectation and historical reality.
10. Guha (1985), however, cites lower-caste myths in which the trader is apotheosised as the destructive and devouring Rāhu, a serpent who consumes the sun or moon during eclipses. This is obviously a genuine parallel to the situation described by Taussig.
11. Indeed, as Vidal points out (1997a: 92), in India indebtedness is seen as much less a mark of failure than as a sign of inability to make the '… social and religious expenditures required by one's status ….' Hardiman (1996: 92–117) suggests that western Indian peasants saw indebtedness as an inevitability, and, in the case of the prosperous, as a sign of credit-worthiness, and hence of social honour.
12. What follows owes much to Nicholas Spykman's helpful exegesis (1925).
13. Simmel erroneously states that Parsis and Ceṭṭis are lower status groups in India.
14. The term *dān* (Sanskrit, *dāna*) refers to ritual gifts (to priests, ascetics, and others) that generate merit. To be efficacious, *dān* should be given without any expectation of return.
15. This phenomenon has been described in various village studies. See, e.g., Mayer 1960.
16. The bids in these auctions are actually given in units of *ghī* at prices that have not been valid since the nineteenth century (Cort 2001: 230 n. 24), suggesting a further separation of these exchanges from mere monetary value.
17. For a rich ethnographic description of Rajasthani traders in Kolkata, see Hardgrove 2002.
18. In this context, the term *dharma* refers primarily to matters of religious doctrine, ritual procedures, and Hindu law.
19. The Osvāls and Porvāls are important Jain castes associated with the Śvetāmbar sect. The Bisā/Dasā distinction is a hierarchical division within some castes, and will be explained later in the book. This latter distinction is extremely important in Gujarat where it is tantamount to a caste division. See Cort, forthcoming.
20. For a valuable discussion of state officials as a class, see Devra 1980.
21. See Hardiman 1996 for a general discussion of trader-peasant relations in western India. For a description of agrarian economics in eastern Rajasthan during the late seventeenth and early eighteenth centuries, see Gupta 1986. For an excellent description of the rural credit networks of Jain traders in contemporary Rajasthan, see Jones 1991.

22. Elsewhere Hardiman makes the point that the relationship between peasant and moneylender was not governed by market relations alone. It was a culturally sanctioned relationship, supported by states, with a deep encrustation of traditional symbolism. But the peasants' understanding of property was nonetheless different from that of the traders (1996: 274–75).
23. For a portrait of the troubled existence of non-Rājpūt state officials in Bikaner (in this case Kāyasths, not traders), see Taft and Devra 1999.
24. Whether there were actual prohibitions is unclear, but we also know that during the late seventeenth and early eighteenth centuries the traders of eastern Rajasthan did not convert their money into land rights (Gupta 1986: 143).
25. This pattern of trader dependency on ruling individuals and groups for protection was a widespread pattern in the region. See Hardiman 1996: 22–23, 32–37.
26. On the point of cultural legitimacy, see also Cadène 1997: 141.
27. Cheesman says that, in nineteenth-century Sind, the Hindu Baniyās had 'no-standing' in the Muslim countryside, however rich they might have been (1982: 453). Our materials suggest that this might have had less to do with Islam than with an inherent feature of the North Indian trader's role.
28. Vidal puts this point nicely by saying that Sirohi's traders had not only a dual monopoly of 'accounting and financing techniques relative to the local population; but also a monopoly of social information about the population relative, this time, to merchants from outside the locality' (1997a: 89–90).
29. Thanks to John Cort for suggesting this connection. These beliefs continue to be acted upon to the present day. On August 31, 1999, *The Times of India* reported an attack on Jain temples by tribals in Rohira, Rajasthan. The attack was motivated by the tribals' belief that, whenever Jain ascetics spend the rainy season retreat (*cāturmās*) in the locality (which was the case in 1999), they block the rain to cause the price of foodgrains to rise. See Hardiman 1996: 165–70 for a general discussion of this issue.
30. Lalit Mehta (1999: 145) reports that some Rājpūtised Osvāls became non-vegetarians in the past, but that they are all vegetarians today.
31. Another example is the Haldiyās, a Khaṇḍelvāl Vaiśya lineage that came into great prominence in the affairs of Jaipur in the late eighteenth century. They were renowned as military commanders and actively participated in many battles (Mishra 1991). Other examples could be cited.
32. I do not consider the extortionate threat of suicide, once a characteristic strategy of Brāhmaṇs, Bhāṭs and Cārans for getting others to do their bidding (Vidal 1997b: esp. 90–112), to be a form of non-violence. In regional culture, the willingness of members of these groups to take their own lives was seen as a guarantee of the truths (religious, genealogical, historical) of which they were the guardians and transmitters. However, despite the fact that Mohandas Gandhi, arguably the most famous trading-caste figure in Indian history, utilised a variant of this technique (ibid.: 111–12), it is not the same thing as trader non-violence. To the degree that it involves a refusal to harm others, it does indeed draw upon the notion of *ahiṃsā*, but the threat of self-inflicted violence puts it in a separate category: a subspecies of violence in which nothing is fundamentally changed except its object. As Vidal points out, it can be located on a continuum that is anchored at one end by the Rājpūt traditions of *jauhar* and suicidal attack by defeated warriors (ibid.: 90). These latter traditions are martial at their core, and merely reverse the normally outward directionality of warrior violence.

As far as I am aware, the threat of suicide has not been a normative tradition among traders (notwithstanding the fact that Muhaṇot Naiṇsī died by his own hand), and it significant that Vidal does not include traders among the castes that engage in the practice. It is true that Jainism, the religious tradition of many traders, puts a strong emphasis on ascetic self-mortification, including death by self-starvation. Such practices, however, are not culturally coded as suicidal, nor is their purpose to put moral pressure on others. Trader non-violence, I suggest, places the emphasis on non-harm as such, not on the redirection of harm.

33. For a brief but vivid portrait of Rājpūt values, see Carstairs 1961: esp. 107–15; also Hitchcock 1959.
34. The first nine days of the lunar months of Āśvin (September–October) and Caitra (March–April), a period considered sacred to the goddess.
35. As an example, see Lévi-Strauss 1963: 72–91.
36. This pattern of mutual interaction seems to exemplify a cultural process first identified and named by Gregory Bateson. Writing of the Iatmul people of New Guinea, Bateson described what he called 'schismogenesis', a process of differentiation of patterns of behaviour that arises from cumulative interaction between two individuals or groups of individuals (Bateson 1958: 175–97). It results from the formation of self-amplifying action-reaction feedback loops between two parties, driving them into even more extreme patterns of behaviour. If the behaviour patterns are identical and mutually stimulating, then the schismogenesis is 'symmetrical'. An example would be the escalation of aggressive displays between two mutually antagonistic parties. If, on the other hand, the differentiation occurs between behaviour patterns that are both different and mutually stimulating, then the schismogenesis is 'complementary'. Dominance and submission can fall into such a feedback loop. The opposition between Rājpūts and traders in Rajasthan exhibits the formal characteristics of complementary schismogenesis.
37. Susan Bayly writes that in British India in the latter part of the nineteenth century the 'interpenetrating worlds of commerce, statecraft and landed privilege were pulling apart', with the traders as the 'new winners' over the seigneurial groups (1999: 210). This trend was less a factor in pre-Independence Rajasthan, although it has now come true with a vengeance (a matter to which we return in the final chapter of this book).

Chapter Three

Sages and Warriors

Social theory comes in multiple flavours. The problem of why and how social things are as they are has presented itself to men and women everywhere, not just to academicians or professional intellectuals, and academic social theory is but one member of a very large family. Indeed, interpretations of society's mysteries are probably as varied as the ethnographic map itself. A society's workings can be imaged mechanistically, organically, spiritually, and surely in many other ways. This chapter introduces a type of social theory that explains social things *ritualistically*. Its explanatory principle is the metaphor of ritual sacrifice.[1]

We shall explore this way of looking at society in two stages. We begin by examining the ancient Vedic rite of sacrifice and its metaphoric social applications. We then turn to the myths of origin of two important Rajasthani communities: the Dāhimā Brāhmaṇs and the Fire Clan Rājpūts. These bodies of myth serve two purposes in this book's overall structure. First, they provide us with preliminary examples of how the sacrificial metaphor can be employed as a myth model for explaining the creation, and thus the character, of social groups. Second, thcy help us understand the nature of the relationship between Brāhmaṇs and Kṣatriyas (i.e., Rājpūts) in ritual–theoretical terms. This method of interpreting mythohistory will be extended to the traders in subsequent chapters.

Sacrifice

The rite of sacrifice (*yajña*) was the principal means by which the ancient Vedic people interacted with their gods. Its antiquity is unknowable, but in some form it certainly predates the coming of the Indo-Aryans to the Indian subcontinent. It emerges into historical visibility in the *Ṛg Veda*, a collection of hymns (the oldest possibly dating from as early as 1,500 C.E.) designed to be sung or chanted in conjunction with the rite's performance. The sacrifice was, or became, a ceremony for all seasons and occasions. It apparently took many different forms and was performed in a great variety of contexts. It could be a simple domestic rite performed by household members, but it was also a grand state ritual sponsored by chieftains and kings and presided over by large numbers of priests. It was in all respects the core ritual of Vedic society, the main ceremonial expression of the most important ideas and values of the culture and era.

It was also a ritual with important social implications. At one level, it brought human worshippers into a beneficial relationship with their gods; at another, it brought the human worshippers into important kinds of relationships with each other. In particular, it bound the Brāhmaṇ and Kṣatriya *varṇas* to each other in a relationship of mutual dependency. The priestly and Veda-knowing Brāhmaṇ was the actual performer of the sacrifice; he was its theorist and also the ceremonial specialist who knew how to manipulate the ritual technology involved in its proper execution. The warrior-ruler Kṣatriya was the archetypal sponsor of the rite (*yajamāna*); he provided both the means and occasion for major sacrifices, and also played an important role in their actual performance. The ideology of the rite, obviously a product of Brahmanical thought, portrayed the Brāhmaṇs and Kṣatriyas as tightly linked, with the Kṣatriyas seen as ultimately dependent (in the ritual sense) on the Brāhmaṇs, and in that respect subordinate to them. Together these two groups clearly constituted a 'ruling class' in relation to the rest of the social order (B. K. Smith 1994: 36–46). Although these ancient social structures no longer exist, the sacrificial complementarity between Brāhmaṇ and Kṣatriya retains symbolic significance to the present day.

The performance of the sacrifice was simple in its essentials, though often quite complex in actual practice.[2] The basic rite consisted of 'a coordinated and extended series of ritual actions, Vedic recitations, and offerings of different kinds' (F. M. Smith 1987: 9). A crucial feature of the rite was that it was designed for the propitiation of deities who were not physically embodied in permanent images in temples (i.e., unlike Sālāsar Bālājī). Instead of a permanent image, the rite's physical focus was a fire, which, in turn, served as the actual medium by which offerings were conveyed to the gods. Offerings included such substances and items as milk products (especially clarified butter), cakes made from rice or barley flour, *soma* (apparently a type of psychotropic beverage), and animal products. Living animal victims were another common type of offering, a fact that will acquire great significance later in this book.

The reasons for the performance of sacrifices were varied and layered. The actual beneficiary of any given rite was the *yajamāna*, the sponsor, and not the priestly performer. The gods responded to the sponsor's rite with boons, and the material benefits conferred by the rite were clearly an important motivation for its performance. But another purpose, one that might or might not have been part of the conscious motivation of sponsors, was embedded in the symbolism of the rite. As interpreted by the *Brāhmaṇa* texts,[3] the purpose of the rite was to perpetuate the created world by recapitulating its creation (ibid.: 13–14). The premise of this recapitulationalist theory of the sacrifice is the idea that the world was created by means of the sacrificial dismemberment of a primordial Cosmic Man, known as Prajāpati or Puruṣa, who was visualised as a creator-deity. This idea is most famously expressed in hymn 10.90 of the *Ṛg Veda*:

> When the gods spread the sacrifice with the Man [i.e., the Cosmic Man] as the offering, spring was the clarified butter, summer the fuel, autumn the oblation.
>
> They anointed the Man, the sacrifice born at the beginning, upon the sacred grass. With him the gods, Sādhyas, and sages sacrificed.
>
> From that sacrifice in which everything was offered, the melted fat was collected, and he made it into those beasts who live in the air, in the forest, and in villages.
>
> From that sacrifice in which everything was offered, the verses and chants were born, the metres were born from it, and from it the formulas were born.
>
> Horses were born from it, and those other animals that have two rows of teeth; cows were born from it, and from it goats and sheep were born. (verses 6–10).

In later verses, the hymn goes on to derive the social order (in a manner to be discussed shortly) and many other features of the cosmos from this same primordial sacrifice.

The recapitulationalist theory of the sacrifice assumes that, after the creation, the cosmos begins to run down, and it is humanity's responsibility to regenerate the creator deity and thereby reenergise the cosmos. By means of the sacrifice, the creator is reassembled in a microcosm, which, in turn, makes possible a reiteration of the primal dismemberment. In the process, the sacrificer achieves a state of immortality; he enters the realm of the gods, participates in creation, and then returns to the human world (F. M. Smith 1987: 20).

In post-Vedic times, the sacrifice diminished in importance, to ultimately become, in F. M. Smith's words, merely one element in 'the spectrum of orthopraxies' (ibid.: 2). The deities who were the focus of Vedic rituals had been shouldered aside by newer gods and goddesses, and the rigorous training required of Vedic priests and the expense of the ceremonies themselves had come to be seen as irksome. Moreover, other later and more specifically 'Hindu' ritual forms (such as the *homa*) were moving into the ritual niche previously occupied by the Vedic sacrifice. The temporary Vedic fire altar ultimately gave way to the Hindu temple and Vedic ritual forms were supplanted by the procedures and ideologies associated with image worship. Nonetheless, the Vedic sacrifice retained an honoured place in the later Hindu scheme of things, though usually in simplified form. It gave rise to internalised or interiorised versions of itself, and also became assimilated to the symbolisms of temple worship. As F. M. Smith puts it, 'One may compare the collective action of the emerging orthopraxies on the Vedic sacrifice to a great river, which gradually cuts away at a mountain, crumbling it into a hill, then a peninsula, and finally a series of disconnected islands' (ibid.: 7). Most important for us is the fact that certain social ideas embodied by the Vedic sacrifice remained very much part of the Indic scene; as this book will show, they are still very much alive today.

The Sacrifice and Social Origins

Readers will already have noted that there is an implicit connection between the sacrifice and the idea of creative power. The sacrifice reiterates the creation of the cosmos and mobilises the creative power responsible for cosmic beginnings. We must now look at this creative process more closely. The cosmogony in question is much more than astrophysics in a Vedic guise. By that I mean that its focus is not merely the physical cosmos; it also concerns the moral and social worlds, and indeed can be said to bring about a fusion of the physical, moral and social dimensions of reality.

We begin with the fact that Vedic thinkers believed the sacrifice to be the source of the social order. Of the creation of society, Hymn 10.90 of the *Ṛg Veda* has the following to say:

> When they divided the Man, into how many parts did they apportion him? What do they call his mouth, his two arms and thighs and feet?
>
> His mouth became the Brahmin; his arms were made into the Warrior; his thighs the People, and from his feet the Servants were born (verses 11–12).

We thus see that the primordial sacrifice gave rise to the four *varṇas*: Brāhmaṇs, Kṣatriyas, Vaiśyas ('the People') and Śūdras ('the Servants'). As idealised by the hymn, these classes form an integrated social system based on the division of labour between social classes. This functional complementation, in turn, rests on the foundation of essential differences between social classes, differences reflecting natural fissures that formed as part of the cosmic dismemberment from which the cosmos emanated at the very beginning of things. Furthermore, the homology between the social classes and the organic unity of the cosmic man's body supports the notion of an organic (and indeed cosmic) harmony between the social classes.

All this being so, it seems logical to suppose that, in a cultural milieu influenced by these ideas, there would exist a general affinity between the idea of the sacrifice and accounts of the origin of social groups other than the *varṇas*. And so there was and is. The sacrifice was (and remains today) the obvious metaphor for expressing the idea of creation of any sort, including the creation of social things.

Sacrifice and Social Inclusion: Dakṣa's Sacrifice

But there is one more point. The resonance between social differentiation and the idea of cosmic dismemberment suggests the possibility that the sacrifice can also stand as a general metaphor for social inclusion and exclusion. Given the implicit homology between the internal harmony of the social order and the unity of the Cosmic Man's body, the sacrifice emerges as an obvious trope for expressing the idea of belonging to the social order; to belong is to exist inside this cosmic entity's 'skin' and to live in harmony with other groups existing there. But if this is so, the sacrifice can also serve as a powerful metaphor for social outsiderhood.

These principles are nowhere better illustrated than in the famous Purāṇic myth of Śiva's exclusion from Dakṣa's sacrifice. Śiva belongs to the triad of pre-eminent Hindu gods—Brahmā, Viṣṇu and Śiva—known collectively as the *trimūrti*. In the cosmic economy, Brahmā creates the world, Viṣṇu presides over its welfare, and Śiva destroys it at the end of each cosmic cycle. Śiva is a complex figure whose chief attributes include asceticism and vast (and potentially destructive or creative) power. Dakṣa, the son of creator-deity Brahmā, is the father of Satī, who is Śiva's wife. The story of his sacrifice (abstracted here from Stella Kramrisch's retelling (1981: 301–30),[4] goes as follows:

> Satī was born in the *tretā yuga*,[5] and was the first of sixty daughters of Dakṣa. But in fact she was the Great Goddess herself, who had taken human shape in order to become Śiva's spouse. Brahmā had connived at this, for unless Śiva could be enticed to marry the goddess, the creation of the cosmos (Brahmā's special function) would not be possible. Satī had longed for Śiva from her childhood days, and, as time passed, she engaged in ever more severe austerities with the aim of uniting with him somehow. In the end, she achieved her goal, for, though reluctant, the great ascetic Śiva agreed to marry her for the sake of his devotees.
>
> One day, Satī and Śiva were attending a sacrifice at Prayāg (Allahabad). When Dakṣa arrived, Śiva did not arise and bow to him. The enraged Dakṣa, who had little love for Śiva in any case, cursed the great god to be deprived of his share of the sacrificial offerings. Actually, this curse merely ratified the fact that Śiva had already been excluded from the sacrifice by the other gods; they had refused to interdine with Śiva, and had also deprived him of a share in any sacrifice. In revenge for this, Nandin—Śiva's chief henchman, who takes the form of a bull—cursed Dakṣa to lead a dissolute and worldly life, and to bear the face of a goat (which is, as Kramrisch points out, the most common victim of blood sacrifice).
>
> Now, a time came when Dakṣa himself held a great sacrifice to which he invited all the gods and goddesses, with one exception. This exception was his son-in-law, Śiva. He excluded Śiva partly because of his general dislike for him, but also because Śiva was an impure, fantastic, horrific,

skull-carrying and lunatic-like figure who wandered about in cremation grounds in the company of ghosts and goblins. When Satī heard about the sacrifice, she asked Śiva to accompany her to it, but he explained that he had not been invited, and so she went alone. When she saw that no portion had been set aside for Śiva, she was totally overcome by rage. To make matters worse, Dakṣa then insulted her by mocking Śiva's strange and unorthodox manner of life. He also informed her that he had agreed to her marriage with Śiva only because Brahmā had importuned him to do so. As it happens, at that time the goddess had agreed to be born as Satī in order to induce Śiva to take a spouse, and she had told Dakṣa that, if he ever insulted her, she would leave her body. That dire moment had at last arrived, and she made good on her pledge by burning up her body by means of her inner yogic fire.

When news of her death reached Śiva, he was mad with grief and fury. He went to the site of the sacrifice and destroyed it, and afterwards cursed Dakṣa to have the head of a goat (an apparent repeat) (In another version he cursed Dakṣa to be born as a Kṣatriya and to sire a son on his own daughter). He then smeared his body with Satī's ashes. Or (in another and very famous version), he took her body (in this version unburned) and danced across the heavens. At the behest of the other gods, Viṣṇu contrived to stop the dance by cutting Satī's body into pieces with his discus. Wherever her body parts fell, there arose a *linga* (the phallic form in which Śiva is usually worshipped) (More usually, the parts are said to have fallen at the locations of the fifty-two *śakti pīthas*, 'places of power' sacred to the goddess).

From Śiva's anger (in yet another variant) was born a demon named Vīrabhadra. To him Śiva assigned the task of destroying Dakṣa's sacrifice as well as Dakṣa himself and his kin. With a vast retinue of demonesses, demons, ghosts, and other ferocious beings, Vīrabhadra attacked Dakṣa and the gods, finally forcing the wounded and defeated gods to flee. The sacrifice itself took flight from the carnage in the form of an antelope, but was caught and beheaded by Vīrabhadra. Vīrabhadra tore off Dakṣa's head and threw it into the firepit as a type of final offering.[6] Or (in yet other versions of the same tale), Śiva himself—not Vīrabhadra—goes on the rampage.

On the advice of Brahmā, the gods, together with Brahmā himself, went to Śiva to seek forgiveness. They asked him to restore both Dakṣa and his uncompleted sacrifice, and also to heal the injuries he had inflicted on them. In return, the gods promised that thenceforth they would allow Śiva a share in the sacrifice. Śiva accompanied this entire group to the site of the sacrifice. There the gods attached the head of a goat to Dakṣa's torso,

> and, at a glance from Śiva, Dakṣa revived. Dakṣa then completed his sacrifice, and gave to Śiva his proper share.

Śiva is notorious as the ultimate outsider, a world-renouncing ascetic who consorts with ghosts and inhabits mountain caves and other marginal places. The narrative we have just seen expresses the idea of Śiva's outsider status in two idioms. We are told, first, that the other gods refuse to have commensal relations with Śiva. Commensality is a universal expression of social relatedness, and this is notably true in the South Asian world, where the presence or absence of commensal exchanges is a fundamental expression of group relations and social hierarchy. But second, our narrative informs us—nearly in the same breath of the gods' refusal to dine with Śiva—that the gods denied Śiva his rightful share of the sacrifice. This is really the same thing as a denial of commensal relationships; here, however, the denial is placed in a special context, that of the sacrifice. Their shared status of sacrifice-receivers and co-consumers of sacrificial offerings defines the community of gods as a community. To exclude from the sacrifice is thus to exclude from the society of the gods. But in the end, as we see, Śiva's furious retaliation gains him a share of the rite, thus including him in the divine community.

Sacrifice as Myth Model

The materials we have seen thus far place before us two themes to which the rite of sacrifice is central. One is a linkage between the sacrifice and notions of creation and creative power. The sacrifice creates things, and this includes social things. The performance of the rite recreates both the cosmos and the social order, both arising from the dismemberment of the paradigmatic Cosmic Man. The second theme, closely associated with the first, is the notion that the rite of sacrifice, as a ritual structure, resonates deeply with the structure of the social order. The rite integrates unlike groups into a single harmonious society on the analogy of the cofunctioning body parts of the Cosmic Man. And, by including the social order within itself, the sacrifice places clear boundaries around society. To be in society is to be included within the rite; to be excluded from the rite is social exile.

Given these connections between the sacrifice and the creation and ordering of social groups, the sacrifice has the potential to be a 'myth model', in Gananath Obeyesekere's (1992) sense of this term, for mythology having to do with the origin and character of social groups. This is a concept that will be with us for the remainder of this book. As noted in Chapter One, Obeyesekere's idea is that a master-myth, informed by a coherent cluster of culturally important ideas, can serve as a pattern, a 'myth model', for other myths. This is what we find in the relationship between the sacrifice and Rajasthani myths of origin. The sacrifice is a powerful theme in these narratives, and the image of the sacrifice and its creative power have become a paradigm for how they depict the creation of social groups. The myths utilise the sacrifice both as a means of explaining how the groups in question came into existence and why they occupy the social niches they do. But as this book will show, the manner in which the myths reflect the sacrificial paradigm varies greatly, and this has much to do with the character of the groups whose origin is being explained.

We now turn to the mythohistories of two actual social groups in Rajasthan. These will serve as preliminary glimpses of how the sacrifice can function as a myth model in origin myths and will also introduce us to two important social categories. We begin with a Brāhmaṇ caste and then move to a famous Rājpūt clan.

Domesticated Sages: the Dāhimās' Tale

The term Dāhimā refers to a specific kind of Brāhmaṇ. As we have seen, the Brāhmaṇ *varṇa* is not an actual group; rather, it is an all-India *category* to which many castes are assigned or assign themselves. A 'Brāhmaṇ caste' may be defined as a caste that claims Brāhmaṇ *varṇa* status and whose claim is acknowledged as valid by others. Every region possesses its own array of castes that are Brāhmaṇs in this sense. The Dāhimās are such a Brāhmaṇ caste prominent in Rajasthan; here they are well known, but in other regions of India they are unknown. We have already met the Dāhimās in the preceding chapter. Readers will recall that the priests of Sālāsār Bālājī temple belong to a lineage of one of the constituent clans of this caste. Although most people refer to the caste as the Dāhimā or Dāymā Brāhmaṇs, the name currently favoured by many among the caste's elite is Dādhīc Brāhmaṇs. This word derives from the name of the caste's eponymous ancestor, a sage by the name of Dadhīci (whom we shall meet shortly).

The Dāhimās are part of a cluster of Brāhmaṇ castes in Rajasthan called the *chah nyāt*, which means the 'six castes'.[7] The 1891 *Marwar Census Report* includes a small mythohistory (Singh 1997: 188) that attributes the origin of the concept of the six castes to Maharaja Jai Singh II, founder of Jaipur. The narrative tells of how the Maharaja had invited Brāhmaṇs from various localities within the region to come to a great *aśvamedh* sacrifice.[8] The Brāhmaṇ castes that came, however, refused to dine together—a reflection of their social distance from each other and also the desire of each to claim higher status than the others. This was a great inconvenience, but the Maharaja was finally able to get six Brāhmaṇ castes from his own kingdom to interdine (though not to intermarry), and they became known as the 'six castes'. The original official list (ibid.) included the Gauṛ, Sārasvat, Dāhimā, Pārīk, Gūjar Gauṛ, and Khaṇḍelvāl Brāhmaṇs.

This small narrative provides us with a preliminary example of how origin narratives utilise the sacrificial theme. The story concerns the creation of a new grouping of castes, and—as we see—the creation occurs as a product or byproduct of participation in a particular rite of sacrifice. This link between the creation of new social entities and the rite of sacrifice will reappear constantly in what follows in this and subsequent chapters. We shall see that whenever a new group comes into existence, the sacrifice is almost always involved in one way or another.

In the past, the Dāhimā caste was concentrated in what is now Nagaur District in the hinterland of the temple that houses their caste deity.[9] This deity is a goddess named Dadhimatī, and her temple is located between the villages of Goṭh and Mānglod, about 38 km to the east (slightly north of east) of the town of Nagaur (see Figure 3.1).[10]

The caste has probably been settled in this area for many centuries. An inscription has been discovered at the Dadhimatī temple that bears the date of G.S. 289 (608 C.E.) and that apparently mentions the Dāhimā Brāhmaṇs (as 'Dadhya' Brāhmaṇs; see Asopa 1988). Over the last century, however, a significant proportion of the caste's membership has migrated to various Rajasthani cities and beyond, and nowadays there are hardly any Dāhimās living in the immediate vicinity of the temple. The Dāhimās are a well-educated community, and have become regionally prominent in such professions as education, law and journalism, as well as government service.

Figure 3.1
The Dadhimatī temple.

We now have a look at the Dāhimā origin myth and the context in which it has assumed its present form.

The *Purāṇa*

In the past, and to a small extent even now, professional genealogists known as Rāvs transmitted the Dāhimas' origin myths. But although the

Dāhimās' genealogists still exist today, their profession has fallen into a state of advanced decay (as is the case with the region's caste genealogists generally). As a result, the most important medium for the transmission of the caste's origin narrative these days consists of the various publications of the caste's national association (the Akhil Bhāratvarṣīya Dāhimā [Dādhīc] Brāhmaṇ Mahāsabhā).

There were probably many variants of the Dāhimā Brāhmaṇ origin story in circulation in the days when traditional genealogists flourished. Now, however, the tale has been standardised in a version that first appeared in the form of a Sanskrit composition called *Śrī Dadhimathī Purāṇam* (hereafter referred to as the *Purāṇa*). This text is an example of what is often called a 'caste *purāṇa*', a purportedly ancient composition that presents an account of the origin and history of a particular caste. It is difficult to say much about how or under what circumstances it was composed. However, its content and organisation suggest that it was created by uniting elements of earlier versions of the caste's origin narrative, presumably as told by the genealogists, with a goodly amount of Puranic boilerplate lifted from other Sanskrit texts. It was probably assembled in the late nineteenth century, although this cannot be known for sure. It was first published in book form early in the twentieth century in the town of Ratlam (in present-day M.P.), and then republished with a Hindi translation in Jaipur in 1981.[11] Though not much read by ordinary members of the caste (and no longer easily available), the *Purāṇa* has been extraordinarily influential. It is one of the principal sources for the abridged versions of the caste's origin narrative that appear from time to time in *Dadhimatī*, the official magazine of the caste's national association, and in numerous pamphlets and booklets. These, in turn, appear to be the main sources for oral versions of the caste's origin myth that can be elicited from most Dāhimās.

What follows is a summary of the *Purāṇa* version of the origin of the Dāhimā Brāhmaṇ caste (translated from the Hindi text):

> From a lotus springing from sleeping Viṣṇu's navel was born Brahmā, and Brahmā produced a son named Atharvā, who became a great sage. Atharvā married a woman named Śānti, and they had a son and a daughter. Their daughter was a goddess named Dadhimatī who later achieved fame by destroying Vikaṭāsur, a ferocious demon. Their son was a great sage named Dadhīci.

Now, Dadhīci was famous for his ascetic practices, so much so that, when a demon named Vṛtāsur threatened the gods, Viṣṇu himself advised them to go to Dadhīci and ask for his body (meaning his bones), which was ripe with the influence of his knowledge, vows and austerities (*vidya, vrat, tap*). From his bones, Viśvakarma, the artisan of the gods, would be able to fashion a powerful weapon (a *vajra*) to be used to defeat the demon. When the gods were on their way to Dadhīci's hermitage to get the bones, Dadhīci's ascetic powers enabled him to know they were coming and what their request would be. Wishing to leave his wife with a son, the sage devised an unusual strategy to give her one. He first deposited some semen in a cloth that he then gave to her for washing. She took it to the Ganges, and there became pregnant while in the water with it. In the meantime, the gods had come and made their request, and Dadhīci had given his life and his bones for the cause.

His wife learned of this only after her return from the banks of the Ganges. When she was about to become a *satī*, Brahmā had to intervene and tell her of the son she carried. But the vow to become a *satī* should not be broken, and so in order to keep it she cut out her womb and entrusted it to Brahmā. Brahmā placed it in the custody of a pipal tree, and from eating the fruit of this tree, Dadhīci's son became known as Pipplād. In time, Pipplād became a great sage in his own right and the father of twelve sage-sons; in time, they also produced twelve sons each, who became sages of great renown.[12]

In those days, there was a Sun-Clan king named Māndhātā.[13] In order to conquer the three worlds, Māndhātā sponsored a great sacrifice, and, on the recommendation of the famous sage Vaśiṣṭh, he called upon Pipplād's 144 grandsons to be the rite's officiants, making them into *ācāryas*. It was a non-violent (i.e., vegetarian) sacrifice, directed at Dadhimatī, and it occurred at what is now the site of the Dadhimatī temple. Pleased by the sacrifice, the goddess herself emerged from the sacrificial firepit (*kuṇḍ*). The 144 priests asked her to be their clan goddess (*kul devī*; in this case the goddess of all the constituent clans of the caste, and thus a 'caste goddess') and to fulfill the king's desires for conquest. These things she agreed to do. She ordered that her sacrifices never involve the killing of animals (as this one had not), and described various benefits that would result from bathing in the firepit. She then stepped into the pit and vanished. Although (as the text makes clear) the 144 officiating sages were not of the sort to make material demands, they nonetheless accepted payment (*dakṣiṇā*) from the king in the form of a village and a bride for each of them. The text then describes how Māndhātā prospered as a result of his worship of the goddess. It closes with a description of her rites of worship together with instructions for their performance.

Figure 3.2
The *kuṇḍ* at the Dadhimatī temple.

The *Purāṇa* says nothing about the building of the temple itself. Rather, the physical focus of the tale (insofar as it relates to the temple) is the sacrificial pit, which Dāhimā Brāhmaṇs believe to have become the bathing *kuṇḍ* adjacent to the temple today (see Figure 3.2); Dadhimatī herself, they say, filled it with power-charged water. As for the building of the temple, a widely known and constantly retold legend maintains that the goddess's image—and in some tellings the temple itself—emerged from the earth (a theme we shall encounter again). The goddess had warned a herdsman that there would be a great commotion when she came out from the ground and that he should not be afraid. But when the moment came, he forgot the warning and fled from the spot (or, in another telling, shouted 'stop mother!' in order to recall his fleeing cows). As a result, only the goddess's skull (some say knee) had enough time to appear, which explains the dome-shaped, aniconic image that is the temple's principal object of worship. Some say that the temple simply emerged from the ground at this time. According to another telling, Māndhātā actually built the temple at the goddess's direction, but it was hidden until she emerged from the earth (Jośī n.d.: 4).

Sacrifice and the Domestication of Sages

Above all else, this text is about the establishment of a line and subsidiary lines of descent. The text shows how the Dāhimā caste consists of clans descended from the 144 sons of the 12 sons of Pipplād.[14] These clans are the basic units of exogamy among the Dāhimā Brāhmaṇs. Pipplād's father was the great sage Dadhīci, who was descended, through Atharvā, from the creator-deity Brahmā. All Dāhimā Brāhmaṇs are thus shown to be agnatically related and to share a distinguished Brāhmaṇ pedigree. The text attaches the goddess Dadhimatī to the genealogy as Dadhīci's sister, thus providing the scaffolding for a perpetual relationship between her and Dadhīci's progeny. The Dadhimatī temple registers this relationship by including an image of Dadhīci in a subsidiary shrine (see Figure 3.3).

The assertion of common patrilineal descent for the Dāhimā Brāhmaṇs gives rise to the obvious question of how caste endogamy, a basic marriage rule, is possible. If there is a common agnatic ancestor for the whole caste, then, on the model of the clans, the caste should be exogamous.[15] I discussed this issue with various members of the caste. Most respondents immediately recognised the point of my query, but seemed to believe that the relationship is simply too distant to matter. One acquaintance, a Dāhimā journalist, responded that King Māndhātā gave the 12 sages (I think he meant the 144 sages) Kṣatriya wives, but it is not clear how this would make any difference because the progeny of the sages would still be agnatic kin.[16] This is clearly not a matter to which Dāhimā Brāhmaṇs give much if any thought. The dilemma is probably intractable in any case; if you wish to trace your descent as a caste to one individual, then you must avert your eyes from the issue of incest. So important, it seems, is the claim of common descent from Dadhīci that it trumps everything else, including this problem.

But then having established a line of descent for the Dāhimās, the narrative has an additional problem to solve—that of how, on the foundation of such a pedigree, to account plausibly for the creation of an actual specific caste. This echoes the case of Mohandās described in the last chapter. In that instance, the issue was the conversion of a celibate Brāhmaṇ devotee/sage's charisma into a form that could be transmitted by patrilineal descent. In this case, the issue is how Brāhmaṇhood, which is indeed transmitted by descent, can be affixed within a niche

Figure 3.3
The image of Dadhīci at the Dadhimatī temple.

in a functioning social system, for although Dadhīci's progeny are indisputably Brāhmaṇs, they are not yet a Brāhmaṇ caste. Their position is actually liminal, somewhere on the boundary of the social order, as suggested by the text's description of them as hermit sage/priests, living in the 'deep forest' (*Purāṇa*, 22: 14). Such sages can have wives, but are never quite householders.[17] The ambiguity of their status is illustrated by Dadhīci's relationship with his wife. It is true he is married, but as a renouncer he cannot physically and socially reproduce himself in the normal way; thus, the semen on the cloth and all the rest.[18] There is a profound dissonance between the world-renouncing, forest-dwelling manner of life of sages and the requirements of fully socialised domesticity.

The narrative visualises this transformation as a *ritual* transformation, and the means by which it is accomplished is the *sacrifice*—in particular, Māndhātā's sacrifice to the goddess Dadhimatī. When Pipplād's grandsons participate in the sacrifice they enter the social order for the first time; in effect, for them the sacrifice is a classic 'rite of incorporation' (van Gennep 1960). They participate by taking the paradigmatic role of Brāhmaṇ priests serving a Kṣatriya patron, and his payment to them, taking the form of wives and land, cements the deal; now they are family men with property. The most significant gift is not the wives; after all, sages do have wives, although the nature of sages' sexuality is always an issue. More crucial is Māndhātā's gift of land, for this not only cements the Brāhmaṇs to the territorial order of the state, but also shifts the focus of their identity from common Brāhmaṇ descent, as such, to that of a bundle of related but distinct clans. The text's suggestion that the Brāhmaṇs are domesticated by means of grants of land is consonant with the fact that actually existing clans of the caste are identified with the villages from which most of them take their names.

The narrative thus accounts for three levels of social segmentation: Brāhmaṇhood in the widest sense, the Dāhimā Brāhmaṇ caste, and the caste's constituent clans. These segmentations are differentiated in relation to a genealogical sequence. Brāhmaṇhood itself takes the lineage back to Atharvā and the creator-deity Brahmā. The text implies that Atharvā is one of the mind-born sons of Brahmā, and Brāhmaṇ tradition proclaims these sage-sons to have been the progenitors of various Brāhmaṇ clans (known as *gotras*). The text then defines the Dāhimās as a particular *kind* of Brāhmaṇs whose identity is defined by common descent from the sage Dadhīci, their own apical ancestor. Finally, the text distinguishes the constituent clans of the Dāhimā caste, called *śākhās* (branches), whose apical ancestors are Dadhīci's grandsons. The group's differentiation into intermarrying descent groups completes the origin of the caste as such. It is precisely at this moment that the goddess Dadhimatī and her temple (or at least the sacrificial pit) come into the picture as embodiments (one metaphysical, the other physical) of the social identity of the Dāhimā Brāhmaṇs.

As envisioned by the narrative, the production of the clans from Dadhīci was a three-step process: first one (Pipplād), then 12, and then 144.[19] Why the differentiation occurred in this way is not entirely clear, but it seems plausible that Pipplād was inserted in the sequence in order to avoid having to explain how superascetic Dadhīci could have multiple offspring. We have seen that he had enough problems producing one. The subsequent squaring of 12 represents the inflationary epoch of the tale; one becomes many in a mere (social) instant, allowing the caste to become completely formed within a scant five generations of the creation of the world.

It should be noted that, apart from the clans, the Dāhimā Brāhmaṇ caste is also divided into 12 supposedly exogamous units called *gotras* that trace descent from Pipplād's 12 sage-sons. The pattern for this is the ancient and all-India Brahmanical tradition of tracing lineages (called *gotras*) to founder sages, for which the seven sages (listed variously) are the prototypes (see Mitchiner 1982).[20] In the Dāhimā case, however, this is a pseudo-segmentation, for although the *gotras* are listed in the caste's literature and are known to some respondents, they do not actually regulate marriage or anything else. I suspect, in fact, that most Dāhimās do not clearly understand the difference between the *gotras* and the actual functioning clans (the *śākhās*). Some say the *gotras* were once exogamous but have lately fallen into disuse, but I know of no evidence to support this contention. I think they were tacked on to an already established system of clans in an effort to make the entire system seem more Brahmanical.[21]

Finally, there is yet another essential element in the narrative, and that is the role of the goddess Dadhimatī. As readers will see, her part in the creation of the Dāhimā Brāhmaṇs is merely one specific example of another widespread myth model, one analytically separate from the sacrificial model but often grafted to it in caste origin myths. The paradigm is one in which goddesses provide crucial assistance at the birth of descent groups—lineages, clans, and in this case an entire caste—with which they then maintain permanent protective ties.[22] Henceforth, we shall refer to this as the 'ancestral goddess' myth model. In the Dāhimā case, we see that the goddess comes to the aid of the caste's ancestors-to-be by guaranteeing the efficacy of Māndhātā's sacrifice; this, in turn, produces the gifts with their consequences. She then binds herself to the group (and the group to her) by a pledge of perpetual protection.[23] When Dāhimā Brāhmaṇs come to the Dadhimatī temple, as they do in large numbers during the spring *navratrī* period, they are reconnecting themselves to these events and thus reactivating the goddess's ancient pledge.

Rājpūts: Birth By Fire

At the mythohistorical moment when the Dāhimā Brāhmaṇ caste comes into existence, the goddess Dadhimatī insists that sacrifices offered to her always be non-violent. Her demand is quite significant. It must be remembered that not all sacrifices are non-violent. As we know, in the regional culture that provides the myth's context, kings like Māndhātā customarily offered buffalo sacrifices to warrior goddesses, and Dadhimatī, a killer of demons, is very much in the mould of warrior goddesses. However, her human constituency does not consist of Rājpūt warrior-kings, but rather a particular caste of Brāhmaṇs. As it happens, the Brāhmaṇs themselves are not completely innocent of associations with blood sacrifice, or at least (as we shall see) this is the Jains' view of the matter. But in present-day Rajasthan, the caste cultures of the Brāhmaṇs are vegetarian. Thus, a warrior goddess who presides over the destiny and welfare of the Dāhimā Brāhmaṇs must herself be a vegetarian. Very different are the clan and lineage goddesses of the Rājpūts and the Rājpūts' relationship to the sacrifice, as we shall see shortly.

But before turning to Rājpūt origin myths, we need to note a few details concerning their clan and lineage structure. The Rājpūt social universe is divided into three great patrilineal divisions often called 'clans': the Sun Clan (*sūryavaṃś*), the Moon Clan (*candravaṃś*), and the Fire Clan (*agnivaṃś*).[24] The Sun Clan claims descent from the sun; the sun's sons included Manu, the first man, and the eldest of his sons was Ikṣvākū, who was the apical ancestor of the Sun Clan. The deity Rāmacandra (whose exploits are recounted in the *Rāmāyaṇa*) was putatively born into this clan. The Moon Clan traces its descent ultimately to Atri, a sage who was a son of creator-deity Brahmā. Atri's eldest son was Soma, the moon; his son, in turn, was Budha (Mercury, not to be confused with the Buddha), who married Ilā, and from this union the Moon line originated. The principal characters of the epic *Mahābhārata*—the Pāṇdavas, Kauravas and Kṛṣṇa—belonged to the Moon Clan. The special circumstances of the Fire Clan's origin place it in a class by itself, as we shall see. These great clans are not exogamous.

The clans, in turn, are segmented into lineages (also often called 'clans' in English). These groups usually trace their descent to some illustrious hero and are the basic units of exogamy among the Rājpūts. As an example, the ruling lines of Jodhpur and Bikaner belong to the Rāṭhaur lineage, which in turn allegedly belongs to the ancient Sun Clan. Another famous line belonging to the Sun Clan is the Kachvāhā lineage, to which the ruling family of Jaipur belongs. The Bhāṭī lineage, which is that of the ruling family of Jaisalmer, belongs to the Moon Clan, and claims descent from the deity Kṛṣṇa. Four great lineages are included within the Fire Clan: the Cauhāns, Parmārs, Parihārs, and Solankis. All of these lineages are, in their turn, further subdivided into lesser lineages and their offshoots.

We now look at the mythohistory of the Fire Clan Rājpūts. In contrast to the story of the origin of the Dāhimā Brāhmaṇs, their origin myth possesses true regional importance. With the exception of the Dāhimā Brāhmaṇs themselves, few Rajasthanis have any real interest in how the Dāhimās came to be a caste, and the same is true of the origin myths of the other castes considered in this book. But because of their importance as a regional elite, the Rājpūts' origin narratives can be considered part of a true Rajasthani cultural patrimony. The story of the Fire Clan's origin is well known in the region and beyond. Many variants of the story exist. In what follows, I endeavour to give the reader a gist of the core story.

Paraśurām

In order to make sense of the Fire Clan origin narrative, readers must first know something about yet another story that serves as its widest narrative frame. This is the myth of the hero-deity Paraśurām. The story is actually a famous Puranic myth of all-India importance, and Paraśurām is generally regarded as the sixth of the 10 *avatāras* of the god Viṣṇu.[25] The link between Paraśurām and the Fire Clan origin narrative thus brings a subcontinental tradition into a regional social landscape.

Paraśurām was the youngest son of a great sage named Jamadagni and his wife, Reṇukā. Though in fact a form of Viṣṇu, Paraśurām was a devotee of Śiva. Śiva trained him in the use of weapons and also presented him with the gift of a great battle-axe. From this incident he got his name, which means 'Ram-with-the-axe'. As told in the *Viṣṇu Purāṇa* (Book 4, Chapter 7, here drawn from Wilson 1868: 16–29), his story begins with a strange aberration of conception:

> It seems there was once a prince called Gādhi, an incarnation of Indra, whose daughter was named Satyavatī. She married a Brāhmaṇ sage named Ṛcīka. Desiring a son, Ṛcīka concocted a special mixture of grains and other things for Satyavatī to consume. At Satyavatī's request, he also prepared a similar mixture for her mother. After Ṛcīka departed, the mother persuaded Satyavatī to trade mixtures. Satyavatī's mixture was designed to produce a Brāhmaṇ, whereas the mother's was designed to produce a world-conquering warrior, and the mother wanted Satyavatī to have the superior son. Upon discovering the switch, the furious Ṛcīka explained to Satyavatī that, because of the trade, her mother would give birth to a pious Brāhmaṇ, and her own son would be a warrior and a killer. Satyavatī then pleaded with him to delay the consequence of her disobedience for one generation. He agreed. Her son was the famous sage Jamadagni, and her mother gave birth to Viśvamitra. Jamadagni married a woman named Reṇukā, and they were the parents of Paraśurām.

Thus far our narrative is a story about *varṇa*, with a sharp focus on the contrast between the fundamental characters of Brāhmaṇs and Kṣatriyas. Because of the switch of potions, Paraśurām is an amalgam of both *varṇas*, a Kṣatriya-like Brāhmaṇ. The circumstances of his conception resulted in a highly significant career diversion. Had Satyavati's mother received the right potion, Paraśurām might have been a world-conquering king.[26] Instead, as we shall see, he becomes a world-conquering sage. The theme of the sage who is a king-who-might-have-been is also a recurrent one in Jainism, though with a very different slant (Babb 1996). Jain myth represents the Tīrthaṅkars as Kṣatriyas who might have become universal emperors had they not chosen the path of spiritual victory instead. In contrast, Paraśurām becomes a world-conquering sage who actually conquers the world. But then, in a sage-like manner, he relinquishes his conquest.

The *Mahābhārata* (Vana Parva: 116.1–117.15) recounts the most famous incidents of his life as follows (summarised here from van Buitenen 1975: 445–47):

> Paraśurām (here 'Rāma') was the fifth but foremost of Jamadagni and Reṇukā's five sons. One day, while all five sons were away from the hermitage gathering fruit, Reṇukā went to a stream to bathe. On her way, she

spied a prince named Citraratha playing in the water with his wives, and as a result she felt desire. Jamadagni, who easily discovered what had happened, ordered his sons, one after the other, to kill her. Paraśurām alone was willing to obey, and he beheaded his mother with his axe. Later, at Paraśurām's behest, Jamadagni restored her to life, forgave the disobedient brothers, and released Paraśurām from the sin of the crime and conferred upon him invincibility in battle.

Now it so happens that, on another day when the sage's sons were absent, King Kārtavīrya ('king of the shorelands') visited the hermitage. Although Reṇukā welcomed him properly, he ransacked the place, smashed down the trees, and made off with the calf of the sacrificial cow. When Paraśurām returned and discovered these outrages, he engaged Kārtavīrya in battle and killed him. In revenge, 'Arjuna's heirs' (Kārtavīrya's sons) attacked Jamadagni when Paraśurām was again away. Jamadagni did not defend himself, and died even as he was calling out for Paraśurām's assistance. While performing his father's last rites, the valiant Paraśurām vowed to avenge his father's death by eradicating the world's 'barons' (Kṣatriyas). In the end, he emptied the earth of them twenty-one times over. Afterwards, he offered a great sacrifice to Indra, and bestowed the earth on the priests. He also made a gift of a golden altar, 'ten fathoms long and nine high,' to the sage Kaśyap. With Kaśyap's consent, the altar was divided into shares among the Brāhmaṇs, who thereby became known as the 'Khāṇḍavā-goers' (share-takers?). He then bestowed the earth on Kaśyap (How this fits with his previous bestowal of the earth on the priests is not clear). Later Paraśurām retired to Mount Mahendra (?) or (the translated text is not clear), having made homage to the Brāhmaṇs, spent a night on the mountain 'and then departed toward the south.'

The Origin of the Fire Clan

The origin narrative of the Fire Clan Rājpūts (in most of its variants) uses this tale as its point of departure. The myth exists in many versions, but uniting most or all of them continues to be the theme of the relationship between Brāhmaṇs and Kṣatriyas.[27] The Rājpūt narratives, however, reverse the values of the Puranic Paraśurām story: far from being the Brāhmaṇs' enemies, the Kṣatriyas now emerge as the protectors of the Brāhmaṇs and the ritual–social order over which they preside. At the crux of the matter is the rite of sacrifice. The point of the narratives is that in the absence of Kṣatriyas, the sacrifice is in danger along with all that it represents.

In his famous *Annals and Antiquities of Rajasthan* (1990; orig. 1829), James Tod presents two versions of the Fire Clan myth, and we begin with these. The question of Tod's sources is somewhat ambiguous, but I think we can safely follow Hiltebeitel in his presumption that Tod's materials reflect authentic local traditions (1999: 452).[28] Version one (summarised from Tod 1990, Vol. 1: 112–13) assumes, but does not actually mention, the story of Paraśurām. The story begins with the fix in which the Brāhmaṇs found themselves in the absence of Kṣatriyas.[29]

> It seems that the Brāhmaṇs were passing their time in the practice of devotion and austerities on Mount Abu. The demons, however, 'raised storms which darkened the air and filled it with clouds of sand, showering ordure, blood, bones and flesh, with every impurity on their rites,' thus extinguishing the sacrificial fire. The sages then reignited the sacrificial blaze and prayed to Mahādev (Śiva) for aid. In response, a figure came striding forth from the fire. He was, however, unwarriorlike, and because of this, he was made into a guardian of the gate (pṛthivī-dvāra), from which was derived the lineage name of his descendants: Pratihār [Parihār]. The second to emerge from the fire was named Cālukya, and he became the progenitor of the Cālukya [Solankī] lineage. The third was Pramār, ancestor of the Pramārs [Parmārs]. These mighty warriors battled the demons, but without success. Then, in response to the prayers and incantations of the sage Vaśiṣṭh (a famous sage whom we have met already and shall meet again), a ferocious warrior, 'lofty in stature, of elevated front, hair like jet, eyes rolling, breast expanded … a bow in one hand and a brand in the other …' emerged from the firepit. Because he was '"quadriform" (Caturanga),' he acquired the name Cauhān, and he was the progenitor of the Cauhān lineage. At Vaśiṣṭh's behest, he attacked the demons. He was aided by the goddess Śakti, who arrived on her lion mount with her trident in hand. She blessed the great warrior, and promised always to hear his prayers in the form of Āśāpūrṇā ('Full of Hope', the Cauhāns' clan goddess). Cauhān thereupon defeated the demons, slaying their leaders and sending the rest of them fleeing in confusion.

Tod's second version (ibid.: Vol. 3: 1441–44), less specifically focussed on the Cauhāns than the first, begins specifically in the aftermath of Paraśurām's rampage:

> After the slaughter of the Kṣatriyas, the Brāhmaṇs held dominion over the earth. 'But,' as the text puts it, 'as the chief weapon of the Brāhmaṇ is his curse or blessing, great disorders soon ensued from the want of the strong arm. Ignorance and infidelity spread over the land; the sacred books were

trampled under foot, and mankind had no refuge from the monstrous brood (of demons).' The sage Viśvāmitra thereupon resolved to recreate the Kṣatriyas, and decided to do so on the summit of Mount Abu where sages and mendicants were congregated. They, in turn, had already taken their complaints about the situation to Viṣṇu. He had instructed them to recreate the Kṣatriyas, after which they had returned to Abu together with all of the deities. They prepared a 'fire fountain,' and Indra, Brahmā, Rudra (Śiva), and Viṣṇu, each in succession, tossed a small image (*putlī*, 'doll') into the fire. As each image went into the flames, a warrior emerged: first Pramār, then Cālukya (Solankī), then Parīhar, and finally Cauhān.[30] These warriors fought the demons fiercely, but wherever the blood of the demons fell, new demons sprang into existence. Then four goddesses ['tutelary divinities, attendant on each newly-created race'] drank the blood and victory was achieved.

To these two versions of the Fire Clan origin myth, I would like to add one more. This is a variant I encountered in a book about the Māheśvari caste (Darak 1923: 4). The book, which will be cited extensively in the next chapter, was authored by a Māheśvarī named Śivkaraṇ Rāmratan Darak and first published in the late nineteenth century. Though mainly concerned with the Māheśvarīs, Darakjī (as his name is usually given in Māheśvarī sources) also reports valuable material on castes other than the Māheśvaris, and what follows summarises his version of the Fire Clan origin narrative. In this variant, Paraśurām and the demons do not appear at all. Their functional niche in the tale is occupied by non-Brahmanical religious traditions.

It seems that a time came when all of the Kṣatriyas gave up their faith in the *Śāstras* and Kṣatriya *dharm*,[31] and became Buddhists (the author adds 'Jains' in parenthesis, apparently not knowing, or fully knowing, the difference). As a result, they lost the qualities of Kṣatriyahood (*kṣatriyatva*). They therefore gave up the sponsorship of sacrifices, and began to trouble and harass the Brāhmaṇs. A large number of Brāhmaṇs thereupon fled to a cave in the eastern corner of Mount Abu where they began to live together, but even here the renegade Kṣatriyas pursued them. Now, among those Kṣatriyas who became Buddhists (or Jains), there were four who were particularly strong, and these heroes had been Vaśiṣṭh's disciples before their apostasy. Vaśiṣṭh purified them in the sacrificial firepit, and when they emerged it was as if they had been reborn. He re-taught them Vedic religion, brought them back into the Vedic fold, and invested them with the sacred thread (which they would not have worn as Buddhists or Jains). He expunged Buddhist teachings from their minds, taught them the

> science of warfare (*astra śāstra*), and returned them to the duties of Kṣatriyas. These great warriors became the ancestors of the four Fire Clan lineages.

There are obviously big differences between these three versions of the Fire Clan myth. In Darakjī's version and one of Tod's versions, the sage presiding over the Kṣatriyas' recreation is Vaśiṣṭh; in Tod's other version, it is Viśvāmitra (in fact, Vaśiṣṭh's archenemy). In Darakjī's version, the framing story of Paraśurām is replaced by another completely different story. Despite their differences, however, the three tales are obviously variations of one basic narrative, and this narrative also has much in common with the Dāhimā myth discussed earlier in the chapter.

The Myths Compared

As in the Dāhimā myth, the sacrificial myth model is central to the storyline of all three variants of the Fire Clan myth. All of these narratives illustrate the theme of the creative powers of the sacrifice, for in each case the sacrifice serves as the crucial context within which social groups come into existence. In each case, moreover, there is a connection between the creation of the group and the role the group is supposed to play in the social order for which the sacrifice stands. In keeping with the generic functions of Brāhmaṇs, the Dāhimā Brāhmaṇs enter this order as ritual officiants. The Fire Clan Rājpūts emerge from the sacrificial pit as protectors of the Brāhmaṇs. By extension, they also emerge as protectors of the entire Brahmanical social order—that is, the social order for which the sacrifice, presided over by Brāhmaṇs, stands as a defining metaphor.

There is another continuity as well, which is the strong assertion of the ancestral goddess myth model. In our Brāhmaṇ and Rājpūt narratives alike, goddesses play key roles in the origin of the social groups in question. In both cases, moreover, the goddess's participation gives rise to a permanent relationship between the goddess and the newly created group. Dadhimatī is directly involved in the creation of the Dāhimā Brāhmaṇ caste. They become a caste as a result of their officiating at Māndhātā's sacrifice, which is offered specifically to her. This forges her relationship with the Dāhimās, and thenceforth they will worship her and she will preside over their welfare as a caste. In Tod's two versions of the Fire Clan Rājpūt myth, goddesses play a similar role, albeit with a martial twist. In these narratives, too, goddesses become the protectresses of social groups, a role that is then perpetuated by patrilineal descent. As subsequent chapters will show, the creation of such permanent relationships between goddesses and lines of patrilineal descent is a common theme in Rajasthani mythohistory.

The variant of the Fire Clan narrative presented by Darakjī has an additional wrinkle that we need to note, for it anticipates issues of great importance later in this book. I refer to the equivalence the story draws between demons and 'Buddhists'. Although Darakjī seems to refer to Buddhism (he uses the Hindi expression *baudh dharm*, but then inserts the term 'Jain' parenthetically), he almost certainly has in mind the Jains, not Buddhists. He would have known little about Buddhists in any case; Jains, on the other hand, he certainly knew well. The narrative stresses Jainism's anti-Vedism and anti-Brāhmaṇism. Furthermore, it places Jains (or Buddhists) in a narrative niche occupied by demons in other versions of the tale. This idea will return in a somewhat different context in the next chapter.

Considered together, the Dāhimā and Fire Clan narratives present us with a highly revealing picture of the relationship between Brāhmaṇs and Kṣatriyas. The Dāhimā narrative emphasises the idea that if Kṣatriyas are to flourish as rulers and warriors they need to sponsor sacrifices. King Māndhātā, therefore, must sponsor such a sacrifice in order to realise his ambition of conquering the three worlds. And to do so, he must enter into a relationship with the Brāhmaṇs, for only Brāhmaṇs can actually perform the rite.

In the world of these narratives, however, Brāhmaṇs can flourish at the margins of the social order in a way that Kṣatriyas cannot. The Dāhimā narrative expresses this idea by stressing that Brāhmaṇs do not have to take *dakṣiṇā*. Furthermore, world-renouncing sage-Brāhmaṇs, who are the best of Brāhmaṇs, do not take it. On the other hand, the sponsor of a sacrifice *must* succeed in giving *dakṣiṇā* to the officiating priests, for unless he does, the rite is inefficacious. And, as the Dāhimā myth shows, if Brāhmaṇs accept *dakṣiṇā*, their acceptance cements otherwise undomesticated seers and sages into the social order as an endogamous caste.

Our tales do not offer a view of 'jungle' Kṣatriyas in symmetry with this. Rather, we see a totally negative picture of Kṣatriyas who move to the social margins. Kārtavīrya epitomises such deviancy; instead of protecting Brāhmaṇ sages, he steals from Jamadagni and wrecks his hermitage. In the end, his sons commit the ultimate sin of Brāhmaṇicide by killing Jamadagni, which is the cause of Paraśurām's bloody rampage.

Darakjī's version of the Fire Clan narrative makes the same point in a somewhat different manner. Here Kṣatriyahood goes sour precisely because Kṣatriyas leave the Brahmanical order, becoming 'Buddhists' (i.e., Jains). The sacrifice is thus brought into danger, which is averted only when Kṣatriyas are brought back to their proper function, which is protection of the sacrifice. It seems that when Kṣatriyas enter the jungle, the world becomes a jungle.[32]

This brings us to a crucial point. In the end, these narratives insist that Kṣatriyas are as necessary as Brāhmaṇs to the social order. The essence of the Kṣatriyas' role is to sponsor sacrifices and to protect the sacrificial social order as embodied by Brāhmaṇs. The Fire Clan origin story presents us with a picture of a world without Kṣatriyas. It is a world in which demons pollute the sacrifice and harass the Brāhmaṇs who perform it. In short, it is a world of social (and indeed cosmic) chaos. In such a world, Kṣatriyas must be recreated, which—as always—requires a sacrifice. Thus the sacrifice becomes a means of recreating an ordered world.

But there is an element missing in this picture. As the last chapter showed, the Kṣatriya–Brāhmaṇ dyad is by no means the only important social pairing in Rajasthan. At least as important, and possibly more so, is the social pairing of Kṣatriyas (i.e., Rājpūts) and traders. How, we may now ask, do traders fit into the sacrificial paradigm our analysis has disclosed? The following chapters explore this issue in detail.

Notes

1. It was A. M. Hocart (1950) who first drew attention to ritual co-participation as a basic principle of caste. The analysis presented here builds on his insights, but takes them in a very different direction. Hocart saw the system as having actually originated in a ritual division of labour focussed on the divine king, which then spread by means of imitation. Our emphasis is on the sacrifice as a metaphor by means of which the workings of the social order are understood from within. I do not want to suggest that this is the only possible Indic social theory. Indian civilisation is complex and intellectually sophisticated, a vast intellectual universe with plenty of room for differing interpretations of social life. For another and very different ('ethnosociological') rendering of Indic social theory, see Marriott 1990.
2. Unless otherwise indicated, the details presented here on the performance of the Vedic sacrifice have been taken from F. M. Smith 1987: 2–35).

3. The *Brāhmaṇas* are ritual manuals appended to the Vedas proper (the *Saṃhitās*).
4. Itself drawn from various sources, especially the *Śiva Purāṇa* and *Mahābhārata.*
5. The *tretā yuga* is the second of the four eras (*yugas*) of the eternally repeating cycle of Hindu cosmic history.
6. As Kramrisch points out (1981: 325), the beheading of Dakṣa echoes Śiva's legendary beheading of Brahmā.
7. Although the number of castes is always six, the specific Brāhmaṇ castes included in the list varies somewhat according to who is doing the listing. As far as I am aware, the Dāhimā caste is always included.
8. An ancient horse sacrifice designed to assert royal authority. In theory, a king would allow a horse to range free for a year, claiming all territories traversed by the horse, and defeating in battle any kings who attempted to defy him. At the end of the year, the horse would be sacrificed.
9. This goddess and her temple play, with respect to the Dāhimā Brāhmaṇs, a role analogous to that of the Shri Chitrapur Matha for the Chitrapur Saraswat Brāhmaṇs as described by Frank Conlon (1977). In contrast to the Chitrapur Saraswat Brāhmaṇs, however, the Dāhimās never had a caste guru. The Matha, moreover, is a recent phenomenon, having been created in the eighteenth century C.E. The Dadhimatī temple is, as will be seen, very ancient.
10. On the Dadhimatī temple, see Cort 2000a, 2000b; Meister 2000, 2002.
11. The Ratlam version might well contain details concerning how the document originated, but I have never managed to see a copy of this edition.
12. Their names: Vṛhadvats, Gautam, Bhārgav, Bhāradvāj, Kaucchas, Kaśyap, Śāṇḍilya, Mahābhāg Atri, Parāśar, Kapil, Garg, Laghuvats (elsewhere also known as Mam).
13. The text identifies Māndhātā as the son of a sun-line king named Yuvnāśva. There is indeed a king of that name and parentage in the Mahābhārata, a renowned conqueror and sacrificer (Vana Parva 126.1–40). Tod (1990: 1629–30) describes a legendary Parmār king by this name who ruled from Dhar and Ujjain. Quite by chance, I came across a reference to a king named Māndhātā, son of a king Yunāśva, in a history of the Jāṭ caste (Vidyālankār 1992: 207); here he is said to be the apical ancestor of a Jāṭ lineage called Gaur. I suspect that he figures in the origin stories of other groups as well.
14. Tradition proclaims that the descendants of one of Pipplād's sons, Laghuvats, became *mlecch* (barbarian foreigners, suggesting conversion to Islam) and left the Brāhmaṇ fold. This is not reported in the *Purāṇa*. The number 144 is pure convention. On the basis of a comparison of several modern compilations, Asopa (1988: 43-67) lists a total of 146 *śākhās* (branches, or 'surnames' as he calls them), most of which have been fitted into the *gotra* scheme (below) but many of which have not. He includes information on the villages after which they are named (e.g., village Pāṭodā for the Pāṭodyas). However, a survey of registrants at a marriage introduction convention (see note 21 below) reveals that only a dozen or so of the listed *śākhās* occur commonly; the remainder are rare or possibly non-existent. I suspect that there has always been uncertainty about whether particular lineages are original *śākhās* or segments of them, but that this became a problem only when efforts to systematise the clan and lineage system (especially in relation to the *gotras*) began early in this century. Despite the existence of published lists, I suspect the system remains somewhat open-ended to the present day.
15. This question arises for other castes as well. A very conspicuous example is the Agravāl caste. As will be seen in a later chapter, all Agravāls are said to be descended

from King Agrasen of Agroha. This does not appear to worry the Agravāls any more than the Dāhimās.

16. When asked how Dāhimā Brāhmaṇs could be Brāhmaṇs in view of the fact that their ancestors had non-Brāhmaṇ wives, he responded with the seed theory of descent in which descent is carried by the seed that is planted in the mother by the father.
17. A status whose ambiguities are registered by the double character (hermits with wives) of the *vānaprasth āśram* (Biardeau 1994).
18. Pipplād's story is similar. After 88 years of meditation (*smaraṇ*) with his wife, he divided his semen into 12 parts and put them into his wife's womb, then becoming passionless.
19. Readers might wonder why Atharvā needs to be interposed between Brahmā and Dadhīci. The answer seems to be that Atharvā and Dadhīci are present as a pair in the *Ṛg Veda*, and thus cannot be severed from each other. Dadhīci is identified with Dadhyañc, who is the son of an Atharvan priest. He was given a horse-head through which he taught the Aśvins; Indra then severed this head, after which the Aśvins restored Dadhyañc's original head (see O'Flaherty 1981: 183–85). This episode is also included in the *Purāṇa* (pp. 122–23). Interestingly, in a genealogical tree displayed at the Dadhimatī temple (and frequently reproduced in caste publications), Dadhyañc is interposed between Atharvā and Dadhīci. The tree's creator has clearly not gotten the message about the identity of this figure and Dadhīci (on which point see Asopa 1988: Ch. 2).
20. The *pravars* represent an additional complication; they are sometimes listed with Dāhimā *gotras*.
21. Respondents said that avoiding commonality of clan on mother's or father's side is the basic rule of exogamy in this caste. An inspection of a list of registrants for a marriage introduction convention (*yuvak yuvati paricay sammelan*) held at Indore in 1994 (Dadhimatī 1994: 10–24) reveals that almost all registrants, male and female, listed only the *śākhās* of mother and father; nobody listed *gotras*. In the introduction to his booklet *Dādhīc Vaṃśotpatti va Gotrāvalī* (V.S. 1981), Śrīnārāyaṇ Vaidya states that his purpose is to provide information that will allow his readers to avoid *gotra*-endogamous marriages. He also refers to a resolution of the caste's 15th annual Mahāsabhā meeting (in Kolkata) against *gotra*-endogamous marriage. This suggests that efforts to insert *gotras* into marriage and systematise the relationship of clans to *gotras* might be a relatively recent development. A conceptual problem with the supposed *gotras* is that they are descended from famous sages who, according to other traditions, are mind-born sons of Brahmā. It is not possible to reconcile these accounts with the Dadhīci-Pipplād version. Respondents acknowledged this difficulty, some responding with casuistic rationalisations.
22. Such goddesses also sometimes enter the affairs of descent groups by intervening protectively at crucial moments of danger. This general pattern has been extremely well-described for Rājpūts by Lindsey Harlan (1992). Male deities can also play this role, as does Bālājī for his temple's priestly lineage.
23. As it happens, Dadhīci himself had already done *tap*, at the suggestion of Śiva, in order to get her to become the *kul devī* of his progeny (*Purāṇa*, pp. 120–21).
24. For more details on these structures, see Harlan 1992: 26–37 and Ziegler 1973: 36–66.
25. Literally meaning 'descent', the term *avatāra* here refers to the forms Viṣṇu took when, on successive occasions, he descended to earth to save the world from some sort of peril. The most famous of these are Rāma (*avatāra* number seven, and not to

be confused with Paraśurām) and Kṛṣṇa (number eight). In its Sanskrit form, Paraśurām would be written as 'Paraśurāma', but I drop the final 'a' in consistency with the Ḥindi milieu of this book.

26. Viśvāmitra was in a similarly ambiguous state. A Kṣatriya by birth, he became a Brāhmaṇ by means of austerities. When she proposes the switch of mixtures, Satyavatī's mother justifies the act by saying that it would be wrong for the Satyavatī's brother to be superior in status to her son. That is, she believes that Kṣatriyas are superior to Brāhmaṇs, and if Satyavatī gave birth to a Brāhmaṇ son, and this would contravene the general belief that an outmarrying woman should bear a son superior in status to her natal family.
27. Alf Hiltebeitel has discussed the evolution of this myth in detail (1999: 439–75).
28. Tod's first version is clearly drawn from Candbardāī's *Prithvīrāj Rāso* (see the extract reproduced in R. B. Singh 1964: 14–15), but the relationship between the Fire Clan myth and this document is itself a complicated story (Hiltebeitel 1999: 447–48). Historian R. B. Singh notes that the Fire Clan myth does not appear in any version of the epic prior to the late sixteenth century. I found a variant of Tod's first version in a locally published work on Rājpūt genealogy (Maḍāḍh 1987: 8–9); this version was also attributed to *Prithvīrāj Rāso*. The origin of Tod's second version is less clear.
29. In my summaries of Tod's versions, I have supplied conventional diacritics.
30. I am omitting details about the derivation of their names and the territories assigned to them.
31. That is, the duties of warfare, protection and sacrificial sponsorship attached to Kṣatriya status.
32. It is, of course, not impossible for a Kṣatriya to be a sage. The most famous example is Viśvāmitra, a Kṣatriya whom tradition holds to have been one the greatest sages who ever lived. However, Viśvāmitra was a Brāhmaṇ manqué, and in the end he won acceptance as a Brāhmaṇ.

Chapter Four

Melted Warriors

Traders are different. Brāhmaṇs and Rājpūts possess clearly defined and stable social identities in relation to the sacrifice. Brāhmaṇs both perform the rite and, as sages, transcend it. Kṣatriyas—in Rajasthan, the Rājpūts—sponsor the rite (or its symbolic equivalent) and protect it and the social order with which it is associated. But in keeping with the contradictory and 'slippery' nature of their relationship with other groups, the position of traders vis-à-vis the sacrifice presents interesting complexities. These complexities reflect marginal aspects of trader identity within the wider social order. Moreover, there are systemic variations in the way the relationship between traders and the sacrificial social order is imaged, and these represent what we might call variant subcultures of social identity. Although each caste presents its own distinctive picture, there are two major subcultures of trader identity, Hindu and Jain. Some trading groups exclude themselves from the rite altogether. These are the Jains. Others, the Hindu or predominantly Hindu trading castes, situate themselves within the symbolic cosmos of the rite, but in a way that reflects the ambiguous character of their historical relationships with regional social and political structures.

This chapter deals with the social identity of three castes belonging to the Hindu cluster of trading castes: the Māheśvarīs, the Khaṇḍelvāl Vaiśyas, and the Vijayvargīyas. The Agravāls, also a predominantly Hindu group, will be treated separately in Chapter Six. The Jain cluster of castes will be the subject of Chapter Five.

In what follows we shall see that at the heart of trading-caste social identity—Hindu or Jain—is the issue of violence. As we noted in Chapter Two, coming to terms with groups that engage in violence is—or was—a significant problem of social adaptation for trading castes. On the basis of what we have learned in Chapter Three about the sacrificial construction of the social order, we now follow this problem into the realm of myth, ritual, and social symbolism. In a situation in which warrior values are held in the highest esteem, in which violence is a pervasive fact of life, and in which martial prowess and its symbolisms lie at the foundation of political authority itself, groups whose social colouration is non-violence must, in accounting for who and what they are, deal with two related problems. They must work out a culturally intelligible relationship with violence, and they must do so in a way that ameliorates marginality and low social honour. As will be seen, this is largely what trader mythohistory is about. We begin with the Māheśvarīs.

Māheśvarīs

The Māheśvarīs are a trading caste found mainly in the eastern and central parts of Rajasthan. Of course, they are also present in force in places where Rajasthani traders spread and settled. They are highly organised at the national, state, and local levels. The Akhil Bhāratvarṣīya Māheśvarī Mahāsabhā, an extremely active caste association founded in 1908, represents them nationally. In the city of Jaipur, they have a local organisation (similar to those in other cities) that manages local Māheśvarī educational institutions and organises various local caste activities such as the celebration of *maheś navmī*, a caste festival (below).

As is the case with all the groups considered in this book, it is impossible to say exactly how many Māheśvarīs there are. Their national association has conducted a caste census, but how rigorously it was done is hard to say. According to a well-connected member of the caste's Jaipur elite, the census yielded a total figure of 1,000,000. This number, my informant added, was considered surprisingly and disappointingly low. The editor of a prominent caste journal, *Māheśvarī Sevak* (not the journal of the national association), told me that the total number of Māheśvarīs is about 2.5 million, but this was probably no more than an optimistic guess. His journal has about 10,000 subscribers; of these, about 4,000 have addresses in Rajasthan, with the remainder in U.P., M.P., Maharashtra, and elsewhere, suggesting the existence of a large diaspora community. According to the same source who told me about the national census, there are currently about 15,000 Māheśvarīs in Jaipur.

The origin of the caste's name is something of a puzzle. The term 'Māheśvarī' is actually one of the many names of the goddess Pārvatī, the consort of the Hindu deity Śiva. This suggests a connection between the caste and the Śaiva tradition—that is, the sectarian tradition of Śiva-worship—and indeed there are also hints of such a connection in Māheśvarī origin narratives, as we shall see shortly. Moreover, images of Śiva are displayed at official caste functions, and his picture is often shown on the covers of caste publications. Śiva is thus an important current symbol of Māheśvarī caste identity. However, the Māheśvarīs are not Śaivas. Rather, as best I could determine, the caste's religious culture is almost totally dominated by the prominent Vaiṣṇava sects of western India. Whatever might have been the past situation, at the present time the caste's Śaiva connection is mostly nominal.[1]

The Māheśvarī caste is segmented in multiple ways. At the highest structural level are cleavages between major caste sections. The caste's most important section, that to which the majority of the caste's members in Jaipur and the state of Rajasthan belong, is called Ḍīḍū or Ḍīḍūvāl. The name implies that this section originated in the town of Didwana. Another section, small but prominent in Jaipur, is known as the Paṭvā Māheśvarīs. The term *paṭvā* means 'bead stringer', and bead stringing was indeed once the occupational specialty of this group. In Jaipur there are about 90 Paṭvā families, many living in a very old colony in the Bapu Bazar area. The main Māheśvarī community kept the Paṭvās in connubial and commensal isolation until (apparently) the 1960s.[2]

The *Marwar Census Report* of 1891 does not refer to the Paṭvās, but does mention four other 'Māheśvarī' groups that it describes as separate 'castes' (*nyāts*) (Singh 1997: 439): the Dhākaṛ, Pokrā, Tūnkvāl, and Meṛtvāl Māheśvarīs. I heard of the latter three of these groups in the course of my research, but I have no material on them. The *Census* theorises that these three originated in Didwana, and, after migrating southward from there, established local roots in (respectively) Pushkar, Tonk, and Merta, thereby becoming separate castes.

The Māheśvarī caste is (or was) also divided into ranked, endogamous subdivisions called 'twenties' and 'tens' (*bisā* and *dasā*), a division apparently common to all the trading castes of the region. The twenties are the superior class and the tens the inferior. It is difficult to judge how important this division is today. In general, informants tend to downplay its current significance, probably because of a general sense that such divisions are unmodern and reflect badly on the caste.

Judging from matrimonial advertisements I have surveyed, the division is probably largely obsolete, at least in Jaipur. In the past, however, the twenty/ten distinction was important indeed, and at one time even inter-dining between the classes was frowned upon.

As are all the castes discussed in this book, the Māheśvarī caste is divided into exogamous clans.[3] In the Māheśvarī case, these clans are known as *khāmps*. The clans, in turn, are further subdivided into lineages known as *nakhs*. Nowadays, many Māheśvarīs derive their surnames from their clans. The clans' greatest significance lies in matters of marriage. Knowledgeable Māheśvarīs have told me that a four-clan rule of exogamy once prevailed in the caste, but it is difficult to judge the truth of this claim.[4] Currently, the normal rule of exogamy is that a spouse may not be taken from one's father's or mother's clan.[5]

The question of how many Māheśvarī clans exist is quite important and will lead us deep into the caste's mythohistory. According to the list published currently by the caste's national association, there are exactly 77 Māheśvari clans.[6] This figure is based on the belief that there were originally 72 clans to which five were later added. The list of 77 appears frequently in the publications of the caste's national association and in other non-official publications, and the number is totally entrenched in the consciousness and affairs of the caste. However, the number 72 (and thus the derivative 77) is purely conventional, and the reality of the Māheśvarī lineage system is far messier than the figures given in caste publications would suggest.

My own survey of 142 matrimonial advertisements from 10 issues (from the year 1996) of the national association's fortnightly magazine, *Māheśvarī*, revealed a wide gap between the idealised scheme and social reality. For example, out of a total of 106 references to the clan of the girl or boy in these advertisements, the names of only 47 of the officially listed clans actually appeared.[7] Whether all of the 77 names would have appeared in a more extensive survey is hard to say, but I suspect not. Moreover, 14 of the clans mentioned in these ads are not on the official list. Twelve of these appear in the standard published list as branch lineages (i.e., *nakhs*) of 'official' clans, and two are total unknowns.

The standard list appears frequently in various caste publications. As in the case of similar lists for other trading castes, the format in which the clans are presented usually provides the basic list along with an index that permits one to find out to which clan any given lineage belongs.[8] The basic list itself has arrived at its present state of canonicity after a long process of copying and recopying both within and outside the ambit of the national association's magazines and other publications. This chain of borrowings ultimately leads back to a single source, which is a book (Darak 1923), mentioned briefly in the previous chapter, written by an extraordinary man named Śivkaraṇ Rāmratan Darak (1808–1887).[9] Māheśvarīs usually refer to him as 'Darakjī' out of respect for his distinguished role in the caste's history. The entire list of Māheśvarī clans and their subdivisions currently reproduced by the national association first appeared in this book (ibid.: 70–96).

The story of Darakjī's interest in questions about the organisation of the Māheśvarī caste provides a window into important transformations taking place in the caste system during the late nineteenth century. It also illustrates how origin mythology articulates with the internal structure of castes, a theme that will be with us throughout the remainder of this book.

Darakjī

Darakjī was a self-taught amateur ethnographer and folklorist who belonged to the Māheśvarī caste and whose principal interest was the social organisation of his caste. He appears to have spent much of his life in Indore where he was the owner of a printing press. First published in 1893, his book on the Māheśvarīs is an excellent example of a type of local history that became quite prominent during this period (see Pandey 1990). These works were mainly concerned with establishing the history and common traditions of various sorts of parochial groups, including castes, on the basis of which these groups could define and publicly project corporate identities. This type of literary activity was one of the chief contexts in which caste identities ultimately crystallised into their modern forms. Fortunately for us, Darakjī provides an account of how his interest in his caste's ethnography began (ibid.: 15–17). What he says is extremely revealing, for it shows how broader social changes taking place in the nineteenth century were affecting the internal affairs of castes like the Māheśvarīs.

As Darakjī describes it, the inception of his interest in his caste was the result of a puzzling conversation he overheard one evening in the lunar month of Bhādrapad[10] in the year 1841. It seems that a group of Māheśvarīs had been sitting together talking in his native village of Mūṇḍvā in Marwar (Jodhpur State). At some point in the evening, a stranger joined them, and he turned out to be a Māheśvarī from Mewar

(Udaipur). Upon being asked to identify himself, the stranger said that he was 'Naugjā Māheśvarī'. This was a surprise to the group because they had never before heard of a Māheśvarī clan of that name. In the course of the ensuing discussion, it soon emerged that in Marwar there were many clans that the visitor had never heard of, and that in Mewar there were many clans that were unknown in Marwar. This was a significant revelation.

In those days, as now, the Māheśvarīs believed that their caste consisted of 72 clans (Nowadays, as noted already, five clans have been added to the list, but the original number is still held to be 72). But when inquisitive Darakjī wrote down a list of clan names from Mūndvā and other nearby villages, the total came to about 160, later rising to 380. How, he wondered, can this be reconciled with the belief that there are only 72 clans? Have some clans gotten mixed in from other castes? Or do some clans have more than one name? Darakjī tells us that it was at this point that he resolved to continue collecting clan names and someday write a book about the Māheśvarī caste.

Darakjī's puzzlement was understandable, given the historical context. As we know, this was a period in which momentous social changes were taking place. By the end of the eighteenth century, India had already become, in Susan Bayly's words, a place 'in which more people than ever before were trading, travelling and making war, and hence exchanging knowledge and information with one another, often in fiercely contentious circumstances. This forging of new links between town and countryside, consumers and producers, worshippers and ritualists, readers and literati, threw many different kinds of Indians into contact with one another, thereby raising fraught questions about where to draw social and moral boundaries, and familiarising substantial numbers of people who were new to them with at least some of the norms and principles of jati and varna' (1999: 94). These transformations, still underway, were very much part of the context in which Darakjī heard the conversation in the village and conceived his mission. The question of what it meant to be a 'Māheśvarī' had to be addressed in a new way reflecting new social conditions.

Indeed, it seems likely that such issues were more salient among traders than among the region's other communities. Darakjī's inquiries began at the threshold of a period in which migrations of Rajasthani traders into other areas of India were occurring on a truly large scale. This not only meant that trading castes were becoming far more dispersed and cosmopolitan than before, but also that their internal organisation was becoming problematic in an entirely new way. The puzzling encounter with the Māheśvarī stranger was probably a typical experience in which Māheśvarīs from previously separated domains of the caste's social space were interacting on a sustained basis for the first time. Members of other trading castes were undoubtedly having similar experiences.

This new cosmopolitanism must have given rise to a range of novel problems related to the fact that people had to interact with caste fellows belonging to subgroups that were difficult or impossible to classify. Judging from Darakjī's own account of his motivations, two issues were at stake. One was marriage and the other was adoption (see esp. ibid.: 26). With regard to marriage, the requirement of clan exogamy meant that certain questions about the organisation of a given caste's descent groups would necessarily arise with new urgency. The question of whether a particular descent group was a clan (i.e., one of the 72) or merely the branch of a clan, and if so which clan, must have frequently confronted those who were attempting to arrange marriages in this new and expanded social universe. Similar questions would have arisen as a result of the preference for adoption to occur within the clan.[11] Dealing with such issues required a systematic overview of the caste's structure, and this was Darakjī's goal.

In the days of Darakjī's youth, of course, no such overview existed. At that time, the principal transmitters of social knowledge were traditional genealogists. In the Māheśvarī case, these genealogists were known as Jāgās, and a particular community of Jāgās specialised in serving only the Māheśvarī caste. They were not themselves Māheśvarīs but belonged to their own separate caste. They were the ones who kept records of the caste's clans and their branches, and they also recorded and recited the caste's origin myth, which (as we see shortly) was directly concerned with the origins of clans. Each genealogist had a group of regular patrons whom he would visit at regular intervals. Such a visit would typically involve the collecting of information about recent changes in the patron's family, and this would be entered into the genealogist's books. The visit would also normally include a recitation of the family's pedigree, and this would be prefaced by a recitation of the caste's origin myth.

The fact that genealogical and mythohistorical knowledge was in the hands of these genealogists meant that such knowledge was necessarily unsystematic and fragmented. Each genealogist had his own books that were copied and recopied as they were passed down from one generation to the next within his own lineage. The accounts of the structure and history of the caste passed down by different genealogists no doubt had a generic similarity, but there was plenty of scope for variation in the details. Thus, the belief that there are exactly 72 Māheśvarī clans could easily co-exist with the fact that far more than 72 names of supposed clans existed. This was possible because the inconsistencies could only come into view if the lists were systematically compared, and this is something that, as far as I am aware, the genealogists never did and would never have thought of doing.

Darakjī's response was to undertake a systematic survey of descent groups and to organise them into a rational scheme based on the existing convention that the caste was divided into 72 clans. He faced immense difficulties in collecting the necessary materials because the Jāgās mostly refused to cooperate with him, despite the fact that he had the strong backing of the Māheśvarī caste leaders of Indore (the caste *pancāyat*) (ibid.: 18–26). The Jāgās were rightly afraid that the existence of a printed 'history' of the caste would render their services redundant. It took Darakjī about 50 years to complete the job.

One of the principal results of his endeavours was the creation of the list of 72 clan names that has remained the caste standard ever since. It is important to realise that Darakjī did not 'discover' the 'real' 72 clans. There was no such reality to discover. Rather, there existed a large number of clan names that Darakjī reduced to 72 by (as best I can judge) listing some of the alleged clans as branches of one or the other of the 72. But the accomplishment was significant, for it meant that Māheśvarīs everywhere would have a fixed, transcaste framework within which to determine marriage (or adoption) eligibility or ineligibility with other Māheśvarīs. When the Māheśvarīs' national association came into existence in 1908, Darakjī's scheme was available to become the foundation for an 'official' rationalised version of how the caste is organised.

Darakjī also rationalised the origin myth of the Māheśvarī caste. That he should have done so was inevitable, for the caste's origin myth is closely connected with the caste's internal clan and lineage structure, which was Darakjī's primary concern. A recitation of the origin myth was, as we have noted, a standard feature of the caste's genealogists' performances for their clients. Darakjī's own version of the caste's origin is probably based on what he was told by several different genealogists and can be regarded as a distillation of more than one of the versions current in his day. Under the aegis of the Māheśvarīs' national association, Darakjī's version subsequently became canonical, and is currently the principal source for all published versions of the story. It is also the basis for a picture depicting the origin of the caste that one sometimes sees in Māheśvarī homes, as a magazine illustration, or in other caste-specific contexts (see Figure 4.2). In addition, it serves as a charter-myth for an annual festivity known as *maheś navmī*. This is a Māheśvarī-only celebration that dramatises the solidarity of local groups of Māheśvarīs by means of processions and cultural performances.[12]

In the meantime, the Māheśvarīs' caste genealogists have largely been pushed out of the picture. This is partly a function of the spatial dispersal of the caste, which has made it extremely difficult for genealogists to conduct their normal periodic rounds of clients' households. But also, the genealogists' role has been preempted by the printed page, which is the means by which information on caste origins and internal structure—though not the genealogies of particular families—tends to be transmitted these days. During the period of my research in Jaipur, a city with a large Māheśvarī population, there was only one very elderly Jāgā of the Māheśvarīs residing in the city. On the one occasion I paid him a call, I discovered that his books were in a state of such total chaos that it is hard to imagine how he could practice his profession in a competent manner. Knowledgeable Māheśvarīs have told me that there are some working genealogists elsewhere in the state, but—in this caste, as in most—the profession is clearly almost dead.

Our next step is to present the Māheśvarī origin myth, and we shall examine more than one version. But before we do this, we need to learn something about its context in cultural geography. The Māheśvarī story involves two main locations, and these will figure importantly in the Māheśvarī case and in other mythic material to be presented in this and the next chapter.

Two Important Places

The first of these locations is an unprepossessing little town named Khandela. Situated in northeastern Rajasthan about 100 km northwest of Jaipur (and about 40 km to the east of Sikar), Khandela is hardly more than a village today. Legend, however, proclaims it to have been a large and important city in ancient times. How large it actually was remains to be shown archaeologically, but it is certainly a very old settlement. Its earliest inscription dates from the third century B.C.E., and it was once an important Śaiva center (K. C. Jain 1972: 261–66).

Figure 4.1
The Sūrya Kuṇḍ at Lohargal.

The second important location is a place called Lohargal (Lohārgal). Located about 20 km to the north-north-west of Khandela in the midst of a cluster of tree-shaded hills, Lohargal is an ancient pilgrimage spot and one of the most important holy places in this part of Rajasthan. Its physical focus is a bathing tank, now completely finished in stone, known as Sūrya Kuṇḍ (see Figure 4.1). Adjacent to the tank are a Sūrya temple (i.e., a temple dedicated to Sūrya, the Sun God) and a shrine for Śiva. The tank is fed from a cliff-side spring located behind the current Sūrya temple. One can imagine that once, before all the recent construction took place, a simple spring flowed forth from the base of a towering cliff into what must have been a charming little pool.

Locals believe the water in the tank to possess miraculous power. It supposedly has curative properties and is also said to have the miraculous power to dissolve metal and bones very rapidly. Any visitor to the place is likely to be shown coins that have supposedly been left in the water and are pitted as a result. I once tested this claim by putting some coins in a bottle filled with water drawn from the tank that I then set aside in my flat in Jaipur. Alas, the coins remained intact, even after several days. It seems possible that whatever dissolves the metal requires continuous replenishment from the spring that keeps the tank filled.

The alleged metal-dissolving property of the water is, in fact, an important component of Lohargal's reputation as a holy spot. According to a local (and false) etymology, the name 'Lohargal' combines two Hindi words: *lohā* (iron) and *galnā* (to melt). The background myth (here taken from Jagannāthdāsjī n.d.: 9, but also in oral circulation) tells of how, after the *Mahābhārata* war was fought, the victorious Yudhiṣṭhira wished to cleanse himself of the sin of the murder of his kin.[13] The great sage Nārad advised him to go with his four brothers on a pilgrimage. They should search, he said, for a place where the water would dissolve mighty Bhīma's club because only that water would be capable of washing away the sin. The brothers wandered fruitlessly from place to place until they finally chanced upon Lohargal. According to the myth, the place was resplendent with hermitages in those days, and Śiva and Sūrya were there in divine person, performing their austerities. With the permission of the sages and deities, the five brothers bathed, and the club dissolved; thus, their great sin was washed away.

This story obviously supports the local etymology of Lohargal with its focus on the dissolving of metal. There is, however, another and more plausible etymology of the name. According to another story (ibid.), Lohargal was created when Viṣṇu placed a mountain named Mālketu, which (or rather who) was Mount Meru's grandson, atop a previously existing pilgrimage spot. Viṣṇu then declared that because Mālketu lies protecting the place like a drawbar of iron, the name of the spot would be Lohargal, thus in this version combining *lohā* (iron) and *argal* (drawbar). This etymology provides a bridge to the Puranic tradition, for the *Varāha Purāṇa* also mentions a placed named Lohargal with similar associations (A. S. Gupta 1981: 639–64).[14] In this text, Viṣṇu describes Lohargal as a place located in the Himalayas, and he further tells of how he kept the gods secure there behind an iron bar while he killed demons that were attacking them. For this reason, the place was named 'Lohārgala' (barred with an iron bar). The image is that of a fortification of some kind, which connects the Puraṇic story with one variant of the Māheśvarī origin myth, as we shall see shortly.

The 'iron bar' etymology is probably the most convincing linguistically, and it therefore seems probable that Lohargal's name was inspired by a Puranic source. However, the 'melting iron' etymology is locally more important, and also bears a deep relevance to the Māheśvarī origin narrative, to which we now turn.

Melting Weapons

We begin with a synopsis of Darakjī's version of the origin of the Māheśvarī caste (Darak 1923: 27–31):

> A certain Cauhān (Rājpūt) king named Khargalsen once ruled Khandela (Darakjī does not specify a period). He was an able ruler and his kingdom flourished, but it was his great misfortune to have produced no son. When he consulted learned Brāhmaṇs about his problem, they told him that Lord Śiva would give him the boon of a son, but only under certain conditions. First, under no circumstances should the boy be allowed to travel northward before the age of sixteen. Second, the boy should never bathe in the Sūrya Kuṇḍ (the main bathing tank at Lohargal). Third, the boy should always honor Brāhmaṇs. Unless these conditions were met, the Brāhmaṇs said, the prince would have to undergo a 'rebirth' (*punarjanam*) in his own body.
>
> The prince was born. He was given the name Sujjānkunvar (spelled variously in different printings) and educated as a ruler. For a time all went well, but when the prince became older, though not yet sixteen, he became a Jain. As a result, he began replacing Śiva temples with Jain temples, and also developed a deep hostility to Brāhmaṇs. He then began traveling around the kingdom to promote his newly adopted religion. At first he avoided the north, but eventually word reached him that Brāhmaṇs were performing sacrifices at Lohargal (which is north of Khandela), and he journeyed there with his seventy-two Rājpūt henchmen. As it turned out, six sages were indeed performing a Vedic sacrifice there. The enraged prince ordered his men to disrupt the sacrifice, which they did. The equally enraged sages responded with a curse that turned the prince and all his men to stone.
>
> When news of this calamity reached the city, the king died of shock, and sixteen of his wives became *satīs*. Taking advantage of the situation, neighboring kings then seized the now rulerless kingdom. On the advice of the Brāhmaṇs, the wives of the frozen prince and chieftains retired to a particular cave where they practiced severe austerities and prayed to Śiva and his consort Pārvatī. After a time, the two deities appeared on the spot. Then, as a result of Pārvatī's sympathetic intervention, Śiva returned the men to life.
>
> But there was a big problem, which was that no kingdom remained for them to rule. Because of this, Śiva declared they would all have to give up the Kṣatriya way of life (*kṣatriya dharm*) and take up the ways of Vaiśyas

Figure 4.2
The creation of the Māheśvarī caste as depicted by a temple wall-painting in Bikaner.

(*vaiśya dharm*). However, their hands were still stiff from their former frozenness, and they were unable to relinquish their weapons. So Śiva then commanded them to bathe in Sūrya Kuṇḍ. When they did so, their swords became pens and their spears and shields became scales, the tools of the trade of businessmen. The descendants of these seventy-two Rājpūt chieftains are the seventy-two Māheśvarī clans existing today.[15] The prince was a special case. He made the mistake of looking at Pārvatī with lust. She cursed him in retaliation, with the result that his descendants became the Māheśvarīs' caste genealogists (see Figure 4.2 for a depiction of some of the foregoing events).[16]

There remained, however, a very important piece of unfinished business. The six sages pointed out that although the king and his henchmen had been released from the curse, the ruined sacrifice itself had not yet been restored and completed. Śiva replied that the now kingdomless erstwhile Rājpūts had nothing to give the sages at that time, but that in the future the new Vaiśyas would give them things whenever auspicious ceremonies occurred in their houses. Śiva added that they—the sages—should 'desire' that the new Vaiśyas abide by their proper (that is, Vaiśya) way of life. Śiva and Pārvatī then departed, and the sages taught the henchmen the proper duties of Vaiśyas. The henchmen then supplicated the six sages, and the sages' descendants later became gurus of the seventy-two Māheśvarī clans. Each sage took twelve disciples, and these disciples are known as *yajmān* (sponsor of a sacrifice). After some time, the new Māheśvarīs departed Khandela and shifted to Didwana, and the seventy-two clans descended from them are therefore called 'Ḍīḍū' Māheśvarī. By the grace of God, and as boon from Śiva and Pārvatī, and from the blessings of the Brāhmaṇs, the seventy-two clans flourished and spread to every region and village.

The Iron Fort

While Darakjī's version of the Māheśvarī myth appears in print more than any other, there exists a slightly different telling that also deserves our attention. I refer to it as the 'iron fort' version for reasons that will be obvious. Whether Darakjī ever heard this myth is impossible to say, but it was certainly in circulation in the nineteenth century because we find it reproduced in Crooke's *Tribes and Castes of the North-western Provinces and Oudh* (1896, III: 407). The retelling given below represents my own abstract of an illustrated version published by Rāmcandra Bihāṇī (1983, among many other printings) of Bikaner, who is also the publisher of the non-official caste magazine, *Māheśvarī Sevak*. Of this narrative's original context, Bihāṇī says only that it comes from a conversation between two individuals named Mangūmaljī Cāṇḍak and Mangnīrāmjī Jāgā that had taken place about 100 years previously, a conversation that was recorded in Sanskrit in a very 'old book'. He provides no additional information about the conversation or book.

As before, this version begins with Khargalsen, the king of Khandela. The period is identified as early in the *dvāparyug*.[17]

Although he had two queens, Khargalsen had no son. When the desperate king told his ministers that he was about to relinquish his duties and retire to a life of austerities in the forest, the famous sage Yājñavalkya informed him that his sonlessness was due to a particular sin (the details need not detain us) that he had committed in a previous birth. The sage further declared that only by recovering a certain buried *śivling* (the phallic form in which Śiva is usually worshiped) and placing it in a temple would he get his wish. The king did as he was instructed, with the result that Śiva and Pārvatī granted him the boon of a son. The prince, whose name was

Sujānsen, grew up, married, and years later succeeded his father who had given up his body at a place near Puṣkar (a major regional pilgrimage center) after practicing austerities for twelve years.

Now, one day Sujānsen went hunting with his men. When they got tired, they rested by a pool in which they washed their bloody weapons. As it happens, a group of sages were performing a sacrifice for Śiva nearby. When one of them came to the pool for water, he saw the blood in the water and became enraged. He then magically created a gigantic and doorless iron fort in which he trapped seventy-two of the king's men plus Sujānsen himself. The men made a great uproar but could not break out. The angry sage then cursed them and they all turned to stone.

The queen's brother took over the affairs of the kingdom. Then one day, a sage revealed to the grieving queen what had actually happened. He explained how Sujānsen had spoiled a sacrifice that six sages had been in the process of performing for eighty-eight years. He further said that the 100-year sacrifice would be completed in twelve years, at which point Śiva would appear to restore the king and his men to their former condition at the behest of the six sages. In the meantime, the kingdom should be given to Khargalsen's younger brother's grandson, Daṇḍadhar, and the queen and wives of the other men should go to the Śiva temple (the one established by Khargalsen) and engage in prayer and other observances. So the queen and the other wives began twelve years of spiritual exercise in seclusion.

Time passed, and at last the six sages completed their sacrifice. When Śiva manifested and offered them a boon, they asked that the king and his followers be returned to life. Śiva said that the men had gotten into trouble because of violence, and that they would therefore have to give up *kṣatriya dharm* and become Vaiśyas. Using ash from the sacrificial fire, Śiva then reanimated the stone men. He told them that they would have to become Vaiśyas, and that the king would record their genealogies and be known as Jāgā. He added that the iron fort would be reduced to ashes and in time the spot would become a place of pilgrimage. Śiva further declared that the descendants of the six sages would be *purohits* (family priests) of the new caste, which would be known as Māheśvarī Vaiśya on the basis of Śiva's name.[18] The god then disappeared, and the men all fell at the feet of the sages.

When news of these events arrived at Khandela, the queen and the wives of the other men came to their husbands. They touched their husbands' feet and worshipped the six sages. Sujānsen anointed Daṇḍadhar as king, and then he and the others bathed in the Sūrya Kuṇḍ at Lohargal. Their weapons dissolved in the water, and in their place appeared scales, pens and inkpots. Sujānsen and the others at first refused to accept their wives

> because they were still Kṣatriyas, whereas the men had undergone a 'rebirth' as Vaiśyas. The women prayed to Pārvatī, who then manifested with Śiva. On the deities' instructions, all the couples circumambulated the divine pair while bound together (symbolic of a remarriage) (In a variant given in the same source, the women are purified of their Kṣatriya nature by bathing in the pool). This is how the Māheśvarī Vaiśya caste (jāti) came into existence.

There remain a few loose ends that also need to be mentioned. First, this version of the myth specifically maintains that Lohargal got its name because its water dissolved the Rājpūts' iron weapons. As in the Darakjī version, the ancestors of the 72 clans leave Khandela and settle in Didwana, thus becoming 'Ḍīḍū Māheśvarīs', and from there spread to other areas. The text also asserts that King Daṇḍadhar was allied with the Kauravas and King Jayant (Sujānsen's wife's brother) with the Pāṇḍavas in the Mahābhārata war. In a version of the same basic story presented by another source (Vyās and Gahalot 1992: 122–24), the sages built the iron fort around themselves (not around the king and his henchmen) for protection in the belief that Sujānsen and his companions were demons. The authors of this source add the observation that even today this fort is famed as '*lohā gaṛh*', which means 'iron fort'. We thus see yet another etymology for Lohargal that must have been floating around the region at the time these various accounts crystallised into their present forms.

The Variants Compared

Although both these narratives specifically connect the Māheśvarī caste to Lohargal, this linkage seems highly problematic. To begin with, both myths place the actual Māheśvarī heartland at Didwana, not at Lohargal. Whether this is historically (as opposed to mythohistorically) true or not is hard to say, but as far as I am aware the region around Lohargal is not a Māheśvarī center in any sense. To the best of my knowledge, there is no special connection at all between the Māheśvarīs and Lohargal outside of the origin myth. Māheśvarīs are not currently a presence at Lohargal, and nothing whatsoever is said about Māheśvarīs in the Lohargal pilgrimage pamphlets that I have been able to see (Bholārām Kyāl 1995; Jagannāthdāsjī n.d.). I once asked the head priest of Lohargal's Sūrya temple if he knew the Māheśvarī origin story. He responded by producing a handwritten copy of Darakjī's version of the myth that he had copied from a Māheśvarī magazine, which suggests that it is certainly not a local tradition at Lohargal. There was a meeting of prominent Māheśvarīs at Lohargal in February 1995. This meeting resulted in the formation of an organisation (the Śrī Lohārgal Māheśvarī Sevā Samiti) that had the precise purpose of establishing a Māheśvarī presence at Lohargal. While this may presage greater involvement of Māheśvarīs in the affairs of Lohargal in the future, it is also an indication of the weakness of the connection in the past.

These considerations suggest that the mythic link between the Māheśvarīs and Lohargal is merely an overlay (possibly quite late) on a more basic mythic substructure (to which we shall return shortly). As we have already noted, the 'iron bar' (*lohā+argal*) etymology makes the most sense on purely linguistic grounds and is probably the actual basis of Lohargal's name. But the 'melting iron' etymology (*lohā+galnā*) is at least phonetically plausible, and it has an inherent attractiveness because it links the place to the *Mahābhārata*. Once established, this notion could have suggested an interesting way of transforming armed Rājpūts into peaceable businessmen. Similarly, the 'iron fort' (*lohā gaṛh*) idea, itself an idea with a Puranic context, would have meshed easily with the 'iron bar' (*lohā+argal*) etymology for both conceptual and phonetic reasons. And in any case, the imaginations of the creators of the Maheśvarī narrative (in whatever specific versions) would have naturally been drawn to the Khandela/Lohargal locale because it figures prominently in the origin narratives of other castes, as we shall see.

The true core of the story, however, is not the locale but the underlying theme, which, in both of the versions we have seen, centers on violence and its taming. The Māheśvarī narrative is really a story about two totally different social personalities—warlike Rājpūts (i.e., Kṣatriyas) and non-violent traders—and the transformation of the former into the latter. In the context of Rajasthani society, the assertion of a Rājpūt pedigree is a denial of marginality or inferior social standing. It situates the Māheśvarīs in the same social space as the Rājpūts by connecting them by means of patrilineal descent. But the problem then becomes that of accounting for Māheśvarīs' non-martial ways. In both versions, this is dealt with in the same basic manner, i.e., by asserting that Rājpūt violence was manifested in a way that went sour, and that this ultimately resulted in a social metamorphosis. The Rājpūts get into trouble, as Śiva says in the iron-fort version, because of violence that is misdirected in that it brings about a disturbance of the sacrifice. This, in turn, results in a total transformation of the group character of the Rājpūts; they take leave of their violent ways and their Rājpūt/Kṣatriya identity, and are transformed into non-violent Vaiśya traders.

The category 'Vaiśya' as employed by these stories, moreover, does not seem to have much in common with the classical idea of Vaiśya (Chapter Two). In this context, it seems to refer to two things: first, to the fact (or mythofact) that the new caste had become *unlike* Rājpūts in their rejection of violence (as symbolised by Rājpūt identity itself, and also the weapons), and, second, to the fact that the new caste would be involved in trade (the weapons having turned to the tools of the trader's craft). The narrative is really more about the creation of 'Baniyās' than Vaiśyas.

As we have learned to expect by now, both narratives employ the sacrificial myth model as their main explanatory principle. The transformation of the Rājpūts into traders is a direct result of their encounter with the sacrifice. The crux of the matter is that it is the wrong kind of encounter. As a result, the power of those who perform the rite, the Brāhmaṇ sages, is mobilised in the curse. And, in the iron-fort version, Śiva utilises sacred ash from the disturbed sacrifice to restore the frozen men to life. The sacrifice thus propels the Rājpūts towards change, brings about the change, and restores the situation to equilibrium.

Violence, as we have seen, is not a sin in the Hindu world. Indeed, Rājpūts are *supposed* to be violent in their culturally sanctioned role as protectors of the sacrifice and the social order it symbolises. But in these stories Rājpūt violence goes bad. The flaw in the Rājpūt penchant for violence is somewhat differently manifested in the two stories. In Darakjī's version, it takes the form of an animosity toward Hindu temples and Brāhmaṇs that results in the attack on the sacrifice. In the iron-fort version, Rājpūt violence is manifested by the celebrated Rājpūt love of blood sport; this results in the inadvertent pollution of the sacrifice. In both cases, the Rājpūts ruin the sacrifice, although this is clearest in the Darakjī version in which the sacrifice is actually left temporarily incomplete.

The concept of the renegade Kṣatriya is a myth image we have already met in the story of Paraśurām. Instead of protecting Brāhmaṇs, Kārtavirya's sons attack Jamadagni's hermitage, killing the great sage in the process. This gives rise to Paraśurām's vengeance, leaving the world without Kṣatriyas altogether, and ultimately leading to the creation of the Fire Clan Rājpūts. This theme is reiterated, albeit in a more parochial context, in the Māheśvarī origin myth. In the Darakjī version, the Rājpūts become demonic under the influence of Jainism (just as they do in Darakjī's version of the Fire Clan origin narrative). In the iron-fort version the corruption seems less severe; it is more a matter of carelessness (and perhaps arrogance) than of culpable sin. But in both cases, the Rājpūt ancestors of the Māheśvarīs are guilty of the sin of Kārtavirya's sons. They oppose and pollute the sacrificial order. The price they pay for the deed is the sages' curse, which can be seen as parallel to Paraśurām's revenge.

In the Māheśvarī story, of course, the delinquent Rājpūts are not actually eradicated, unlike the unfortunate Kṣatriyas of the Paraśurām myth. Instead, they are transformed. The first stage of their transformation is physical immobilisation. It is as if they are dead. A powerful deity's divine power then returns them to life, but they have had to relinquish their Rājpūt character; no longer warriors, now they are Vaiśya (i.e., Baniyā) traders. The bath in the Sūrya Kuṇḍ serves as a clear marker of the final transition. The alteration is profound indeed, and is vividly symbolised by the metaphor of melting weapons being converted to the tools of trade. It can be said that the warriors themselves have been melted down and transmuted into a totally different social type.

But although they have offended against it, they are not actually expelled from the sacrificial order. Instead, the Māheśvarīs-to-be leave one niche within the social order, that of Kṣatriyahood, only to return to the sacrificial social order in the end, albeit on a completely new basis. Their return is symbolised by their reestablishment of a relationship with Brāhmaṇs. Once again they are *jajmāns* (sponsors of sacrifices), but in a different social role: now they are traders who will support Brāhmaṇ priests with their wealth. When, in the Darakjī version, the Brāhmaṇ sages complain to Śiva that the sacrifice has not yet been completed, I think we may take it that they are really saying that *dakṣiṇā* (payment) has not yet been given, for the deity responds with a promise of future largess from the new traders. Underlying this exchange is the idea, already encountered by us in the Dāhimā Brāhmaṇ narrative, that without *dakṣinā* (payment to the priests) a sacrifice cannot be efficacious. Thus, when the new traders become rich, all will be complete; Brāhmaṇs will have patrons (though of a sort different from the Rājpūts), and the sacrifice will be restored to efficacy.

As in many other Rajasthani origin myths, females have a key role to play in the creation of the Māheśvarī caste, and here we find at least an echo of the ancestral goddess myth model. Pārvatī's contribution is pivotal. Also crucial is the part played by the queen and wives of the king's henchmen. In the end, it is their intervention that makes possible the revivifying of their frozen husbands. It so happens, however, that the theme of female participation does not, in this narrative, generate any caste or lineage goddess. Māheśvarī clans (and probably their lineage segments) are linked with numerous goddesses, but these are not mentioned in the versions of the Māheśvarī origin myth that I have seen (although they are frequently named as part of the information, often appended to printings of the origin myth, concerning the original 72 clans). It is quite possible that the Māheśvarī origin narrative was linked with some of these goddesses in local versions formerly transmitted by traditional genealogists, but I have no evidence on this point. As far as I am aware, no single goddess plays a role analogous to that of the Dāhimā's Dadhimatī among the Māheśvarīs. On the other hand, the fact that the caste bears Pārvatī's name is a possible hint of such a relationship in the past.

The Māheśvarīs, as we have said, are an example of a caste that possesses a canonical origin narrative. It is true that there are currently two versions in printed circulation, the Darakjī and iron-fort variants, but the Darakjī version holds sway in the official publications of the caste's national association, and the two versions are quite similar in any case. We now turn to the Khaṇḍelvāl Vaiśya caste and a decidedly more chaotic situation.

Multiple Pasts: Khaṇḍelvāl Vaiśyas

It must be clearly understood that there is no such thing as a 'Khaṇḍelvāl' caste, despite the widespread impression in Rajasthan and beyond that such an entity exists. This label, which means 'of Khandela', is borne by at least four separate castes (and probably more): a Brāhmaṇ caste, a carpenter caste, and two separate castes of traders.[19] One of the trading castes is the Khaṇḍelvāl Jains, to be discussed in the next chapter. The other, and the one that concerns us here, is the Khaṇḍelvāl Vaiśya caste, a group that is entirely Hindu. It is certainly possible, even likely, that these two castes share a common past, but to the best of my knowledge there is no connection between them today.[20] An instructive contrast is provided by the Agravāls (to be discussed in Chapter Six). The membership of this caste consists of both Hindus and Jains, and intermarriage takes place between the two religious groups. This means that we can speak of a single Agravāl caste, despite the sectarian division. As far as I am aware, however, there is currently no intermarriage at all between Khaṇḍelvāl Vaiśyas and Khaṇḍelvāl Jains. That is, they are separate endogamous castes.

A highly placed official of the Akhil Bhāratvarṣīya Khaṇḍelvāl Vaiśya Mahāsabhā (the Khaṇḍlevāl Vaiśyas' national caste association) informed me that there are roughly 500,000 Khaṇḍelvāl Vaiśyas in India, with about 80,000 in Jaipur. The reliability of these figures, however, is questionable. The caste is present in significant numbers in the Rajasthani cities of Jaipur, Alwar, Kota, Ajmer, and Dausa. Dausa appears to be a Khaṇḍelvāl Vaiśya epicenter. This caste is significantly less prosperous than the Māheśvarīs, or at least this appears to be the case in Jaipur. Here they seem to have mainly occupied the economic niche of shopkeeping, especially as sellers of sweets and groceries. Only relatively recently have they been able to establish a foothold in the lucrative gemstone trade. Many are also in service occupations in Jaipur. In villages they are almost entirely shopkeepers and moneylenders.

Their national caste association was founded in 1914, and its current headquarters are in Jaipur. In Jaipur, there is also a separate local association (the Śrī Khaṇḍelvāl Vaiśya Hitkāriṇī Sabhā) that manages schools, a college, and two temples in the city. At the time of my research, both organisations were in a state of disorganisation and disarray, the apparent result of power struggles and disputes. The Khaṇḍelvāl Vaiśyas have a caste-only festival analogous to the Māheśvarīs' *maheś navmī*. It occurs on the same date as the Hindu spring festival of *vasant pancmī*, and was once celebrated with processions and other public events in Jaipur. But when I participated in the event in 1997, it was celebrated in an extremely desultory manner in the confines of the national association's office. Participants consisted of a few association bigwigs and office staff.

Religious figures have been an important element in this caste's collective sense of itself. A famous seventeenth century Dādūpanthī poet-saint named Sundardāsjī, born of Khaṇḍelvāl Vaiśya parents in Dausa, is a major caste icon and symbol of caste pride.[21] The national association has made efforts (as yet unsuccessful at the time of my research) to have a postage stamp issued in his honour. In recent times, another significant focus for Khaṇḍelvāl Vaiśya spiritual energy and caste identity has been a Vaiṣṇava guru named Balrāmdāsjī. He was born in 1911 in Jaipur State to Khaṇḍelvāl Vaiśya parents, and was still living at the time of my research. Although his headquarters are in Lodra in Gujarat, he makes periodic visits to Rajasthan where he has a large following among the state's Khaṇḍelvāl Vaiśyas.

The caste's national association has formulated an official list of 72 Khaṇḍelvāl Vaiśya clans (called *gotras* in this case). The list is frequently reproduced in caste publications, and is conspicuously displayed in large lettering on an interior wall of the association's Jaipur headquarters. A survey of matrimonial ads in five issues of *Khaṇḍelvāl Mahāsabhā Patrikā* (the national association's bimonthly journal) from late 1996 to early 1997 yielded a total of 50 clan names. Of these, 42 overlapped with the national association's official list, suggesting that the rationalised version of the clan system fits only incompletely with social reality. As among the Māheśvarīs (and all the trading castes considered in this book), the clans are the basic units of exogamy. The Khaṇḍelvāl Vaiśyas follow a two-clan rule of exogamy, as shown by the fact that almost all matrimonial advertisements seen listed only the father and mother's clans for the prospective bride or groom.[22] As among the Māheśvaris (and other castes), there was once a strong Ten/Twenty distinction in this caste. It is said to be only of marginal importance today.

The pattern of consulting caste genealogists is on the wane among the Khaṇḍelvāl Vaiśyas, but is in a somewhat healthier state than among the Māheśvaris. As do the Māheśvarīs, the Khaṇḍelvāl Vaiśyas call their genealogists Jāgās. I have had the privilege of meeting several of them (see Figures 4.3 and 4.4). Of the ones I met, the most active currently was a middle-aged man living in Tūngā, a village in eastern Jaipur District with a population of about 8,000. He had numerous patrons in Dausa town from whom he was evidently making a very good living. His books were in excellent order, and he claimed that his college-educated son intended to follow in his footsteps. Probably more typical of the current situation, however, was a group of Khaṇḍelvāl Vaiśya genealogists living together in a colony in Lavān, a small town in western Dausa District with a population of about 20,000. One of them, the man I had come to see, was the then-elderly genealogist of the family of a Khaṇḍelvāl Vaiśya friend who lived in Jaipur. This man had stopped coming to his patron's urban home some years back because of illness, and nobody had taken his place. His books, however, were in good condition, though obviously not fully up to date.

I mention these encounters because they are of a piece with the currently unsystematised character of the Khaṇḍelvāl Vaiśyas' mythohistory. The reason for the current disorder is not totally clear, but at least in

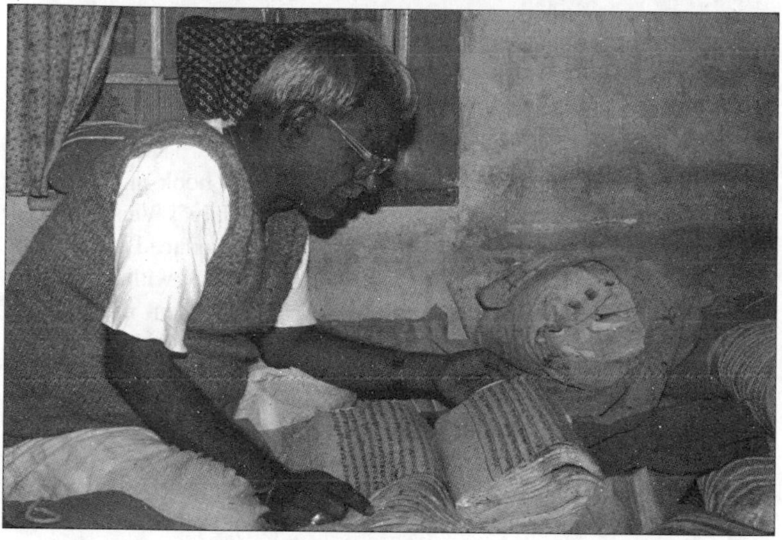

Figure 4.3
A genealogist who serves members of the Khaṇḍelvāl Vaiśya caste.

Figure 4.4
A traditional genealogist's book with wrapper.

part it seems to reflect organisational problems in the national association. The genealogists are not quite out of the picture yet, but—and in contrast to the situation among the Māheśvarīs—the caste's national association has proven incapable of settling on an origin narrative that can be woven into a wider project of rationalising the caste's structure and social identity. There is no equivalent to Darakjī's influential book in this caste's collective life. There is indeed a book on Khaṇḍelvāl Vaiśya history (Motīlāl Gupt n.d.), but the most important myth reproduced by this book (and retold below) has never achieved general currency within the caste. Rather, we are dealing here with a congeries of different narratives of varying degrees of mutual resemblance. In the midst of this variation, however, we can discern some common themes.

Khaṇḍelvāl Vaiśya Origin Myths

We begin with a version told by the elderly genealogist of Lavān (above). One of his patrons (my friend) had transcribed his oral telling of the story some years earlier and published it in *Khaṇḍelvāl Mahāsabhā Patrikā* (M. C. Khaṇḍelvāl 1984). When I met this genealogist in 1996, he was kind enough to recite the story orally for me. There are some significant differences between the published version and the one I heard, which I will discuss. We begin with a summary of the published version. The story returns us to the town of Khandela and to nearby Lohargal.

> In ancient times, there lived a king of Khandela by the name of Khargal. One time, this king sponsored a sacrifice that was performed by a great sage named Durvāsā. Sages from many different places had been invited to the sacrifice, and among them was the famous Jamadagni Ṛṣi, who came with two disciples from Lohargal. While on the way to the sacrifice, Jamadagni killed a deer, and he unwisely brought the dead deer into the place of the sacrifice. Durvāsā lacked the power to revive the dead creature, and (presumably because of this) when he saw the body in the place of sacrifice he became extremely angry. He thereupon cursed Jamadagni and his disciples, turning them into stone. When news of the curse reached Jamadagni's wife in Lohargal, she became angry. She came to the place of sacrifice where she threatened a counter-curse if her husband were not restored to life.
>
> Now, King Khargal, fearing that the sacrifice might not be completed, became very uneasy. He pleaded with Jamadagni's wife not to curse

> Durvāsā, but she remained determined. So the king then begged Durvāsā to return Jamadagni and his disciples to their former state. Durvāsā agreed, but only under the condition that Jamadagni would no longer be a Brāhmaṇ, but would be allowed to live on the earth as a Vaiśya, and that his descendants would be called Khaṇḍelvāl Vaiśyas. He also commanded that the descendants of one of Jamadagni's disciples would become the Khaṇḍelvāl Brāhmaṇs, who would serve the Khaṇḍelvāl Vaiśyas as priests. The other disciple's descendants would become the genealogists of the Khaṇḍelvāl Vaiśyas, and serve them by recording and reading their genealogies. Ultimately, the different clans within the caste developed and separated from each other, acquiring their names on the basis of locality and the names of individual ancestors.

Before moving on, a few words about the dramatis personae of the story are in order. Jamadagni we have already met in the previous chapter; he is the father of Paraśurām, who, as we now see, figures prominently in regional mythology. Durvāsā (or Durvāsas) is a sage, said to be an incarnation of Śiva, who is famous for his sensitivity to insult and violent temper. Even the gods fear him. In our story, we see an example of his propensity to anger. Both sages are well known figures in the Puranic and Epic traditions, but as far as I know the events recounted in this narrative belong to local tradition alone. Finally, King Khargal looks a lot like King Khargalsen of the Māheśvarī myth. We may surmise that the genealogists of various castes drew from a common store of names and myth images in formulating these narratives.

It should also be noted that although this myth posits a special relationship between Khaṇḍelvāl Vaiśyas and Khaṇḍelvāl Brāhmaṇs, no such relationship exists today (if it ever did). The point is important to the story, however, for it illustrates the idea that the Khaṇḍelvāl Vaiśyas, now ex-Brāhmaṇs, would no longer officiate at sacrifices, but would sponsor them in the future, for which they would need Brāhmaṇ priests.

Finally, something should be said about the locale of these events. As we know, the link between the Māheśvarīs and Khandela and Lohargal is tenuous at best. In this case, there is at least a nominal connection with Khandela, for the name 'Khaṇḍelvāl' actually signifies that the group comes from Khandela. As far as I know, there is no monument or special place of pilgrimage for Khaṇḍelvāl Vaiśyas at Khandela, although some members of the caste have clan or lineage deities there. Nor, as far as I am aware, is there any local tradition at Lohargal connecting the place with the Khaṇḍelvāl Vaiśyas. Lohargal is, however, physically close to Khandela.

The story, as we have seen it thus far, contains two central assertions. The first is that the Khaṇḍelvāl Vaiśyas were originally Brāhmaṇs. This is a significant departure from the far more common belief (as this book will show) that trading castes are descended from Rājpūts, a belief that we have already encountered in the Māheśvarī case. The second assertion is that their transformation from Brāhmaṇhood to trader status was connected with the rite of sacrifice, and more specifically with a change in the nature of their relationship (or that of their putative ancestor) to the sacrifice. What begins as Jamadagni's positive relationship with the rite—his invitation to participate—turns negative when he pollutes the site of the rite with an act of violence. In this we see a direct parallel with the sacrifice–disruption and hunting incidents in our two versions of the Māheśvarī narrative, and the parallel is continued with the freezing of the sage and his disciples into immobility and their subsequent change of social essence.

As in the Māheśvarī case, the change of social personality ends with a reunion with the rite of sacrifice, albeit on an entirely new basis. Jamadagni's descendants will no longer be Brāhmaṇs. They will return to the sacrificial order, but as sponsors of the rite, not as performers. They will therefore need the services of priests, who will be the Khaṇḍelvāl Brāhmaṇs.

When the same genealogist and one of his colleagues recited the same story orally for me in 1996, there were some interesting differences from the published version. In this telling,[23]

> Jamadagni and his wife, Reṇukā, had two sons. One was Paraśurām, who had no issue because he was celibate. The other was Khaṇḍilya Ṛṣi, who married and had twenty-eight sons. The king of Khandela sponsored a sacrifice that was attended by all the kings of the area. Durvāsā had come from Lohargal for the sacrifice, which (if I understood the somewhat confused and hard-to-follow telling rightly) was actually performed by Khaṇḍilya Ṛṣi, who was the 'King's *ṛṣi* (sage)'. Durvāsā objected to the animal sacrifice entailed by the rite, and so he said to the twenty-eight sons of Khaṇḍilya Ṛṣi that they should worship God, protect all life, and take up business. And they thus became the 'Khaṇḍelvāl Baniyās'.

The two reciters of the story then added elaborations of the myth dealing with the origin of the other trading castes of the region:

> There was in those days a certain King Maheś who had 24 sons and those sons also attended the rite. They became the 'Māheśvarī Baniyās'. King Agrasen's 17 sons also came, and they became the Agravāls. From

> Osagarh (meaning Osiya) came 175 sons, and they became the Osvāls. From Vijaygaṛh came 21 sons, who became the Vījavargīs (Vijayvargīyas). The 28 sons of Khaṇḍilya Rsi produced 84 sons, and they became the progenitors of 84 clans (i.e., of the Khaṇḍelvāl Vaiśyas). But 12 of these began to deal in alcohol, and they were forced out of the caste; they became the Śungas.[24]

Here the basic pollution-of-sacrifice theme is extended to a theory of the origination of trader castes as an entire category. When I asked the two genealogists about the origin of the Khaṇḍelvāl Jains, they responded (possibly improvising) that some Agravāls and Khaṇḍelvāls became Jains because of the powerful influence of 'Rājā Jain' (for whom they gave a date of V.S. 1133 [1076 C.E.]). At that time, they said, the Khaṇḍelvāls split into the Vaiṣṇava and Jain sections. When asked about the Khaṇḍelvāl Brāhmaṇs they replied (again, possibly improvising) that Khaṇḍilyā Ṛṣi came from Ayodhya, where he had another group of sons, and they became the Khaṇḍelvāl Brāhmaṇs.

The two variants of the story are quite different in some respects, despite the fact that they come from the same source. This should be a lesson in the malleability of such narrative materials. But the important themes are quite stable: the Brāhmaṇ origin, the sacrifice, the violence, and the transformation. It should be noted, however, that other trading castes are supplied with what seem to be Kṣatriya ancestors (the kings) in the oral version. In the oral version, the hunting episode is absent, and the violence is placed within the sacrifice itself, but the idea is the same. There is no curse or freezing in the oral version, but in this case, too, Durvāsā's objection to violence brings about the transformation. In the oral version the ex-Brāhmaṇs become Khaṇḍelvāl 'Baniyās' instead of Khaṇḍelvāl Vaiśyas. I believe that this reflects more natural usage in Rajasthan.

Although our first narrative (in both its versions) supplies the Khaṇḍelvāl Vaiśyas with a Brāhmaṇ pedigree, other narratives trace the caste's ancestry to Rājpūts. An example is the following (summarised here from Motīlāl Gupt n.d.: 9, but almost certainly originating from a caste genealogist):

> There were four brothers who were soldiers. They were hunting one day, and by mischance they killed a deer beloved by a certain ancient sage. The sage was enraged and was about to curse them. But they pleaded with him, and assured him that they would give up the military profession and hunting. The sage was mollified, and withheld the curse. From that day

onward, the brothers' military life was over, and their descendants became the Khaṇḍelvāl Vaiśyas.

Although the word Rājpūt or Kṣatriya is not actually used in the above text, Rājpūt descent for the Khaṇḍelvāl Vaiśyas is clearly implied. The context in which Motīlāl Gupt offers this narrative is a discussion in which he tries to make the point that '*kṣatriyatva*' (kṣatriyaness) is an integral part of Khaṇḍelvāl Vaiśya character. He notes that they have distinguished themselves in various wars and cites the conspicuous heroism of the Haldiyā lineage (ibid.: 8–9).

A single article in *Khaṇḍelvāl Mahāsabhā Patrikā* published in 1984 (Rāmānand Khaṇḍelvāl 1984: 16–17) presents no fewer than six separate Khaṇḍelvāl Vaiśya origin myths. The author of the article attributes them to the writings of someone named Dāmodardās Khaṇḍelvāl (about whom I have no information), and provides no other context. Clearly, however, they represent a range of narratives that must once have been in active circulation. I present them in the order in which they appear in the article:

1) At the end of the *dvāpar yug*, King Pāṇḍu sponsored a sacrifice in Hastinapur. While on their way home afterwards, twenty sages and four kings heard that a Vaiśya Seṭh named Khaṇmal was holding a sacrifice. They decided to attend. On the way, they killed a deer that belonged to the sage Durvāsā. Durvāsā was performing austerities at the time, and when he opened his eyes and saw the dead deer he cursed all 24 to become stone. When Seṭh Khaṇmal heard about this, he asked Durvāsā to be merciful to his guests. The sage partially relented, but insisted that all 24 become Vaiśyas. Seṭh Khanmal thereupon brought all the new Vaiśyas together. He declared that they would henceforth be a new caste (*jāti*) with 72 clans, and that they would be called Khaṇḍelvāl Vaiśyas. They settled in Khandela, and the Brāhmaṇs of that town became their *purohits* (i.e., their family priests, presumably thereby becoming the Khaṇḍelvāl Brāhmaṇs).
2) Four brothers went hunting and they killed the tame deer of a sage. The sage cursed them to have to give up soldiering and hunting and become Vaiśyas. (This seems to be identical to the 'four soldiers' version given previously).
3) A certain Seṭh Dhanpat Mahārāj of Khandela had four sons: 1) Khaṇḍū (from whom the Khaṇḍelvāls came), 2) Maheś

(from whom the Māheśvarīs came), 3) Sunda (from whom the Sarāvgis [i.e., Jains, specifically Khaṇḍelvāl Jains] came), and 4) Bījā (from whom the Bījāvargīs [i.e., Vijayvargīyas] came).

4) Ṛṣi Paraśurām sponsored a sacrifice at Lohargal. Having broken up a golden *vedī*, he gave it as *dān*. Those who bought the gold (presumably from the recipients) were called Khaṇḍelvāl Vaiśya, and the place they began to live was called Khandela. (We shall encounter this story again below).
5) Khāṇḍal Ṛṣi performed a sacrifice, and those people who collected things for it were called Khaṇḍelvāl Vaiśyas.
6) One time in Khandela City, a king named Khaṇḍprasth sponsored a vaiśya yajña (a sacrifice, presumably in the 'Vaiśya' or non-violent mode). There the people of eighty-four castes ate together. The king had *pakkī* and *kaccī* prepared separately, and told the people they should eat wherever they wanted.[25] The Khaṇḍelvāl Brāhmaṇs and Khaṇḍelvāl Khātīs (carpenters) took *pakkī*, and the Khaṇḍelvāl Mahājans (i.e., the trading caste) took *kaccī*. (For reasons that are unclear to me, this story seems to suggest that Khaṇḍelvāl Vaiśyas have lower status on the commensal hierarchy than the Brahmans and carpenters who bear the same name).

Our final example of a Khaṇḍelvāl Vaiśya origin myth, a longer version of number 4 above, comes from Motīlāl Gupt's (n.d.) history of the caste. No longer living, Gupt was a Khaṇḍelvāl Vaiśya academician who lived in Jodhpur. Although the Khaṇḍelvāl Vaiśya Mahāsabhā in Jaipur had published the book, by the time I had begun my enquiries in 1996 nobody at the Mahāsabhā's office could recall when it was published. Indeed, I discovered to my astonishment that no copy of the book was available at the office, although there were some tattered fragments of a photocopy of a portion of the text. Portions of it have, however, been reprinted in the Mahāsabhā's magazine. I was finally able to borrow a copy from a friend's friend. I mention these details to stress the currently total nascent state, if it can be said to exist at all, of the Khaṇḍelvāl Vaiśyas' quest to rationalise a single mythohistorical construction of their identity. Given the role of the Mahāsabhā in the original publication of Gupt's book, one can imagine an alternative scenario in which it might have played a role analogous to that of Darakjī's book for the Māheśvarīs. This might indeed happen some day, for the principal myth reported in Gupt's book is certainly an ideal candidate for a canonical version of Khaṇḍelvāl Vaiśya mythohistory. But as far as I know, this has not happened yet.

In his book, Gupt reports several narratives of Khaṇḍelvāl Vaiśya origin, and these include the six given in Rāmānand Khaṇḍelvāl's article to which we have just referred.[26] The account Gupt foregrounds, however, is the following (here paraphrased from ibid.: 11–16), which he traces to the 'Revā Khaṇḍ' of the *Skanda Purāṇa* (chapters 35–40). The story takes as its point of departure the legendary rivalry between two great sages, Viśvāmitra, a Kṣatriya, and Vaśiṣṭh, a Brāhmaṇ. The rivalry was rooted in Viśvāmitra's inability to achieve the highest state of sagehood (*brahmarṣi*, a status he ultimately achieved), which is denied to all but Brāhmaṇs. To avenge an insult that Vaśiṣṭh had directed at Viśvāmitra, Viśvātmitra's 100 sons attacked Vaśiṣṭh's hermitage. In response, Vaśiṣṭh created demons who killed all 100 of Viśvāmitra's sons. Later, the sage Bharadvāj gave his own 100 mind-born sons to Viśvāmitra in substitution, and the Kṣatriya sage raised and educated them, and married them to daughters of other sages.

> One day Viśvāmitra came to a sacrifice that was being performed by the famed Hariścandra in order to cure his dropsy. Hariścandra had purchased the son of a poor Brāhmaṇ as a sacrificial offering. The victim's name was Śunahśep, and he just happened to be the son of Viśvāmitra's sister. Viśvāmitra thereupon rescued Śunahśep, and afterwards told his 100 sons that Śunahśep would be counted among his sons, would receive a share of his wealth, and that they would have to accept him as their elder brother. Of the 100 sons, 50 refused to accept this, and Viśvāmitra turned them into *mlecchs* (i.e., non-Aryan barbarians). The remaining 50 did accept the arrangement, and for this they received their father's blessing. The eldest of them was named Madhuchand, and consequently they are collectively known as the 'Madhuchandādi' Sages.
>
> Now, in atonement for his twenty-one-fold killing of the earth's Kṣatriyas, Paraśurām performed a Viṣṇu sacrifice (*viṣṇu yajña*) at Lohargal. The principal officiants were Kaśyap and Vaśiṣṭh. The Madhuchandādi Sages were staying on a hilltop overlooking Lohargal, and they served as *ṛtvik* priests. When Paraśurām distributed *dakṣinā*, they refused to accept it. The Sage Kaśyap, however, urged them to take it, for without *dakṣinā* the sacrifice would remain incomplete. At last they relented, but by the time Paraśurām heard the good news, he had already given everything away in *dān*. All that was left was the golden sacrificial altar, so he divided it into 49 pieces, each of which he gave to one of the sages. For this reason, they became known as the 'Khaṇḍal' (fragment or piece) *jāti*, and among them

> the 50th, who got no piece of the vedi, was held (at the order of a voice from the sky) in special honor. This how the Khāṇḍal Vipras (more commonly known as the Khaṇḍelvāl Brāhmaṇs) got their name.

When he turns to the origin of the Khaṇḍelvāl Vaiśyas specifically (ibid.: 15–16), author Gupt presents variations on a single theme: that the apical ancestor (*adi puruṣ*) of the Khaṇḍelvāl Vaiśyas was none other than Śunahśep. In one version, based on chapter 39 of the 'Revā Khaṇḍ', a Vaiśya named Śunahśep bought the altar pieces, and because of this he and his descendants came to be called 'Khaṇḍal, Khāṇḍal, or Khaṇḍelvāl'. In the 40th chapter we find a different take on the same basic tale. Here Śunahśep and someone named Bohrā were not included in the sacrifice; they therefore got no golden pieces, and as a result (not fully explained) became known to the world as 'Vaiśya'. Apparently editorialising, Gupt opines that Śunahśep was clearly a Brāhmaṇ, but one who, out of pride, did not want to take *dakṣiṇā*. He was wealthy enough, however, to buy the pieces from those who did take them. He then began to be called Vaiśya because of his proclivity to trade ('*len den*').

Finally, Gupt mentions another slightly different version of the same basic story. In this variant, when the 49 altar pieces were given to the 49 sages, Śunahśep and one other sage were left out of the picture. They bought the 49 pieces and started doing business (presumably with these pieces as capital). From taking the pieces 'as dān,' the Brāhmaṇs became known as Khaṇḍelvāl and the purchasers became known as Khaṇḍelvāl Vaiśyas. The town of Khandela, in turn, got its name from them because they started to live there.

Readers will recognise this entire narrative as based on a version of the story of Paraśurām's destruction of the world's Kṣatriyas that we already encountered in Chapter Three. In that version, taken from the Vana Parva of the *Mahābhārata*, the golden altar is also divided among the Brāhmaṇ priests. Clearly, this variant merely localises an Epic/ Puranic narrative by attaching it to Lohargal and a Brāhmaṇ caste of regional importance.

Narratives in Flux

The Khaṇḍevāl Vaiśya myths represent an extremely mixed bag. As we have said, there is no dominant origin narrative for the Khaṇḍelvāl Vaiśyas. Instead, we find several competing narratives in various kinds of circulation, and there are undoubtedly more in existence than the ones retold here. In fact, the current Khaṇḍelvāl Vaiśya situation is probably a good indication of how things were among Māheśvarīs at the time Darakjī conducted his research. There are obviously certain 'myth-atoms' that stick to one another in varying molecular combinations and permutations: the respectable pedigree, the sacrifice (spoiled or not), Durvāsā, becoming stonelike, Paraśurām, Khandela, Lohargal, and so on. Also, it is clear that, in the conceptual world in which these narratives took shape, four castes formed a natural cluster: the Māheśvarīs, Khaṇḍelvāl Vaiśyas, Khaṇḍelvāl Jains, and Vijayvargīyas.

One narrative stands out as most clearly different from the others. This of course is the Śunahśep version. There are two big differences between this and the other versions. First, it is far more embedded in Epic/Puranic tradition. Second, its true main focus is Brāhmaṇs, not traders. As I was able to discover, the story of the 50 sages is in fact the core of the origin myth of the Khaṇḍelvāl Brāhmaṇs (or Khaṇḍelvāl Vipras, as they prefer to be called) currently being promoted in their caste publications (see Pīpalvā 1997). The traders seem to be tacked on as an afterthought at the end of this tale.

But despite the immense variation of these narratives, we can see familiar themes in many of them, and this includes the Śunahśep version. The most important is the image of transformative encounters with the sacrifice. The sacrifice is not mentioned in all of the narratives, possibly because some of them are incomplete fragments. But it is the key episode in most of them. We see again that when basic changes occur in the social essence of groups, the sacrifice is likely to be involved in one way or another. This notion is particularly salient in the Śunahśep narrative. The point of this story is clearly that *who* you are depends on the *nature of your relationship* with the sacrifice. Śunahśep leaves the Brāhmaṇ fold precisely because he does not take *dakṣinā* in the normal way. He buys it and sells it, and in this way becomes a trader. Another key theme, though not present in all of the narratives, is the repudiation of violence in or around the sacrifice. Paradigmatically—and as we have already seen in the Māheśvarī case—an act of violence pollutes a sacrifice or offends a Brāhmaṇ. This sets in motion a social transformation.

In one respect, however, the Khaṇḍelvāl Vaiśya tales—though not all of them—depart from the Māheśvarī pattern. The claim of a Brāhmaṇ pedigree, as opposed to a Rājpūt pedigree, is an important trend in this group of narratives. We shall return to this point after taking a brief look at origin narratives of the Vijayvargīyas.

Vijayvargīyas

The Vijayvargīya caste is small and obscure in comparison to the Māheśvarīs and Khaṇḍelvāl Vaiśyas. Even some of my well-informed friends in Jaipur's business community were under the impression that the Vijayvargīyas are a subgroup of some kind among the Khaṇḍelvāl Vaiśyas. They are, however, an endogamous caste with their own traditions and group identity.

In numbers they are few. A knowledgeable acquaintance deeply involved in the caste's organisational affairs gave me an estimated total of around 100,000, but stressed that this is no more than an educated guess. Members of the caste seem to be concentrated in Jaipur, Dausa and Kota Districts, and in the cities of Jaipur, Kota, Tonk, Ajmer, Malpura and Indore. They have their own modern caste association, the Akhil Bhāratīya Vijayvargīya Vaiśya Mahāsabhā (founded in 1920) that produces the usual array of publications, and organises caste affairs in a manner similar to that of other caste associations among traders.

Until recently, the Vijayvargīyas appear to have languished at the periphery of the region's commercial life. In the past (and to some extent nowadays), they were specialists in the perfume business, but many were not involved in trade of any kind. Insiders told me that until 25 or 30 years ago they were a poor community relative to the other trading castes, mostly living in villages where they were small businessmen, moneylenders and farmers. The caste has become much more urbanised since 1960 or so, but many still live in rural areas.

They were apparently never as prominent in state service as the other trading castes, a fact noted by the 1891 *Marwar Census Report* (M. H. Singh 1997: 440). In this connection, the report also notes an interesting legend about the caste connecting them with the famed sixteenth-century poetess-saint, Mīrābāī. According to the well-known story of her life, she married a prince of Mewar. Her conjugal family, however, despised her because of her devotion to Kṛṣṇa. Her father-in-law (or husband, or brother-in-law, depending on the telling) attempted to kill her by sending her a cup of poison disguised as *caraṇāmṛt* (water used to wash the feet of a divine image). When she drank it, Kṛṣṇa intervened and changed the poison into genuine *caraṇāmṛt*. Now, according to the legend reported by the *Census*, the poison was actually given to her by one Kālūrām Bījābargī, a Vijayvargīya who was the king's chief minister. Mīrābāī then cursed the caste. They would henceforth be excluded from state service, and in families that had food there would be no children, and in families with children there would be no food.

The Vijayvargīyas are culturally and socially similar to the Māheśvarīs and Khaṇḍelvāl Vaiśyas. They are mostly (if not entirely) Vaiṣṇava, with especially strong ties to the Rāmsnehī sect. Informants tell me that they were once divided into Twenty and Ten sections, but the distinction apparently has little saliency today. Their system of clans and rules of exogamy are the same as other trading groups we have seen. They are unique, however, in the sheer number of exogamous clans they claim. Caste publications list a total of 172. This large number is possibly a by-product of the relatively small size of the caste. In theory, at least, a small number of clans could raise the level of difficulty in finding marriage partners not excluded by the rules of exogamy, especially in a small caste spread thinly on the ground. That is, from the standpoint of any given family, the smaller the number of clans, the larger the proportion of total caste membership exluded as potential marriage partners by clan exogamy. This circumstance could have led to a pressure to elevate more lineages to the status of separate clans. The very large Agravāl caste (to be discussed in Chapter Six), with its mere 18 (or, according to the telling, 17 and one half) clans, represents the opposite situation. In all events, in the Vijayvargīya case it appears that someone has simply placed a '1' in front of '72', the latter figure being a culturally conventional number (as we have seen among the Māheśvarīs and Khaṇḍelvāl Vaiśyas).

Origin Myths

While it is probable that caste genealogists of the Vijayvargīyas continue to pursue their craft in rural areas, I was unable to meet any. However, narratives obtained from caste genealogists (known as Rāvs or Jāgās among the Vijayvargīyas) are available in various caste publications. The materials I was able to obtain are thin, but they are useful in comparison with the origin narratives of other Hindu cluster castes.

One source is an essay (R. Vijayvargīya 1969) on the origin and development of the Vijayvargīya caste published as part of the souvenir volume for the national association's 1969 meeting. Its author states that when the national association met for the first time in Ajmer in 1920, efforts were made to scrutinise the traditional genealogists' books for clues about the caste's origin. Those involved in this effort also decided—either at this meeting or soon thereafter—to standardise the caste's name to Vijayvargīya. In the genealogists' books, the name had been commonly written as Vījāvargī, Bījābargī or Bījāvat, but these were rejected as corruptions of what was said to be the original and proper 'Vijayvargīya'—which the author says means, 'Those who obtain victory'. As we know, this sort of effort to rationalise a caste's identity was typical of the time, and it is of interest that recovering the caste's mythohistory was high on the association's agenda from the very start. It demonstrates the great importance that such materials were to assume in the efforts of modern caste associations to project corporate identities for the castes they represented.

The article's author presents a Vijayvargīya origin narrative (ibid.: 10) that he obtained from a caste genealogist. It traces the caste's descent to the year 301 (calendar unspecified, but likely to be the Vikram era).

> It seems that there was once a certain Pāl Śāh who had two sons: Khāṇḍā and Bījā. Bījā conquered Ranthambhor (near the modern town of Sawai Madhopur), and from seventy-two 'beings' (the author uses the term *prāṇī*) made the Vijayvargīya caste, so-called because of their victory (*vijay*). From these seventy-two came the caste's seventy-two clans (here called *gotras*).

Pāl Śāh is not identified further in this very brief passage, nor is anything said about how 72 clans can be squared with the 172 claimed today by the Vijayvargīyas. Clearly the other son, Khāṇḍā, is supposed to be the founder of the Khaṇḍelvāl Vaiśyas, although this is not actually said.

I was able to find one other useful source. This is an essay on Vijayvargīya history published in a 1993 caste directory (Āśārām Vijayvargīya 1993). The author reproduces brief synopses of several versions of the caste's origin narratives. Two of these are as follows:

1) He cites an article appearing in a caste magazine (*Sacitra Vijayvargīya*, year 1, no. 1) published in Kolkata in 1921. The author of this article provides the following narrative (context unknown):

> In the year V.S. 363 (no reason for this year is given), the ruler of Khandela was a Cauhān Kṣatriya. His son's name was Jayantsiṃh. His minister was Dharmpāl or Puṇyapāl, who was an adherent of the Vaiśya *dharm*. He had four sons, Sūṇḍā, Khāṇḍā, Maheś, and Bījā. From them came four castes: the Sarāvgis (i.e., Khaṇḍelvāl Jains), the Khaṇḍelvāls (Khaṇḍelvāl Vaiśyas), the Māheśvarīs and the Bījābargīs (Vijayvargīyas).

2) He also cites an account presented in the Jodhpur 1891 Census (see M. H. Singh 1997: 439–40). This story, which he reports accurately, returns us yet again to Khandela:

> It seems in Khandela there once lived a Mahājan named Dhanpāl. He had four sons from whom emerged the Sarāvgis, the Khaṇḍelvāls, the Māheśvarīs and the Bījābargīs. Now, Bījā went with the King's son to Ranthambhor. There, as a boon from Ganés,[27] the prince became king and Bījā became his chief minister. The Bījābargīs (i.e., Vijayvargīyas) are his descendants. But then, when Ranthambhor came under Muslim rule, the Bījābargīs dispersed to Delhi and various towns and cities such cities as Ajmer and Nagaur.

On the basis of the four-brothers motif, the article's author declares that it can at least be concluded that the origin of these four castes occurred in Khandela. We, of course, have seen this motif already in connection with the Khaṇḍelvāl Vaiśyas. Using the four-brothers story as a point of departure, and apparently on the basis of a caste genealogist's narrative, he then continues with what he regards as a reasonable reconstruction of the origin of the Vijayvargīya caste:

> Because of the growing influence of Jainism, the Māheśvarīs went to Didwana, and thus became a new caste (i.e., the Ḍīḍū Māheśvarīs). Among the remaining Khaṇḍelvāl Vaiśyas, not all agreed with Jainism. The king had already fallen under the Jains' influence, which led to a break between king and his prince, Jayantsiṃh. The Viṣṇu-worshiping section of the Khaṇḍelvāl Vaiśyas supported the prince in his ambition to establish a separate kingdom. Their first stop was in Lakheri; then they went to the place now known as Ranthambhor. Here an image of Ganés manifested. With the god's assistance, Jayantsiṃh, his minister Bījā, and seventy-one supporting families of supporters defeated the king of the Bhils, who then ruled that place, and established a new kingdom. Because of Bījā's valor, he created a new caste out of the seventy-two families collectively. They were the Bījābargīs or Vijayvargīyas.
>
> From the very beginning the '*sanātan dharmi*' (i.e., Hindu) castes—namely the Māheśvarīs, Khaṇḍelvāl Vaiśyas, and Vijayvargīyas—all had seventy-two clans. But because the Vijayvargīyas had established a new kingdom, additional population was added from Khandela for the purpose of strength in numbers (thus explaining the larger number of Vijayvargīya clans). In the years 1049–50 C.E., one Pīthāśāh (about whom nothing else is said) invited the whole caste to a sixteen-day meeting in Pīplū village in Tonk district. The meeting established sixteen temples, and, in recognition of his efforts, the meeting changed Pīthāśāh's clan name from Sūrṭhoṭh to

Caudhrī. The meeting called a Gujarati Brāhmaṇ and recognized him as 'Rāv' (genealogist); they presented seventeen books to him for the recording of genealogies, and arranged for his support and proper respect (dān, *mān* and *sammān*).

The attribution of Brāhmaṇ ancestry to the genealogist in this last account betrays the milieu of professional genealogists from which its basic elements must have originated. The reference to the origination of the Caudhrī clan's name suggests that the story was probably part of the repertoire of a lineage of genealogists who served families of this clan. The story leaves a few loose ends, most conspicuously that of the fate of the Khaṇḍelvāl Vaiśyas.

With these rather scattered and disorganised Vijayvargīya materials now in the mix, let us turn to a general analysis of the mythohistorical materials presented in this chapter.

Sacrifice and the Creation of Traders

Ancestry

Between these three castes there are clear differences in the nature of the ancestry they claim. A powerful trend among the region's traders generally is to trace the descent of their castes to Rājpūts. Whatever else this might mean, in Rajasthan it is a clear bid for co-participation in the high social status of Rājpūts as well as the assertion of a special social link with them. That link was in fact an important reality in the former social and political systems of the region. This tendency is particularly pronounced among the Jains, as the next chapter will show. Of the castes considered in this chapter, the Māheśvarīs are the clearest case in point, for both versions of their origin myth unambiguously claim Rājpūt descent. The Khaṇḍelvāl Vaiśya and Vijayvargīya cases are less clear.

In the Khaṇḍelvāl Vaiśya case, we have seen that only one narrative (the 'four soldiers' story) claims, or seems to claim, Rājpūt descent. Another (the 'Seṭh Dhanpat' story) points to Vaiśya descent. The Śunahśep narrative posits Brāhmaṇ ancestry.[28] The remaining Khaṇḍelvāl Vaiśya narratives, discounting ambiguities, prefer Brāhmaṇ ancestry. A Brāhmaṇ pedigree is certainly a distinguished one, but it lacks the element of connection with the Rājpūts that seems to be an important theme in trader cultures of identity. The reasons for the Brāhmaṇ claim are not clear, but I suggest that it might have something to do with the 'Khaṇḍelvāl' label this caste bears in common with the Khaṇḍelvāl Jains. Stressing a Brāhmaṇ heritage would accentuate their separateness from the Jain caste, given the anti-Brahmanical flavour of Jainism. Amidst these variations, however, it can at least be said that most of the Khaṇḍelvāl Vaiśya narratives, though not all, *reject* a Vaiśya pedigree for the caste.

The Vijayvargīya materials also present ambiguities. In accepting Vaiśya ancestry for the caste, these narratives appear to diverge from the trader norm. But then we find hints of Rājpūt/Kṣatriya ancestry entering through the back door. For example, although the 'Pāl Śāh' Vijayvargīya myth does not claim Rājpūt status for Bījā, the founder of the caste, the portrait of his behaviour as conqueror of Ranthambor certainly suggests Rājpūt traits. The other narratives of this caste that we have seen posit (or seem to posit) Vaiśya ancestry, but two of them also impute Rājpūtlike behaviour to ancestor Bījā in connection with the conquest of Ranthambhor. Moreover, the caste's modern name, with its stress on the central notion of victory (*vijay*) seems to reflect a martial idea.

But it has to be said that, on the whole, the Vijayvargīya narratives seem more comfortable with the notion of Vaiśya ancestry than those of any of the traders considered thus far. Why this is so is not clear. However, it seems possible that of all the trading castes considered in this book, the Vijayvargīyas were the least employed in state service. As we know, a legend (the one connecting the caste with Mīrābāī) exists to explain this apparent fact. And if this were true, then the Vijayvargīyas would have been, of all the trader castes, the least present in Rājpūt social space. In such a context, the symbolic assertion of a relationship with the ruling martial aristocracy might have been a less pressing symbolic issue than for other traders. Perhaps, too, the acquiescence in Vaiśya ancestry merely reflects the relative marginality of the Vijayvargīyas among the region's trading groups. Maybe for them—the smallest and probably the poorest of the trading castes—the claim of Vaiśya ancestry was grand enough to satisfy what were their (or their genealogists') relatively modest expectations, and perhaps a claim of a Rājpūt pedigree would have exceeded the limits of credibility. Or possibly materials more complete than the ones we have would alter the picture.

There is another distinctive trait of the Vijayvargīyas' origin myths. Alone among our narratives, these stories make no reference to the sacrifice. This might merely reflect the thinness of the materials at hand.

I would like to suggest, however, that it might be connected with their acceptance of Vaiśya ancestry. From this standpoint, it could be argued that the Vijayvargīya narratives are not really *origin* narratives at all. The origin narratives of the other trading castes describe a fundamental change in the social essence of the groups in question. This involves a radical break with the past and a subsequent transformation in the social personality of the group. Crucial to this dynamic is contact with the sacrifice. But in the Vijayvargīya case, the element of transformation is not present, or at least is only minimally stressed. And if there is no transformation, there is no need for the sacrifice.

The Sacrifice

This brings into sharp relief the principal theme of the other Hindu-cluster narratives, which is the role of the sacrifice as myth model in depictions of social creation and change. The narratives link the sacrifice with the subthemes of violence, illegitimate violence, and the amelioration of violence. The Māheśvarī narrative exemplifies the general paradigm. The group that is to be transformed (that is, the ancestor or ancestors of the new-caste-to-be) first enters a negative relationship with the rite of sacrifice. This negativity has something to do with wrongfully directed violence. In the Māheśvarī case, violence is directed against the sacrifice itself by Rājpūts. The Khaṇḍelvāl Vaiśya myths are far less uniform, but in virtually every one of them a sacrifice is involved in one way or the other in the caste's creation. Not all of these myths involve violence, but in those that do, the miscreants are Brāhmaṇs *or* Rājpūts, and violence—the dead deer or violence perpetrated within the sacrifice itself—precipitates the action. In both Māheśvarī and Khaṇḍelvāl Vaiśya cases, the violence offends or enrages a powerful Brāhmaṇ sage or group of sages, which ultimately brings about the group's change.

The misdirection of violence in these narratives involves violations of the code that governs the normative character of the group in question. In the Māheśvarī case, the protagonists ignore the requirement that Rājpūts use violence solely to protect the sacrifice and the social order of which it is the core. In the Khaṇḍelvāl Vaiśya case, the issue is, in part, that Brāhmaṇs should not be violent at all. The Brahmanical subculture of contemporary Rajasthan is deeply vegetarian, and thus for Brāhmaṇs to engage in hunting (in the case of one narrative), a characteristically Rājpūt activity, is for them to act outside the normal norms of Brāhmaṇhood. And in the contemporary cultural milieu of the Hindu traders to whom these narratives belong, for a Brāhmaṇ to preside over animal sacrifice (in the case of one of the Khaṇḍelvāl Vaiśya tales) is also problematic. As we shall see, however, the Jains see animal sacrifice as a natural Brāhmaṇ trait.

These violations bring on the curse. The curse results in a period of separation from any normal social status, as dramatised (in the Māheśvarī narrative and one of the Khaṇḍelvāl Vaiśya narratives) by a condition of stonelike immobility and non-interactivity. The group is then returned to the social order, but in a new condition and status. The transformation is registered in a shift of the group's relationship with Brāhmaṇs, i.e., those whose distinctive domain is the sacrifice. The Māheśvarīs resume the sponsorship of sacrifices, but no longer as Kṣatriyas. In the case of one of our Khaṇḍelvāl Vaiśya narratives, the traders-to-be begin as Brāhmaṇs and lose their Brāhmaṇ status. No longer officiants of the sacrifice, they become patrons of sacrifices performed by *other* Brāhmaṇs.

Of all the narratives discussed in this chapter, the Śunahśep version of Khaṇḍelvāl Vaiśya origins stands most clearly apart from the others. This is because it is actually an origin myth of the Khaṇḍelvāl Brāhmaṇs onto which a Khaṇḍelvāl Vaiśya spur has been grafted (and of course the Khaṇḍelvāl Brāhmaṇ myth itself was laid over an even older narrative). In this myth, too, the theme of violence is present, but in a manner that differs from the other narratives. In this case, the violence is not committed by traders-to-be; instead Paraśurām inflicts it on the Kṣatriyas, whom he kills in vengeance for his father's death. As in our trader narratives, however, this violence distorts the code of conduct natural to the group to which the perpetrator is born. Paraśurām, a Brāhmaṇ, acts like a Kṣatriya (reflecting, as we know, a flaw in his own ancestry). The violation brings about a disequilibrium. Harmony is ultimately restored, as we now know to expect, *by means of a sacrifice*. Paraśurām's sin is expiated, and in the process two castes are created: Khaṇḍelvāl Brāhmaṇs and Khaṇḍelvāl Vaiśyas.

There is also an interesting echo of the Dāhimā Brāhmaṇ narrative in the Śunahśep myth. As in the Dāhimā Brāhmaṇ case, the Khaṇḍelvāl Brāhmaṇ caste arises from Brāhmaṇ sages, now domesticated by their acceptance of *dakṣiṇā* as recompense for their role in the rite. The Khaṇḍelvāl Vaiśyas come into existence when a Brāhmaṇ does *not* take *dakṣiṇā*—i.e., a priestly sort of transaction—but instead buys and sells the pieces of a sacrificial altar, a more commercial sort of transaction.

Key female figures sometimes play a role in the mythohistorical creation of the groups considered in this chapter, but the myth model of the ancestral goddess is weak by comparison with the previous chapter. It is strongest in the Māheśvarī case; in their narratives, the roles played by the frozen men's wives and Pārvatī are pivotal. In the Khaṇḍelvāl Vaiśya case, Jamadagni's wife's brief moment on stage is the extent of what we have, and in the Vijayvargīya narratives there is no trace of the theme at all. It is not that clan and lineage deities do not exist in these castes, for the pattern of clan-goddess worship is a widespread feature of Rajasthani society, and is strongly present in all three castes. But the pattern has not been the basis of a caste-wide goddess cult in these castes on the order of Dadhimatī for the Dāhimā Brāhmaṇs. A possible reason for this is that the cultural space that might have been occupied by a caste-goddess has been filled by the various Vaiṣnava sects that are so prominent a feature of the religious cultures of the region's Hindu or predominantly Hindu trading castes.

Finally, a striking feature of some of the narratives discussed in this chapter is an underlying plot movement that clearly reflects the logic of the rites of passage as discovered and analysed by Arnold van Gennep (1960). A negative relationship with the sacrifice brings about a separation from a previous social status (Rājpūt/Kṣatriya or Brāhmaṇ). Then follows a period of betwixt-and-between liminality; in some of our narratives, this is vividly expressed by the curse-caused and death-like immobility of the traders-to-be. Then follows a social reincorporation, a rebirth of the group into a new social niche. The group in question dies to the social order, and then rejoins it on a new basis. That is, the group now has a completely new relationship with the sacrifice and the Brāhmaṇs who preside over the rite.

But this gives rise to a question. Is it possible for the sequence to be changed? In particular, is it conceivable that a group could undergo separation and liminality *without* a reincorporation into the sacrificial order? The answer is yes. As it turns out, this is precisely what it means, at the level of mythohistorical symbolism, to be a Jain.

Notes

1. On the apparently widespread Vaiṣṇava overlay on an older Śaiva base, see Eck 1991.
2. A Paṭvā acquaintance showed me a collection of letters sent by Jaipur's Māheśvarī caste association to felicitate marriages in his family. The earliest of these was dated

1984, suggesting that the formal isolation of the Paṭvās had ended by then, but what happens in practice is harder to say.

3. Paṭvā informants maintain that all the Māheśvarī clans are found in their community.
4. According to the four-clan rule, one should not marry into one's own clan, one's mother's clan, one's father's mother's clan, or one's mother's mother's clan. For a discussion of this rule, see Vatuk 1972: 93–96. I do not believe that this rule is actually followed by any of Rajasthan's trading castes.
5. I have occasionally seen matrimonial advertisements seeking grooms for Māheśvarī girls that specifically state that Agravāl boys would be acceptable. This suggests the possibility of an emerging marriage rapprochement between Māheśvarīs and Agravāls, and thus a breakdown in rules of caste endogamy. Cort (forthcoming) reports that six distinct trading castes of Gujarat seem to be moving in the direction of marital mergers, especially in Mumbai.
6. Some sources, list 75. Seventy-seven, however, is the current standard.
7. In this sample the most cited *khāmps* were Mālpāṇī, Mūndhṛā, Rāṭhī, Sāṛrā.
8. These lists also typically include information about the *gotra*, *mātā*, *veda*, *pravar*, *bheru*, *ṛṣi*, and *guru* of the listed clans. This information is inherited from Darakjī, who in turn must have obtained it from the genealogists who were his sources. The terms *mātā* and *bheru* refer to clan or lineage goddesses and gods; the current validity of these links seems to be questionable, but I have no systematic data on the issue. The other terms refer to features of Brahmanical social structure that have no relevance to the actual clan and marriage systems of the Māheśvarīs currently. When queried about the terms, Māheśvarī respondents were at a complete loss to explain them.
9. My source for these dates, and the only source I came across, is Baruā 1985: 54.
10. The sixth month of the Hindu lunar calendar (August–September).
11. Adoption was commonly practiced by those without male issue. Ideally, the adoptee had to be a close agnate. More generally, the adoptee had to belong to the same clan as the adopting family. However, another acceptable adoptee was a daughter's (not a sister's) son.
12. It is a public-space celebration, and not (as far as I know) celebrated privately. One informant, born in 1933, remembers it from childhood as celebrated in the village of about 5000 in which he grew up. It seems a reasonable surmise that the festival was invented around the turn of the century as part of the caste revival and consolidation taking place then.
13. The *Mahābhārata* culminates a dynastic war won by Yudhiṣṭhira and his four brothers against their cousins. In another telling of the Lohargal myth, Yudhiṣṭhira wishes to rid himself of the sin of killing his great teacher, Droṇa.
14. In a section dated by Hazra (1975: 105–6) as not later than 1500 C.E..
15. As noted before, an additional five are added to contemporary listings. The notion of 72 original clans, however, remains embedded in the system.
16. This detail seems to be a sign of the myth's origination with the genealogists. They would naturally prefer to inflate their own pedigree (tracing it to the prince), but at the same time would have to account for their relatively lowly status.
17. The third of the great ages (*yugas*) of the Hindu cosmic cycle.
18. The sages' names are as follows: 1) Parāśar (Pārīk), 2) Dadhīcī (Dāhimā, 3) Gautam (Gujar Gauṛ), 4) Khādik (Khaṇḍelvāl), 5) Sukumārg (Sukvāl), and 6) Sārsur (Sārasvat).

Thus, the myth also accounts for the creation of the 'six castes' of Brāhmaṇs (in one version of the list).

19. The Khaṇḍelvāl Brāhmaṇs, however, do not accept the notion that they acquired their name because they once lived in Khandela. The caste's association prefers to use the term Khāṇḍal Vipra instead of Khaṇḍelvāl Brāhmaṇ in self-designation. According to the currently officially favoured origin narrative, the caste acquired this name because it was created when its sage-ancestors each received a piece (*khaṇḍ*) of a golden sacrificial altar as *dakṣīṇā* after they served as priests in a sacrifice (Pīpalvā 1997: 11–12). This was the sacrifice offered by Paraśurām in expiation of his massive act of Kṣatriyacide, and (according to this narrative) it occurred at Lohargal. This is yet another example of the tendency to connect the creation of a social group to the sacrificial rite. In the *Mahābhārata*, as we know, the priests who officiate at Paraśurām's sacrifice are indeed given fragments of a golden altar in payment, with the result that they come to be called Khaṇḍavāyana Brāhmaṇs. This story also becomes the basis of a variant Khaṇḍelvāl Vaiśya origin myth, as we shall see below.
20. One writer, Rāmballabh Somānī (1997: 3/3), says that it 'is said' that Jain and non-Jain Khandelvāls once intermarried as Jain and non-Jain Agravāls do today, but that intermarriage came to an end because of a quarrel of some kind in Amber. He gives no source for this story. In the same article he lists the earliest extant inscriptions mentioning the Khandelvāl Jains; the earliest of these bears the date of V.S. 1162. My own comparison of published lists of *gotras* for each caste (from Paṭodiyā 1986 and Kāslīvāl 1989) reveals hardly any overlap.
21. His dates are V.S. 1653–1746. For details on his life, see Motilal Gupt 1972: i–iv.
22. See p. 100 and Note 4 above.
23. The genealogist of Tūngā told me a somewhat similar story.
24. The Śungas are said to be a trading caste that deals in liquor. I never met any and do not know where they are to be found. They are mentioned in the English version of the 1891 Census Report (Singh, M. H. 1986: 154) but apparently not in the Hindi version (Singh, M. H. 1997).
25. This passage refers to the North Indian distinction between *kaccā* and *pakkā* food. To take *kaccā* food—which is ordinary, daily fare—from another suggests either great intimacy or great hierarchical distance between the giver and the receiver. *Pakkā* food—which tends to be feast-food—has much weaker implications of hierarchy when exchanged.
26. Probably one got it from the other, and it seems likely that Gupt's book was the original source.
27. An elephant-headed deity, son of Śiva and Pārvatī.
28. Elsewhere in his book, however, author Gupt refers to the notion that Śunahśep might have been a Kṣatriya in disguise; at the time of Paraśurām's slaughter of the earth's Kṣatriyas, Śunaśep would have disguised himself as a Brāhmaṇ (n.d.: 24).

Chapter Five

Warriors Exiled

If traders bear a culturally distinctive identity as a class, this is even truer of the Jains as a subclass of traders. In their case, too, social identity is constructed from images of violence and its control, but the Jains pursue these themes more intensely than the Hindus and push them in a somewhat different direction. The result is a distinctive subculture of identity, one that also possesses its own internal variations. The Jains' relationship with violence is even more deeply negative than that of the Hindu traders. The energy of this negativity not only propels them into a non-violent social identity, but into an identity that is, in significant ways, external to the surrounding sacrificial–social order. In consonance with the socio-historical position of traders, the Jains are—from the standpoint of the analytical categories of this book—in a state of symbolic self-imposed exile.

This chapter focusses on the three most prominent Jain castes of the Jaipur area: the Khaṇḍelvāl Jains, Osvāls, and Śrīmāls. The Agravāls, a predominantly Hindu caste with a significant Jain minority, will be treated separately in the next chapter. The origin myths of these groups exhibit deep thematic continuity with the materials we have already seen. There is, however, a fundamental difference in the way these narratives approach their subject. The Hindu narratives must account for the creation of trading castes from other *kinds* of castes. The Jain narratives, however, must couple the creation of the castes in question with an account of *religious conversion*, because the identity of a Jain caste is sectarian as well as social. The universal scenario adopted by these narratives is one in which a Jain caste comes into existence when a previously existing group adopts the non-violent ways of Jainism under the influence of a Jain mendicant. As will be seen, the group in question is invariably a Rājpūt group, and the rite of sacrifice is both the catalyst and medium of the transformation.

Jains in Rajasthan

We must begin by saying something about the nature of Jainism and its relationship with Hinduism. This issue is by no means clear-cut. The terms 'Jainism' and 'Hinduism' are English locutions that suggest the existence of two distinct and internally coherent systems of belief. The on-the-ground reality, however, is multipolar and devoid of clear boundaries.

The term 'Jainism' affixes the English suffix 'ism' to the Indic term 'Jain'. A 'Jain' is an adherent of the teachings of the *Jinas*. A Jina is a 'victor' or 'conqueror', by which is meant one who has attained victory over the desires and aversions that keep souls in the world's bondage. The Jinas, also known as Tīrthaṅkars, are human teachers who teach the means of achieving liberation from the bondage of rebirth and the suffering it entails. Jains believe that the Tīrthaṅkars who have existed, exist, and will exist are infinite in number, and that they have always taught, and will always teach, precisely the same basic doctrines throughout infinite time. The last such teacher in our part of the cosmos was Mahāvīr, who attained liberation about 2,500 years ago. He and his predecessor, Pārśvanāth, are the only actual historical figures among the Tīrthaṅkars.

All forms of Jainism share certain core beliefs. One such belief is a rigid dualism holding that matter and souls (infinite in number) are equally real and completely distinct from each other. Another is the concept of *karma* as a form of matter that adheres to the soul and prevents its liberation by obstructing it from realising its true nature, which is omniscient bliss. Jain teachings couple these ideas with a vision of the soul's tortured wanderings through the cosmos from beginningless time. Liberation requires a cessation of the accumulation of karmic matter and the removal of previous accumulations. The belief that violence is a powerful source of karmic accumulation is the theoretic justification for the extreme emphasis Jains place on non-violence. The belief that self-denial can rid the soul of karmic accumulations is the source of the well-known Jain proclivity for ascetic practices.

These beliefs lend a consistent tone and emphasis to a distinctively Jain style of life centering around non-violence and asceticism.[1] It must be said that neither non-violence nor asceticism is uniquely Jain. Many other communities, especially trading groups (as we know), hold non-violence in high esteem, and asceticism has always had an honoured place in the Indic world at large. Nonetheless, the Jains see themselves, and I believe are generally seen by the people of Rajasthan, as epitomising these values. Their commitment to the protection of life is significantly and visibly greater than that of other communities, and Jains are particularly renowned for the rigour of their ascetic practices, both monastic and lay.

But under the umbrella of universally accepted Jain ideas and values are numerous sectarian and social fissures that divide Jains from each other. Foremost among these is a fundamental disagreement on a crucial issue of monastic discipline, which is the question of whether male mendicants should wear clothing. This disagreement divides the Jain world into two major branches: the Svetāmbar (meaning 'white clad') and Digambar (meaning 'space clad') sects. Male and female Śvetāmbar mendicants wear white clothing, whereas the most advanced male Digambar mendicants wear no clothing.[2] Each of these great branches is further subdivided. The mainstream branch among the Svetāmbars is known as *mūrtipūjak* (image worshipping) or *mandirmārgī* (temple going). These are Śvetāmbar Jains who worship images in temples. They, in turn, are divided into what I shall call 'disciplic' lineages of mendicants and their lay followers. Disciplic lineages are based on the principle of spiritual descent from teacher to disciple, typically traced back to a founding *ācārya*; filiation to such a lineage is achieved by means of initiation. Two of these mendicant lineages are particularly important in Rajasthan: the Khartar Gacch and the Tapā Gacch.[3] In addition to the image-worshippers, there are two important non-image-worshipping sects among the Śvetāmbars: the Sthanakvāsīs and the Terāpanthīs. Among the Digambars, we find an important division between the mainstream, orthoprax branch, known as Bīspanth, and a dissenting branch known as Terāpanth.[4] It should be noted that affiliation to these various sectarian and subsectarian divisions is mainly determined by one's birth in a particular family, lineage, or caste, and is not, for most people, a matter of individual choice. The same is true of Hindu sects.

There is no question that a division exists between Jains and Hindus as religious communities, but the boundary is not always very clear. The principal reason for this is that although Jainism can be considered a single—if internally subdivided—religious tradition, Hinduism possesses no such internal unity. Rather, it is best described as a bundle of traditions that share certain family resemblances. The question of how substantial these resemblances actually are is beyond the scope of this study, but it should be noted that some Hindu traditions actually have much in common with Jainism. For example, Śaiva Siddhānta, an important

Śiva-worshipping Hindu sect, holds views of the nature and object of liberation that bear a striking resemblance to Jain teachings (Babb 1996: 181–84). And as we know, both non-violence and asceticism—values stressed by the Jains—are Hindu values as well. Furthermore, the ritual cultures of Jain and Hindu traditions are quite similar, although there are certain key differences in the way some ritual transactions are conducted and understood (ibid.: 176–81, 186–94). The vagueness of the boundary between the two traditions is illustrated by the fact that Jains sometimes identify themselves religiously as 'Hindu', especially in contexts in which politics are involved.

Moreover, 'Hinduism' is not an operating category in the origin myths of Jain trading castes. As we shall see, these narratives portray Jain castes as coming into being when their ancestral groups *adopt Jainism*, but this transformation is not characterised as *ceasing to be 'Hindu'*. Rather, the essence of the change is an alteration in the group's relationship with the sacrifice and with Brāhmaṇs as a class of ritual specialists. The term 'Hindu' is not used at all in the materials with which I am familiar. Instead, the 'other' of what these groups become when they become Jains is usually said to be 'Rājpūt' or 'Śaiva' (worshipper of Śiva). In ordinary discourse today, Jains often use the term 'Vaiṣṇav' (worshipper of Viṣṇu) to describe what they are not, which in fact is an accurate characterisation of the religious orientation of most non-Jain traders.

On one point, however, there is indeed a clear difference between Jain and Hindu traditions, one that has great importance from the standpoint of the narrative material presented in this chapter. This is the contrast between Jain and Hindu relationships with Brāhmaṇs. Jainism originated as a dissenting, anti-orthodox tradition. That is to say, Jains rejected and continue to reject the religious authority of the Brāhmaṇs, whereas Hindus accept it. It is true that nowadays Brāhmaṇs often serve as priests in Jain temples, but Jains see this as a lowly and menial function, and nothing worthy of special respect. As we shall see, the radical break between Jains and Brāhmaṇs is, in Jain origin mythology, at the heart of what it means to be a Jain. Brāhmaṇs, of course, were and are closely identified with the rite of sacrifice and the social order associated with the sacrifice. Thus, rejection of Brāhmaṇs and rejection of the sacrifice come in a single symbolic package. As this chapter will show, the sacrificial myth model plays a central role in the social identity of Jain castes, but in a far different manner than we have seen in the case of trading castes of the Hindu cluster.

Crosscutting the Hindu/Jain division are important caste differences. The question of the relationship between Jain identity and caste identity presents its own complexities because the relationship is not always one-to-one.[5] An example of a one-to-one match is the Khaṇḍelvāl Jain caste; the entire membership of the caste is (as far as I am aware) Digambar Jain and mostly Bīspanthī. Śvetāmbar Jainism plays a similar role among the Śrīmāls, who seem to be (in the Jaipur area) entirely Jain. Very different is the Agravāl case; the caste is mostly Hindu in Rajasthan, but there is a small minority of Digambar Jains. (Agravāl Jains are quite prominent in Delhi.) In this case, religious identity seems to be almost entirely trumped by caste identity in the sense that intermarriage occurs between the two religious groups while the caste itself is endogamous. The Osvāl case is somewhat similar; there are both Hindus and Śvetāmbar Jains among the Osvāls of Rajasthan, and there is no bar to intermarriage. But here, in contrast to the Agravāls, Jains constitute the majority and Jainism is central to the caste's origin myths.

We begin this chapter with the Khaṇḍelvāl Jains, and then shift focus to the Śrīmāls and Osvāls.

The Sin of Human Sacrifice: Khaṇḍelvāl Jains

The Khaṇḍelvāl Jains are numerous in the Jaipur region and constitute the largest Jain caste in the city itself. As noted above, they belong entirely to the Digambar sect, which means that, from a Jain point of view, Jaipur is essentially a Digambar city. They are often called 'Sarāvgīs'. This word derives from the term *śrāvak*, which literally means 'listener' and is commonly employed to denote a Jain layman. It should be noted again that despite the 'Khaṇḍelvāl' label held in common, the Khaṇḍelvāl Jains and Khaṇḍelvāl Vaiśyas are separate endogamous castes.

Well-informed insiders have told me that the total number of Khaṇḍelvāl Jains is about a million, with roughly 200,000 living in Jaipur. I do not know how these figures were obtained. Although a few of Jaipur's most prominent business families belong to this caste, it does not have a reputation for great wealth. In Jaipur, most members of the caste are in service occupations, and they have been especially prominent in government bureaucracies. Insiders tell me that more than half of the Khaṇḍelvāl Jains belong to the mainstream Bīspanthī sect, but the dissident Terāpanthī sect has the allegiance of a sizeable minority.[6] There was once a close connection between Digambar castes and the domesticated Digambar clerics known as Bhaṭṭāraks, and in their heyday the Amer and later the Jaipur Bhaṭṭāraks were closely associated with the Khaṇḍelvāl Jain caste and were a focus for caste identity (Cort 2002). Another important focus for the identity of the caste has been a nationally important Digambar pilgrimage center called Mahāvīrjī (on English maps, 'Mahaveerji'). Located east of Jaipur in Sawai Madhopur District, its governing board is totally dominated by Bīspanthī Khaṇḍelvāl Jains.

Over the past century, the caste has been represented, or partially represented, by various modern organisations. In the early twentieth century, the caste's principal association was the Khaṇḍelvāl Mahāsabhā. This organisation was caste- rather than religion-oriented; that is, it emphasised caste identity over Digambar Jainism. It was also deeply conservative, and opposed intercaste marriage and other social innovations advocated by the reformers of those days. In the 1920s, another organisation, the more liberal Digambar Jain Pariṣad, came into existence. The Pariṣad still exists, but has been shouldered aside by the Digambar Jain Mahāsamiti, another relatively liberal organisation that emerged as a direct result of the celebrations of the 2,500th anniversary of Mahāvīr's liberation in 1974.

The ostensible focus of these latter two organisations is Digambar Jainism, not the caste as such, but the Digambar community in Jaipur is hardly distinguishable from the Khaṇḍelvāl Jain caste. In Jaipur, the Digambar organisations support and manage schools, including a famous Sanskrit academy, a library, and other institutions. In the meantime, the Khaṇḍelvāl Mahāsabhā has reemerged as the Digambar Jain Mahāsabhā, an organisation retaining the social conservatism of its predecessor, though now flying the flag of Jainism, not caste. The general trend has been a downplaying of explicit caste identity in favour of Digambar Jain identity, and this has in fact generated an on-the-ground reticence to discuss caste. On sundry occasions, Khaṇḍelvāl Jains have refused to acknowledge their caste affiliation to me, insisting that they are merely 'Digambar Jain'.

Khaṇḍelvāl Jains acknowledge a total of 84 exogamous clans (called *gotras*), a convention that is apparently centuries old (Kāslīvāl 1989: 72). I do not know whether an official list of any kind has ever existed, but the list given in Kastūrcand Kāslīvāl's history of the caste seems to enjoy semi-official status (ibid.: 88–91). A close examination of this list in the company of two knowledgeable caste members revealed that roughly 45 of these clans are currently extant. A survey of personal data from 46 matrimonial advertisements (26 males, 20 females) found in a publication of a Digambar women's organisation in Jaipur (in which the father's and mother's clans were listed for each candidate) yielded 25 clan names. Of these, eight do not appear on Kāslīvāl's list. Obviously the Khaṇḍelvāl Jains' clan system has yet to be fully systematised, but it is clearly the same kind of system that we find in other trading castes. In this caste, there is also a hierarchical division similar to the Ten/Twenty division in other castes; the higher stratum is called *bar sājan*, the lower, *lohar sājan*. Informants state that this distinction is mostly ignored nowadays.

Origin Myth

There might once have been professional genealogists who served the Khaṇḍelvāl Jains in the same manner as the genealogists of other castes we have discussed; indeed, they might still exist. In Jaipur, however, I was unable to discover any contemporary traces of such an institution. Instead, Digambar Jain authors and manuscript repositories appear to have long ago become the principal means by which this caste's mytho-historical heritage is transmitted. In this caste, we can say, Jainism itself has provided the institutional and intellectual contexts in which mytho-historical knowledge has been socially reproduced.

A single basic (or at least prevailing) Khaṇḍevāl Jain origin myth appears to have been in circulation for centuries. Whether it has dominated the scene for that long is another question and one to which I do not know the answer. Its most recent published version is to be found in Kāslīvāl's caste history (ibid.: 1989). He has drawn his material, in part, from manuscripts available in Digambar Jain temple repositories, and of these the earliest cited is dated 1573 C.E. Another of his sources is a book by Bakhatrām Śāh titled *Buddhi Vilās* and dated 1770. A Khaṇḍelvāl Jain himself, Bakhatrām Śāh was a ferocious polemicist whose best-known work is *Mithyāva Khaṇḍan Nāṭak* (1763). This work is a critique of a Digambar reformist movement known as Adhyātma, but it also contains material on the Khaṇḍelvāl Jain caste.[7]

Though centuries old, this origin myth is also current. It is quite familiar to many ordinary members of the caste, and has become especially salient recently because of the efforts of some Khaṇḍelvāl Jain leaders to revive and bolster caste consciousness by renovating a Digambar temple in Khandela, the caste's supposed place of origin. To what degree the goal of heightened consciousness was achieved is unclear, but the temple, consecrated with great éclat in May 1997, stands as a material embodiment of the narrative we are about to examine. A problem confronted by the organisers of this event was that no Khaṇḍelvāl Jains were actually living in Khandela at that time (although there is a sizeable community in nearby Sikar). This is a serious difficulty because of the requirement that all consecrated Jain images be worshipped once per day. In contrast to Śvetāmbars, Digambars will not allow non-Jains to perform this daily worship. Some rich donors ultimately stepped forward to offer monetary rewards to Khaṇḍelvāl Jain families willing to settle there (how successfully I do not know).

The narrative (summarised here from Kāslīvāl 1989: 64–69) takes us once again to ancient Khandela:

> A king named Khaṇḍelgiri once ruled Khandela. He was a Jain,[8] but his ministers and priests were Śaivas, and he was sympathetic to Śaivism. A time came when a great plague afflicted the city and the people began to flee. The situation was desperate, and the king's Brāhmaṇ advisors said that a human sacrifice would certainly bring the epidemic to an end. The king refused to have such a thing done, but the Brāhmaṇs were determined and would not be deterred. As it happens, a group of 500 Digambar Jain monks had recently come to Khandela and were meditating in a garden just outside the town. The priests went there in the night, seized some of the monks, and fed them into the sacrificial fire. As a result, the plague attacked the city with renewed fury.
>
> When Aparājit Muni (a prominent Digambar *ācārya* of the time) came to know of these events, he dispatched a distinguished monk named Jinsen to the scene. When Jinsen arrived, he called all the town's Jains to a certain place outside the town. There the goddess Cakreśvarī protected them, and in this way all the Jains of Khandela were saved. In the meantime, King Khaṇḍelgiri himself fell victim to the plague. All other remedies having failed, he went to meet Jinsen at the Jains' retreat. On the monk's advice, the king stayed with him for seven days, purifying his diet and manner of life, and praying to the Tīrthaṅkar. At the same time, Jinsen prayed to Cakreśvarī. The king recovered, and Jinsen announced that from that time forward the king would be under the protection (*śaraṇ*) of the Tīrthaṅkar, and that the king would publicly declare himself to be a Jain.

King Khaṇḍelgiri then returned to his palace. There, in 44 C.E. (in some versions, 55 B.C.E.), he and 13 of his Rājpūt (Cauhān) feudatory lords became initiated Jain laymen in the presence of Jinsen and his mendicant followers. These 14 nobles became the apical ancestors of the original 14 of the 84 exogamous clans of the Khaṇḍelvāl Jain caste.

After retelling this story, author Kāslīvāl presents material on the origin of the caste's 84 clans (ibid.: 85–142). The prevailing view seems to be that one of the 84 clans (the *śāh gotra*) is descended from the king himself and the rest from his feudal lords, although different accounts disagree on certain details. The clans get their names from the villages of their apical ancestors.

Sacrificial Violence

The Khaṇḍelvāl Jain origin myth is a story about the relationship between Rājpūts and Brāhmaṇs. It is also, and necessarily, about the sacrifice and sacrificial violence, which it places at the heart of the relationship between the king and his Brāhmaṇ priests. Its approach to sacrificial violence, however, is very different from anything we have seen thus far.

The Māheśvarī narrative that we saw in the last chapter portrays violence as *external* to the rite of sacrifice, *brought to the rite* by errant Rājpūts. The reason for this approach is clear. Māheśvarīs are nonviolent, but they are not Jains. Because they are not Jains, they do not reject the sacrifice and the authority of Brāhmaṇs who are its human agents. They remain part of the sacrificial order, albeit on a different basis than before their transformation. This scenario requires as a premise that the sacrifice (and Brāhmaṇs) not be inherently violent. This same theme is echoed in the Khaṇḍelvāl Vaiśya myths. In these narratives, errant Brāhmaṇs or soldiers pollute a sacrifice and/or offend a temperamental Brāhmaṇ sage by killing a deer. It is true that one Khaṇḍelvāl Vaiśya myth (the oral version of the Jāgā's tale) does envision animal sacrifice. In this case, however, it is precisely because of a *Brāhmaṇ's* (Durvāsā's) objection that the animal sacrifice is abandoned.

In contrast, the Khaṇḍelvāl Jain narrative assumes that the sacrifice is an inherently violent act, and that those who sponsor and perform it, Kṣatriyas and Brāhmaṇs, have a propensity for violence. This, of course, is deeply resonant with Jainism's fundamental rejection of Brahmanical religious authority. In the story, violence leads to hyperviolence, the consignment of Jain mendicants to the flames. The resulting disaster exposes the pretensions of the Brāhmaṇs, which leads to the king's break with them and the socio-religious system they represent. This separation is dramatised by the king's departure from the city to join Jinsen at the Jains' rural retreat. It is then rendered into an institutionalised reality when the king and his henchmen become Jains, thus separating themselves permanently from the Brāhmaṇs and the sacrificial order.

As always, the sacrifice plays a key role in this transformation. It should be noted that the Jains do not accept the view, as given in hymn 10:90 of the *Ṛg Veda*, that the cosmos and the social order arose from a primordial sacrifice. They attribute the creation of three of the four *varṇas* to Ṛṣabh, the first Tīrthaṅkar of our region and era; his son, in turn, created the Brāhmaṇs. Thus, the Jains reject the specifically Brahmanical version of the link between the sacrifice and the creation of social groups. Nevertheless, despite the fundamental difference in attitude toward the sacrifice, there is a deep similarity between the Khaṇḍelvāl Jain narrative and the Hindu narratives with respect to the transformative role of the sacrifice, for in both instances the sacrifice is the root of social change. The big difference is that, in the Jain case, the sacrifice's creative energy is *repulsive* in nature rather than inclusive and attractive.

As in the Hindu scenario, the group about to be changed first enters a negative relationship with the rite. In the Khaṇḍelvāl Jain case however, the negativity is greatly accentuated by the murder of saintly mendicants. Then follows a liminal period in which the king and his henchmen are neither what they were before, nor yet what they are to be. The sin of the initiating act mainly stains the Brāhmaṇ instigators/perpetrators, with the clear implication that a break with them, and with the sacrifice over which they preside, cannot be repaired.[9] Thus, instead of culminating in a renewed and readjusted relationship with the social and religious order represented by the sacrifice, this narrative propels the Jains-to-be outside that order altogether.

After a betwixt-and-between sojourn in the retreat outside the city, the king returns to his palace: his brief separation from the social order is over. What now occurs, however, is not a reincorporation, but a neoincorporation, for the king does not return to an old order on a new basis, but to a completely new order. There is no re-establishment of relations with Brāhmaṇs, which would signify a return to the Hindu/Vedic social order of which they are both the apex and emblem. Instead, Jain mendicants replace Brāhmaṇs as the defining ritual 'others' in the situation, thus transforming Rājpūts into a Jain caste. Brāhmaṇs and their sacrifices are out of the picture; Jain monks are in, and martial Kṣatriyas have become non-violent Jains.

As in origin myths we have seen already, the myth model of the ancestral goddess is implicated in the transition. In this case, she takes the form of the Jain goddess, Cakreśvarī. As in other myths, she enters a permanent relationship with the newly created group, for she is a protective goddess for Jains in general and apparently was once an actual clan goddess for some Khaṇḍelvāl Jain clans.[10] This is another example of how the presence of such a goddess can serve to ratify the heritability of the transition that has been made; what has been created are not merely new Jains, but ancestors of descent groups that together form a new caste. In the Khaṇḍelvāl Jains' conventional clan lists, specific clan goddesses are listed for each clan (ibid.: 96–97), and these associations appear to be quite old. Cakreśvarī is listed as clan goddess for 17 clans, but 21 other clan goddesses are also mentioned.

As best I have been able to determine, however, the tradition of ancestral goddess worship is extremely weak among the Khaṇḍelvāl Jains of Jaipur nowadays, probably as a result of having been squeezed out by the ritual culture of Digambar Jainism as such, which is particularly strong in this caste. For the Khaṇḍelvāl Jains, the principal image at the pilgrimage center at Mahāvīrjī, a major ritual focus for the caste as a whole, occupies the functional niche of a caste deity (such as Dadhimatī for the Dāhimā Brāhmaṇs).[11]

The origin myth of the Khaṇḍelvāl Jains will serve as our paradigm for understanding the narratives of other Jain trading castes. It is not the case that all Jain groups understand their origin in exactly the same way, but there a single, basic theme that informs all their origin myths. This is a deep hostility to the sacrifice, which is seen as inherently violent. From the perspective of these narratives, what it *means* to be a Jain is to belong to a group that defines its identity by means of a *rejection* of the sacrifice. We now shift our attention to two Śvetāmbar castes whose origin myths illustrate this same paradigm, though in somewhat different contexts: the Śrīmāls and the Osvāls.

Animal Victims: Śrīmāls

The Śrīmāls and Osvāls are the principal castes of the Jaipur's Śvetāmbar Jain community and are preeminent in the city's important gemstone business. Their lifestyles are very similar, intermarriage between them is common, and their origin myths are intertwined. In Jaipur, both the Śrīmāls and the *mandirmārgī* (image-worshipping) Osvāls tend to be strong supporters of the *mandirmārgī* mendicant lineage known as the Khartar Gacch, and the link between the Śrīmāls and the Khartar Gacch is especially strong. In this section of the chapter we look at origin myths of the Śrīmāls; we turn to the Osvāls in the next section.

Whether or not one can speak of a single Śrīmāl caste is an open question. Ostensibly, the largest concentration of Śrīmāls is in Gujarat (under the name Śrīmālī), where they are one of the regionally dominant trading castes. The Śrīmāls of Jaipur, however, belong to what appears to be a separate Śrīmāl group mainly distributed in eastern Rajasthan (especially Bharatpur, Jaipur, and Jhunjhunu), with significant numbers also in Delhi, Lucknow, and Kolkata. These are the Śrīmāls with whom we shall be concerned in what follows. Jhunjhunu appears to be a caste epicenter for this group, with Osvāls more prevalent towards the west in Churu District. I am not fully convinced that these 'northeastern Śrīmāls', as we shall call them, are actually part of the same social universe as the Gujarati Śrīmāls. As far as I am aware, there are no significant marital exchanges between the two groups, and the northeastern Śrīmāls appear once to have had their own origin traditions, as we shall see shortly.

According to a senior member of Jaipur's Śrīmāl community, a man well versed in Śrīmāl affairs, there were exactly 227 Śrīmāl houses in Jaipur in 1995. A list of 135 Śrīmāl clans (usually called *gotras*) has appeared in various publications, and probably first appeared in print in 1910 (Rāmlāljī 1910: 109–10). I was unable to obtain any marriage listings or other source that would enable me to assess the relationship between this list and on-the-ground reality. However, oral queries revealed that the social world of the northeastern Śrīmāls probably contains no more than 35 or 40 clans. Some of the most prominent of these appear on the published list, but some do not. These points suggest that the published list has at least some relation to the social reality of the northeastern Śrīmāls, but that the clan system is as yet only partially rationalised.

The Śrīmāls of Jaipur currently intermarry with the Osvāl caste. Some informants say that the Śrīmāls formerly would take brides from, but not give brides to, the Osvāls, an asymmetry that, if real, would suggest Śrīmāl superiority. I strongly suspect that the Ten/Twenty distinction once prevailed among them and it might still function informally to some degree, but I was unable to obtain any firm evidence to support this.

There appears to be no national Śrīmāl organisation within the social horizon of the Śrīmāls of Jaipur. They do, however, have an organisation at the Jaipur level—the Śrīmāl Sangh—that manages two temples. One of these is a lavish temple in the Johari Bazaar area of the walled city, and the other a Dādābāṛī (a type of shrine focussed on the worship of distinguished deceased mendicants) located on Moti Dungri Road. Jaipur Śrīmāls, however, are also deeply involved in the affairs of the local laymen's organisation of the Khartar Gacch, which also includes Osvāls. The Khartar Gacch is the dominant Śvetāmbar mendicant lineage in Jaipur. It is my strong impression that Śvetāmbar Jainism and the Khartar Gacch have tended to be the principal context for this caste's corporate identity. I met no Jaipur Śrīmāls belonging to the non-image-worshipping sects, although I am told that the Śvetāmbar Terāpanthī sect has a Śrīmāl following in Jhunjhunu.[12] In general, the Śrīmāls see themselves, and are seen by others, as among the Khartar Gacch's most steadfast supporters.

An important symbol of Śrīmāl identity in Jaipur in the past was the local branch of the 'Rangsūri' mendicant sublineage, which in turn was a branch of the Khartar Gacch. Rangsūri was a seventeenth-century Khartar Gacch monk (born in 1607) who became the apical disciplic ancestor of the mendicant sublineage that bore his name.[13] He was a Śrīmāl, and although many of his successors to the leadership of the branch were Osvāls, the sublineage he established appears to have had a close relationship with the Śrīmāl caste, and its branches flourished in areas of Śrīmāl settlement, such as Jaipur.

The Rangsūri sublineage consisted mainly (probably even entirely) of *yatis*. The term *yati* denotes a type of male Śvetāmbar mendicant and ritual functionary whose vows are less complete than those of fully initiated monks. As a result of twentieth-century reforms, *yatis* have become a dying breed, and there are very few remaining in the Khartar Gacch today. However, once they were numerous, and in the past they were probably the only kind of mendicants with whom most lay Śvetāmbar Jains actually came into contact. The fact that they could stay in fixed residences meant that *yatis* could develop extremely close ties with local communities, with the result that the segmentation of *yati* mendicant sublineages could easily parallel the physical and social segmentation of lay communities.

Although the Jaipur branch of the Rangsūri sublineage had many Osvāl followers, its staunchest supporters were Śrīmāls, and its physical seat was at the Śrīmāl-owned temple in the walled city. The sublineage appears to have once functioned as the focus for local Śrīmāl caste solidarity, and to some degree still does. To this day, the city's Śrīmāls have an annual community festival at one of their temples (the Dādābāṛī) in Rangsūri's name, and the extreme loyalty of the Śrīmāl community to the Khartar Gacch undoubtedly represents a contemporary remnant of this former association.

The Bhinmal Variant

The most widely known Śrīmāl origin myth traces the caste to the ancient city of Śrīmāl, now known as Bhinmal. Although other versions of the origin of the Śrīmāl caste have circulated in the past, this story—we shall call it 'the Bhinmal variant'—appears to have become the current default Śrīmāl origin myth. Versions of it are reproduced repeatedly in various caste histories,[14] and it has been retold by a prominent Jaipur Śrīmāl in a small booklet on Śrīmāl history (R. K. Śrīmāl n.d., probably published in the late 1980s). It seems to represent the prevailing view of Śrīmāl caste origin among those Śrīmāls of Jaipur who have opinions on the matter.

Jain mendicants almost certainly originally composed and subsequently transmitted this narrative. Genealogists who were not Jain mendicants once served the Śrīmāl and Osvāl castes, and still do in some areas. However, Jain mendicants also played a major role in the recording of their genealogies. As among the Khaṇḍelvāl Jains, Jainism and its key institutions thus provided one of the most important contexts for the social transmission of mythohistorical knowledge about these Śvetāmbar castes. The mendicants in question had an interest in linking particular clans and lineages to their own mendicant lineages. This connection was established by means of attributing the conversion of the group to Jainism to the activities of an *ācārya* belonging to the mendicant lineage in question. In theory, the tie between the two entities—one a mendicant lineage, the other a lay lineage, clan, or entire caste—would then be reproduced in subsequent generations resulting in a perpetual tie (Granoff 1989).

The retelling of the Bhinmal story to be presented below is abstracted from a book written by a Khartar Gacch *yati* named Rāmlāljī (Rāmlāljī 1910). This narrative requires us to shift geographical focus far to the west and south of the Jaipur region. Bhinmal, a town in what is now

Jalor District, is one of the most famous places in regional mythohistory. As noted above, it is said to have once been a great city called Śrīmāl. The best-known groups to trace their origins to this ancient city are two: the Śrīmālī Brāhmaṇs and the Śrīmālī or Śrīmāl traders. Our version of the traders' origin myth (ibid.: 103–10) begins with a king:

> At the time when Lord Mahāvīr was still on earth and teaching, a king named Śrīmall, who was a follower of Vedic religion, ruled Śrīmāl City. His only child was a daughter named Lakṣmī. When the time came to find a match for her, he told his learned Brāhmaṇ advisors that a *svayamvar* (a marriage in which a woman chooses her husband) was out of the question. If such an event were held, he said, the kings who came, overwhelmed by her beauty, would fight and kill each other. So the Brāhmaṇs advised him to sponsor an *aśvamedh* sacrifice (a horse sacrifice) instead. Many Brāhmaṇs would attend, and the king would have the benefit of their advice. He would gain merit from the rite, and his daughter would obtain a groom like Indra (the king of the gods).
>
> Now as it happens, Lord Mahāvīr himself was at Śatruñjaya (a major Jain pilgrimage site in present-day Gujarat) at that very time. Knowing that violence was about to be inflicted on hundreds of thousands of creatures in Śrimall's sacrifice, he sent his chief disciple, Gautam, with 500 other monks to avert the carnage. Hundreds of thousands of Brāhmaṇs had been invited to Śrīmāl City for the sacrifice, and a horse had been taken on a tour of various countries and brought to the site of the ceremony. Large numbers of other captive animals were also waiting there to be burnt in the sacrificial fire. But then, at the very last moment before the sacrifice was to begin, Gautam appeared and began to impart Jain teachings. Conversions resulted, and the sacrifice was abandoned.
>
> Gautam's teachings influenced two different groups, Brāhmaṇs and Rājpūts. Most (but not all) of the Brāhmaṇs who came for the sacrifice—whom Rāmlāljī characterizes as the 'relatives' of Gautam and his 500 disciples[15]—gave up lethal sacrifice. They became '*samyaktyukt vrat dhārī*' Brāhmaṇs, by which author Rāmlāljī apparently means that they actually took the vows of lay Jains. Among them were the Śrīmālī Brāhmaṇs, who were Brāhmaṇs from Śrīmāl City. In addition, other Brāhmaṇ sages had come from distant places, and they, too, gave up lethal sacrifice and the consumption of meat and liquor.[16] On the Kṣatriya side, the king and 125,000 Rājpūts accepted Jainism, and they became the Śrīmāl caste, which was divided into 135 exogamous clans (here called *gotras*). The converted Brāhmaṇs and Rājpūts became devotees (*sevaks*) of Gautam, and began to perform his *pūjā* (i.e., worship him).

This story also has an important sequel:

> At a later point, King Bhīmsen of Sirohi besieged Śrīmāl City. King Śrīmall had no son, and his daughter Lakṣmī was still unmarried. So, in order to avoid the sin of the annihilation of hundreds of thousands of people in warfare, the king gave Lakṣmī in marriage to Bhīmsen, and gave his kingdom as well. Bhīmsen then produced three sons: Upaldev, Āspāl and Āsal. Bhīmsen gave Āsal in adoption to Śrīmall, but designated him as successor to the throne.[17] Śrīmall himself ultimately went to Gautam, took initiation as a monk, and later acquired omniscience and attained liberation. Āsal was a Jain only in name, with no knowledge of Jain teachings and conduct, and Bhīmsen and his other two sons were followers of the *vām mārg* (which in this context I take to mean they were Śaivas or Śāktas, i.e., devotees of Śiva or the goddess).
>
> Presumably because of the city's non-Jain atmosphere, the Jains of the Śrīmāl caste (here called *śrīmālvaṃś*) gradually migrated from Bhīmsen's kingdom to Gujarat, Gaudwar, Malwa, and elsewhere, and the city's name changed from Śrīmāl to Bhinmal. Upaldev and Āspāl ultimately departed to found the city of Osian where Ratnaprabhsūri (whom we will meet below) later converted them to Jainism.[18] The Śrīmāl merchants of Gujarat came to be known as Dasā and Visā Śrīmālīs (that is, they were hierarchically divided into the usual Tens and Twenties), and lost knowledge of their clans (*gotras*).[19] Under the influence of Śankarācārya[20] they later gave up Jainism and became Vaiṣṇavas and Śaivas, but were returned to the Jain fold by Hemācārya.[21] The Śrīmālīs of Delhi, Lucknow, Agra, Jaipur, and Jhunjhunu were reconverted from Śaivism by Jincandrasūri,[22] and they all belong to the Khartar Gacch.

Comparison with the Myth of the Khaṇḍelvāl Jains

This narrative is obviously very similar to the origin story of the Khaṇḍelvāl Jains, despite differences in its cast of characters, locale, and sectarian context. It, too, is a story about violence and its centrality to the relationship between Brāhmaṇs and Kṣatriyas. Although the narrative does not take us to the extreme limit of human sacrifice, it does project an image of innocent animal lives about to be extinguished in a sacrificial rite sponsored by a king at the instigation of Brāhmaṇs. As in the Khaṇḍelvāl Jain case, the radical rejection of the rite leads to a social transformation of the Kṣatriya sponsor; where there was a warrior aristocracy before, now there are non-violent Jains. There are further twists and turns to the story including a territorial transition, which may reflect the theme of transitional liminality. At last, however, the 135 clans settle in Gujarat and elsewhere as Śrīmālī/Śrīmāl Jains.

There is another similarity with the Khaṇḍelvāl Jain myth that emerges when both are compared with the non-Jain narratives of the previous chapter. In the non-Jain narratives, trade itself often (though not always) plays some role in the depiction of the transition from old status to new. In the Jain narratives, however, not much is said about trade or commerce. The entire transition is focussed on the sacrifice, violence, and the role of Brāhmaṇs in promoting the killing of innocents in the rite. In the non-Jain narratives, the transition is from one relationship with the sacrifice to another, accompanied by a shift in occupation. In the Jain narratives, the shift is from a relationship with the sacrifice to no relationship with the sacrifice, with little emphasis on any change of occupation.

But there are also some significant differences between this narrative and the Khaṇḍelvāl Jain myth. Chief among them is the fact that, after the rejection of the sacrifice, Brāhmaṇs continue to play a role in the Śrīmāl tale. Not only do the Kṣatriyas become Jains, but some Brāhmaṇs also become Jains or fellow travellers of the Jains as a result of the newly acquired aversion to the sacrifice. Author Rāmlāljī probably feels obliged to keep the Brāhmaṇs in the picture for two reasons. One is the regional prominence of the Śrīmālī Brāhmaṇs, whose role in the whole affair therefore needs to be explained. The other reason, probably the most important, is the fact that Gautam, famously a Brāhmaṇ by birth, plays a leading role in the story. This naturally gives rise to the question of Gautam's relationship with other Brāhmaṇs, and also renders plausible the notion that Brāhmaṇs are not incorrigible (an apparent implication of the Khaṇḍelvāl Brāhmaṇ tale).

But then Rāmlāljī must face a difficulty, for having said that various Brāhmaṇ groups became Jainlike (if not actual Jains), he must account for the fact that they are non-Jains today. With regard to the Śrīmālī Brāhmaṇs specifically, he says that they were brought back to the Vedic fold by Śankarācārya. In the text he concedes that they do not actually eat the meat of sacrificed animals today, but he nonetheless claims that at least some Śrīmālī Brāhmaṇs sacrifice small replicas of buffaloes (made of *lapsī*, a sweet pudding made from cracked wheat and raw sugar) on Dassehrā and other occasions, which they then consume as *prasād* (food sanctified by virtue of having been offered to a deity) (ibid.: 108).

I believe one implication of this to be that Brāhmaṇs are never fully redeemable as long as they retain any connection with the sacrificial social order, which is to say, as long as they remain Brāhmaṇs.

The ancestral goddess myth model is not strongly present in this narrative, or at least not in this version of it. There certainly are traces of the idea, however, in the role the princess Lakṣmī plays as the catalyst for the ultimately rejected sacrifice. Rāmlālji himself says that the princess became the goddess of the Śrīmālī Brāhmaṇs, and in fact the Śrīmālī merchants and Śrīmālī Brāhmaṇs of Gujarat consider the goddess Lakṣmī to be a caste deity (Cort 2001: 37, 164). At least some Śrīmāls of Jaipur identify Lakṣmī as their *kul devī* (clan or caste goddess), but I do not know how widespread this idea is.

The Bharatpur Version

I would now like to introduce a very different account of the origin of the Śrīmāl caste. This version falls within the same pattern as the other Jains myths we have seen, but it presents familiar ideas in a somewhat more rustic or folkish idiom. We shall see, however, that idiom aside, the narrative is deeply similar to the other Jain narratives we have encountered thus far.

I discovered it in the form of a photocopy of a disintegrating hand-written manuscript entitled *History of the Śrīmāls* (*Śrīmālõ kā Itihās*; M. S. J. Śrīmāl n.d.) that was put in my hands by a Jaipur Śrīmāl with a strong interest in the history of his caste. Its author is Mangal Siṃh Jain Śrīmāl of Bharatpur, who evidently collected the material from local sources. It bears no date. According to another source, however, in 1879 the Maharana of Udaipur invited to his kingdom a Śrīmāl named Śrī Mangal Siṃhjī from Bharatpur, whom he installed as a high official in Bhilwara in 1880 (R. K. Śrīmāl n.d.: 32). Were this our author, as I strongly suspect, it would establish the period in which this specific account was collected as the late nineteenth century. The narrative (here summarised from the manuscript) brings us back to the eastern part of modern Rajasthan and the vicinity of Jaipur:

> It seems that, in the year 862 C.E., a certain Cauhān Rājpūt ruled a place called Moran (apparently near Lalsoth, about 40 km south of modern Dausa). He had received a son as a boon from Śiva, and when the boy reached the proper age, the king had married him to two brides: a Rājpūt

girl and a Mahājan's daughter (As we know, the term Mahājan refers generally to members of the trading castes; we are not told the exact caste). The marriage with the Mahājan girl occurred in the following unusual way: One day, the King had gone hunting. Some girls of several castes were playing *gharua* (a game, apparently played with a miniature house) on a street in the middle of the city. One was a Mahājan's daughter. When they saw the king's vehicle coming, the other girls fled, but the Mahājan girl bravely covered the house with her shawl and sat down. When the king asked the girl why she would not move, she replied that she wanted to protect her house. The king ordered that the house be left intact. Then, after returning to the palace, he began to think about the girl. She seemed somehow to be in God's favor, and it occurred to him that his son might obtain blessings by marrying her. He thereupon called the girl's father and proposed the match. The Mahājan answered that such a marriage would be impossible because he was a Vaiśya and the king a Kṣatriya, but the king paid no heed, and the marriage took place.

One night, the king's son was sleeping with both his wives in the palace. The braid of the Mahājan girl was hanging down from the bed, and a snake climbed up her braid and bit the prince. When the two wives awoke and saw their husband dead, the Rājpūt's daughter began to wail. To the Mahājan girl, however, came that special power known as *sat*.[23] She caught the snake and put it in a pot. Her intention was to become satī and to avenge her husband by burning the captured snake as well. While on the way to the funeral pyre, she chanced upon a Jain *yati*.[24] She said to the *yati* that she would give him anything he wanted except three things: her husband's body, her own body, and her enemy (the snake). The *yati* said, 'I am a *yati*; you are *satī*. For both of us, it is appropriate to protect life. So let the snake go'. The 'satī' (as the text now refers to her) said, 'Mahārāj, how can I leave alive an enemy that took away my *suhāg* (her status as a married woman)?' The *yati* then assured her that she would have her husband back.

Then the king arrived, and he said that he would serve the *yati* in any way he asked. The *yati* said that if the king wanted his son to live, he would have to accept Jainism, and the king agreed. Using a special *mantra* (a powerful spell), the *yati* then ordered the snake to suck the poison out from where it had gone in, and the prince was revived. The king accepted Jainism, and the *yati* decreed that the prince's progeny (presumably through the Mahājan's daughter) would be called *sirīmāl* (Śrīmāl).[25] When the king died, the prince, who had also become a Jain, succeeded him. The son's son in turn, Ugrasāh, was greatly attracted to Jainism, and (apparently because of this) completely gave up the ways of Kṣatriyas (*kṣatridharm*) (How this fits with the fact that his father and grandfather were also Jains is not clear). He entered the service of the king of Hastinapur, and there he had six sons. They gave rise to six Śrīmāl clans, of which the highest is Śrīsrīmāl.[26]

Analysis

This 'Bharatpur version' of Śrīmāl caste origin represents a tradition that is both differently located and much more parochial than the Bhinmal version. The geographic focus of the Bhinmal version is mainly the southwestern part of what is now Rajasthan plus Gujarat, whereas the geographic focus of the Bharatpur version is to the east of Jaipur.

This difference seems to mesh with another point. As we have seen, Rāmlālјī regards the Śrīmāls of 'Delhi, Lucknow, Agra, Jaipur, and Jhunjhunu' as a community different from other Śrīmāls. As I have noted above, I suspect that the group to which the Bharatpur version refers is in fact different from the Śrīmāls (or Śrīmālīs) to the west, despite the name held in common. The absence of exogamous clans among Gujarati Śrīmālīs, a point mentioned by Rāmlālјī, is an indication that the single label 'Śrīmāl/ Śrīmālī' conveys a misleading impression of unity. Whether these northeastern Śrīmāls should even be considered a 'branch' of some larger Śrīmāl caste seems doubtful to me. The northeastern Śrīmāls have a very strong traditional connection with the Khartar Gacch, which suggests the possibility that they were originally proselytised separately by Khartar Gacch mendicants (as Rāmlālјī suggests). And their location suggests that they acquired their identity as a Jain caste independently of the western Śrīmāls.

The Bharatpur narrative seems likely to have been an authentic origin myth of the northeastern Śrīmāls, perhaps one among many. Probably as a result of a general widening of social horizons occurring in the twentieth century, the northeastern Śrīmāls have come to identify with the western Śrīmāls under an all-inclusive 'Śrīmāl/Śrīmālī' label. This has resulted in the shouldering aside of the Bharatpur version of Śrīmal origin (and perhaps others like it) by the Bhinmal version, which now seems to hold uncontested sway. Whether this merging of identities has been paralleled by the development of actual social bridges is a question I do not have adequate evidence to answer.

At first glance, the Bharatpur narrative looks quite different from the other Jain origin myths we have seen. For example, nothing is said of the sacrifice. Brāhmaṇs, moreover, are nowhere in evidence. Nonetheless,

I suggest we are dealing with the same basic Jain narrative pattern that we have seen before. The difference is one of idiom, not of substance.

Let us begin with the obvious fact that this narrative, too, is about an act of violence that was averted because of a Jain monk's teachings. Here, as in our other stories, we find victims about to be burnt: in the first instance the snake in the pot (to be sure, not an innocent victim), but also the prince's wife, on her way to self-immolation. It is true that the term *yajña* (sacrifice) is not employed in the text at all. Nonetheless, there are traces of the theme of sacrificial death in this story. To begin with, there is certainly a physical resemblance between the between the fiery deaths facing the snake and the *satī* and the burning of offerings in Vedic sacrifices. The degree to which this resemblance extends to symbolic homology is obviously a debatable point. Still, there seems to be little doubt that the burning of widows is seen as a 'sacrificial' offering, a point lucidly made by Weinberger-Thomas (1999: 83–84, 86–88). Among Rājpūts, moreover, the immolation of a *satī* is associated with animal sacrifice, specifically with the buffalo sacrifice.[27] And although Brāhmaṇs are not actually mentioned, it seems likely that an unstated assumption of the myth is that Brāhmaṇ officiants await the *satī* and her unwilling passenger at the end of their journey.

Why is the sacrificial metaphor expressed so indirectly in this story? A possibility is that this story was, unlike our other Jain materials, transmitted by non-Jain genealogists, and not by Jain mendicants. This might account for the absence of the powerful anti-Brāhmaṇism characteristic of our other stories and for the relative weakness of the sacrificial theme. But in any case, the basic narrative movement of this story is familiar. A crisis is resolved by means of a Jain mendicant's power and teachings. Sacrificial violence, or at least something resembling it, is averted. When the prince comes back to life, equilibrium is restored, but it is an altered equilibrium because Rājpūts have now become non-violent Jains.

As do many other origin myths, the Bharatpur tale places a key female figure at the center of the creation of the new group. In this narrative, she is not a goddess but a virtuous human woman, a *satī*, pledged to follow her husband into death. But the ancestral goddess myth model is definitely at work here. Prior to her immolation, a *satī* is an embodied protogoddess in the sense that she possesses that special quality of supernormal purity and virtuous character known as *sat*. After her death, she becomes an object of worship, a goddess to her conjugal lineage. In fact, *satīs* and clan or lineage goddesses are worshipped on the same periodic occasions—normally either or both of the twice-yearly *navrātrī* festivals that are dedicated to the worship of the goddess. Thus, it is not unreasonable to speculate that the Mahājan's daughter (who, though unnamed in the manuscript, might well have possessed a name in the original myth) might have once been an actual object of worship to some of the northeastern Śrīmāls. Indeed, given her relationship with the caste's apical ancestor, she was structurally positioned (as in-marrying female) to become a worship-worthy *satī* to the entire caste. In the story she comes across as more courageous than the Rājpūt wife, thus possibly emphasising the point that although Jains are non-violent, they are neither cowardly nor weak.

Taming the Goddess: Osvāls

Osvāls are found in large numbers in both Rajasthan and Gujarat. As in the case of the Śrīmāls, however, whether Rajasthani and Gujarati Osvāls are the same community in any meaningful way is, in my view, doubtful. In Jaipur, the Osvāls (with the Śrīmāls) are quite prominent in the gemstone and jewellery business and have the reputation of being very wealthy.

It is impossible to say how many Osvāls exist. As far as I am aware, there is no established national organisation of Osvāls, or at least none that encompasses Jaipur's Osvāls, that could be a source of authoritative information (or guesses). In Jaipur, the Osvāls are a relatively small community, numbering (according to locals in the know) only a few thousand. As far as I am aware, there is no Osvāl caste association as such in Jaipur. Instead, this functional niche is occupied by various organisations focussed on Śvetāmbar Jainism. There is a Śvetāmbar Sangh for all Śvetāmbar Jains (i.e., including the image-worshippers and dissident sects), but it is weak. For the image-worshipping Śvetāmbars there is an all-India Khartar Gacch organisation headquartered in Delhi with a Jaipur branch. This organisation includes Śrīmāls as well as Osvāls, and its local branch manages three temples in Jaipur. The Sthānakvāsīs and Terāpanthīs have their own local organisations.

From the standpoint of religion, the Osvāls of Rajasthan present a far more mixed picture than the northeastern Śrīmāls. While most Rajasthani Osvāls are probably Jains, there are many Osvāl Hindus, particularly in Jodhpur and Udaipur. Also, and unlike the Śrīmāls, Osvāls have been strong supporters of the non-image-worshipping Sthānakvāsī and Terāpanthī sects. In the Jaipur area, the image-worshipping Osvāls are mostly associated with the Khartar Gacch, although the Tapā Gacch (the mendicant lineage dominant in Gujarat) has a temple in the heart of the old city. In Jaipur there is also a small community of Digambar Osvāls who migrated from Multan, now in Pakistan, at the time of the partition of the subcontinent between India and Pakistan.

The caste's internal organisation presents a somewhat confused picture. Nobody really knows how many Osvāl clans (in this caste usually called *gotras*) exist. Historian Bhūtoṛiyā (1995, vol. 1: 189) has reproduced a number of estimates that range from a few hundred to 1,444 (a figure attributed to traditional genealogists). Such figures have little meaning except to indicate that the there has been no unifying context in which an organising mind could create a rational system by designating some of these groups as subordinate branches or segments of others. That is, there has been no Osvāl Darakjī, nor has there (apparently) been a national organisation, as among the Māheśvarīs and other trading castes, that could publicise and promote a rationalised system.

Some Osvāl lineages have maintained longstanding intimate relationships with the Rājpūt aristocracy whose states they served in high offices, and as a result have adopted Rājpūt dress, manners, and customs, including the drinking of alcohol. Some, indeed, left Jainism to become Vaiṣṇava Hindus. To some extent these lineages have become a recognisable subgroup within the Osvāl community. Members of this subgroup tend to regard their social standing as superior to that of ordinary Osvāls, and I am told that their disdain for Osvāls in business is expressed in a tendency to avoid intermarriage with business families. However, I have no systematic information on this point. According to Lalit Mehta, some of these Rājpūtised Osvāls actually adopted a non-vegetarian diet in the late Mughal period, but later returned to vegetarian ways (1999: 145). Vegetarianism is certainly normative today (though what individuals choose to do in private is always another matter). The extent to which similar incipient sectioning between business-conducting and non-business-conducting subgroups has arisen within the region's other trading castes is a question worthy of further investigation.

Informants say that Osvāls formerly adhered to the four-clan rule of exogamy. Whether this is true or not is hard to say, but a large number of clans would have made such a rule easy to obey. As among traders generally, the two-clan rule prevails today. The usual hierarchical distinction between Twenties and Tens was once strong among Osvāls, but has largely disappeared in Jaipur today. I have, however, seen many references to the distinction in matrimonial advertisements in a state-wide newspaper. The Twenty/Ten distinction appears to be strong in Udaipur where Twenties have tended to be associated with government service and Tens with business (Singhi 1991: 140, 155).[28]

Osvāl Origins

The Osvāl caste possesses a body of mythohistorical knowledge far vaster and more complex than anything we have seen yet.[29] This is partly a consequence of the size and regional spread of the caste, and partly of the multiplicity of institutional conduits for the transmission of the caste's genealogies. Traditional genealogists, usually known as Bhāṭs in this context, once served some Osvāl lineages. They differed little from the genealogists we have met in connection with other trading castes. These specialists still exist and practice their profession in some areas. There is also a special class of Osvāl record-keepers known as Mahātmās. No longer active in the genealogical profession (as far as I know), they are clustered in Bikaner, and are believed to be descendents of non-celibate *yatis*. Jain mendicants also played a crucial role as creators and transmitters of Osvāl mythohistorical knowledge. For them, origin myths served a crucial purpose. As noted above, by linking the creation of specific groups to the proselytising activities of particular mendicants, such narratives provided a charter for a permanent relationship between the groups in question and the mendicant lineages of the proselytisers.

Material from all these sources has been pulled together in a number of twentieth-century works dealing with Osvāl history and mythohistory. Among the earliest examples is a book authored by a Khartar Gacch *yati* (Rāmlāljī 1910) that has been much utilised by later writings (and is also the source of the Bhinmal version of Śrīmāl origin given above). A fully initiated monk named Jñānsundarjī wrote another highly influential work, published in 1929, that will be the source of the Osvāl narrative retold below. Lay authors have also written important compilations (Bhaṇḍārī, et al. 1934, Bhansālī 1982, Bhūtoṛiyā 1995 and Nāhṭā and Nāhṭā 1978).[30] Most of these works present Osvāl origin myths as well as origin myths of some of the more important Osvāl clans. Lay authors tend to present these materials in juxtaposition to the insights of modern historians, whereas the mendicant authors that I have seen do not, but there is a great deal of overlap in the actual narrative material presented.

I have chosen Jñānsundarjī's book as the source for the Osvāl origin myth to be presented here because of its powerful influence on Osvāl perceptions of their history. Drawn itself from various older sources, it is the principal source of many subsequently published works on Osvāl origins, and is the basis for the story of Osian, the Osvāls' putative place of origin, that the temple authorities there are currently promoting.[31] An Osvāl by birth and an extremely erudite man, Jñānsundarjī was the last-but-one fully initiated (i.e., non-*yati*) mendicant belonging to a mendicant lineage called the Upkeś Gacch.[32] The origin myth he presents credits this mendicant lineage with the creation of the Osvāl caste. He produced many published works and was a tireless promoter of the Osvāl caste and the town of Osian as a religious and cultural center for Osvāls.

Two locations figure prominently in this story. The first is the ancient city of Śrīmāl (i.e., contemporary Bhinmal), which we have already encountered. The second is the town of Osian, located in Jodhpur District about 45 km north of Jodhpur. At the present time, the town is notable for the presence of two important temples.[33] One is a Jain temple dating from the eighth century C.E. that houses a particularly beautiful image of Mahāvīr. Until its restoration in the twentieth century, this temple languished in total desuetude, and even today it has yet to become a leading destination on the Śvetāmbar pilgrimage circuit. The other temple, also dating from the eighth century (although the current structure is later) and located on a nearby hill, houses a goddess known as Sacciyā (or Saciyā, or Saccikā). Both temples figure prominently in the origin myth of the Osvāl caste.

Jñānsundarjī's account of the origin of the Osvāls is organised around the disciplic genealogy of the Upkeś Gacch. The genealogy and story (here summarised from 1929: Ch. 3) begins with Pārśvanāth, the twenty-third Tīrthaṅkar and Mahāvīr's predecessor. Jñānsundarjī refers to the Upkeś Gacch as Pārśvanāth's *santān* (progeny). The tale traces disciplic succession from Pārśvanāth to Ācārya Śubhdatt (one of Pārśvanāth's chief disciples), to Haridattsūri, Āryyasamudrasūri, Keśīśramaṇācārya (who lived during the period of Mahāvīr), and finally Svayamprabhsūri, Pārśvanāth's fifth successor. Except for the reference to Mahāvīr's period, the narrative is dateless.[34] Although all these *ācārya*s are represented as great proselytisers of Jainism, identifiable convert-castes enter the picture only when we get to Svayamprabhsūri.

Jñānsundarjī's Story

> Once when Svayamprabhsūri was at Mount Abu with his followers he met some businessmen from Śrīmāl City. They told him that hundreds of thousands of innocent animals were being killed in sacrifices there, and invited him to the city. He arrived at a time when preparations were being made for a great sacrifice. When his disciples entered the city in search of alms and saw how matters stood, they returned empty-handed, saying that the city was an unfit source of food for Jain mendicants. Svayamprabhsūri thereupon gave a sermon that convinced King Jaysen and his subjects to release the animals and become Jains. Their descendants became the Śrīmāl caste.[35] Then came news that a similar sacrifice was about to be held at Padmāvati (a city near Mount Abu). Svayamprabhsūri went there with the same result, thereby creating the Porvāl caste (a Śvetāmbar trader caste not discussed in this book).

Svayamprabhsūri's successor was named Ratnaprabhsūri, and he was the creator of the Osvāl caste. He came on the scene in the following fashion:

> One time when Svayamprabhsūri was giving a sermon to the goddesses Cakreśvarī, Ambikā, Padmāvati and Siddhāyikā, a wizard by the name of Ratnacūḍ was flying overhead. His celestial vehicle came to an abrupt stop over the great mendicant's head. Then, in order to pay proper respect, Ratnacūḍ descended and listened to Svayamprabhsūri's discourse, after which he requested and received initiation as a Jain mendicant. Later, in the 52nd year after Mahāvīr's liberation, he became an *ācārya* himself (thus acquiring the name Ratnaprabhsūri) and ultimately succeeded Svayamprabhsūri as head of the mendicant lineage.

In the meantime, important events had occurred at Śrīmāl City, to which our story now returns. One of Jaysen's sons, Bhīmsen, had become king; he was a non-Jain, and the Jains had left the city entirely in order to escape persecution. Bhīmsen had two sons, one of whom was named Upaldev.

Because of a quarrel with his elder brother, Upaldev left the kingdom. His companion was Uhaṛ, the younger brother of Bhīmsen's minister. After many a twist and turn, they found their way to a spot just north of Mandor where they founded the town known as Osian today.[36] In time, large numbers of people from Śrīmāl City followed the prince to settle there, and it became a large and flourishing city.

In the 400th year before the start of the Vikram era (i.e., 457 B.C.E.), and at the urging of the goddess Cakreśvarī, Ratnaprabhsūri journeyed to Osian with 500 disciples. The monks made camp on the hill known as Luṇādrī (a short distance from the present-day Sacciyā temple) where they completed a month-long fast. At the end of the fast, a few of them went into the town in search of food. The inhabitants of the town were meat-eaters, drinkers of alcohol, and devotees of the ferocious goddess Cāmuṇḍā. This goddess, who figures prominently in events to come, was non-vegetarian and a great lover of animal sacrifices. As a result, there was no food suitable for Jain monks available, and Ratnaprabhsūri decided to move on. But Cāmuṇḍā was quite distressed when she heard about their impending departure, for it would be disgraceful not to receive with proper hospitality a distinguished monk sent by Cakreśvarī. She therefore asked him to remain for the rainy season retreat, saying that his stay would be highly beneficial. He did so with thirty-five of his hardiest disciples.

Then one night a venomous snake bit King Upaldev's daughter's husband (in fact the son of Uhaṛ, now Upaldev's minister) as he was sleeping. He appeared to be dead, but when the king and his subjects were carrying the body to the burning grounds, a Jain monk accosted them—actually the goddess Cāmuṇḍā in disguise—and asked why they were about to burn a living person. The monk thereupon vanished. The people then recalled that there had been a group of monks on the hill outside the city, so they all went there with the body. There the boy was brought back to life by being sprinkled with Ratnaprabhsūri's footwashings (see Figure 5.1).

Ratnaprabhsūri rejected all the king's offers of material rewards. Instead, he declared that the king and the others would gain great benefits in this life and the next by becoming Jains. Upon their agreeing to do so, Ratnaprabhsūri delivered a sermon. The sermon was long and covered many points, but one of its main themes was the great evil of sacrifices and of the *pākhaṇḍīs* (hypocrites, here referring primarily to Brāhmaṇs) who promote and perform sacrifices, and whose actual motive for doing so is not piety but the desire to eat meat (a common assertion in Jain writings). He said that he would teach a pure and non-violent sacrifice that would burn away the *karmas* that have bound the soul from beginningless time. Using sanctified powder (*vāskṣep*; a yellow powder used by Jain mendicants

Figure 5.1
The revival of Upaldev's son-in-law.

to confer blessings[37]) supplied by Cakreśvarī herself, Ratnaprabhsūri then initiated the king, his minister and others as lay Jains. He converted Brāhmaṇs, Kṣatriyas, and Vaiśyas, bringing them all together in a single 'Mahājan Sangh'. This group much later became known as the Osvāl caste.[38]

At the time of the conversion, Minister Uhaṛ had been in the midst of building a temple for the god Nārāyaṇ (Viṣṇu). But whatever he built each day would fall to the ground the following night. The problem was finally solved when, in mid-construction, he changed his project into a temple for Mahāvīr, and this is the Mahāvīr temple in Osian today. The goddess Cāmuṇḍā herself fashioned an image of Mahāvīr for the temple under the ground from sand and milk. Unfortunately, the eager new Jains unearthed the image before it was fully formed, with the result that there were two lemon-shaped, knot-like flaws on its chest.[39]

Despite her central role in these events, Cāmuṇḍā was left in the lurch. She had been present at, and was much pleased by, the conversions to Jainism. At that time, however, she had asked Ratnaprabhsūri if the conversions meant that she would have to give up her beloved animal sacrifice, and his answer was ambiguous. As a result, the people became very anxious as the

> date of the autumn *navrātrī* came near. This is a festival at which Cāmuṇḍā would expect animal sacrifices, which, as Jains, they would be unable to provide. In the end, Ratnaprabhsūri intervened, with the result that Cāmuṇḍā gave up meat and liquor, accepted vegetarian offerings, and became a proper Jain goddess.[40] Ratnaprabhsūri renamed her 'Saccikā' because she had spoken 'truthfully' when she told him that a rainy season stay in Osiaṇ would prove beneficial. For her part, Cāmuṇḍā promised to protect her devotees in the town (by implication the inhabitants at that time and their descendants) who worship the image of Mahāvīr in Osian's Mahāvīr temple and who serve Ratnaprabhsūri and his descendants (by which she meant the Upkeś Gacch).[41] She also became the protective goddess of the Mahāvīr temple.
>
> These events culminated in the consecration of the Mahāvīr temple. As it happens, the 465 monks who had not stayed with Ratnaprabhsūri at Osian had gone to the town called Koraṇṭpur for their rainy season retreat. The people there (whom Svayamprabhsūri had originally converted to Jainism) had also built a Mahāvīr temple, and its consecration had been set for the same day as that of the Osian temple. Because he was a wizard, Ratnaprabhsūri was able to preside bilocationally at both consecrations, which occurred in the year Vīr 70 (i.e. seventy years after Mahāvīr's liberation, which tradition places at 527 B.C.E.). He had done so, however, in his *nij* (true) form only in Osian, and when the people of Koraṇṭpur came to know of this, they were quite angry. In their pique, they conferred *ācārya* status on one of the monks who had spent the rainy season retreat with them, and this was the origin of the division between the Upkeś Gacch and the Koraṇṭ Gacch.

According to Jñānsundarjī, King Upaldev later built a Pārśvanāth temple at Osian. Jñānsundarjī claims that this same temple is currently Osian's Sacciyā temple. He maintains (ibid.: 91, f.n.) that the temple's principal goddess image was originally located in a shrine outside the main temple, and was shifted to Pārśvanāth's place after the Jains had begun to abandon the town (below). Jñānsundarjī probably feels he needs to make this point because it would seem odd indeed for a Pārśvanāth temple never to have been built in a place to the history of which the Upkeś Gacch is so important.[42]

There is an important sequel to the conversion story (ibid.: Ch. 5). In Jñānsundarjī's text, the thread that connects this sequel to the occurrences just described is a line of disciplic succession. The context in which the story is given is an account of the career of the Pārśvanāth's thirteenth successor, an *ācārya* named Kakksūri.

Figure 5.2
Having chiselled off the Mahāvīr image's flaws, the artisan is killed by the flow of blood.

In Vīr 373 (that is, 303 years after the original consecration), some young men of the town were worshipping the image in the Mahāvīr temple when they noticed the flaws on its chest. They foolishly had them chiseled off. This infuriated the goddess Sacciyā, and blood immediately began to flow from the image, killing the artisan who did the work (see Figure 5.2). Word of this was sent to a famous Upkeś Gacch *ācārya* named Kakksūri, then at Girnār, and when he arrived he began a fast. On the night of the fast's last day, the goddess appeared and explained what had happened, adding that the *jāti* (the Osvāl caste) would be destroyed as a result of the outrage. The *ācārya* was able to mollify her, and in the end she agreed to end the

> disturbance, but said that a special rite, a *śāntipūjā* (a peace-inducing rite), would be required.
>
> Noting that there are many different kinds of *śāntipūjās*, Kakksūri then asked the goddess, of what sort it should be. He added that it should use locally available materials. The goddess responded by saying that he, Kakksūri, could use only *vāskṣep* powder to bestow peace, but that this rite should be one in which others (meaning laypersons) could take part. The great mendicant replied that it would be inappropriate for him to teach any such new rite without support from the scriptures, and thereupon sent her to Mahāvideh Kṣetra to obtain instructions from Sīmandhar Svāmī.[43] This she did. It was an image-bathing rite (and Jñānsundarjī's text includes instructions for its performance). Under Kakksūri's supervision, the lay participants were arranged by their clans, of which there were eighteen; nine were stationed to the image's left and nine to the right. When the rite was performed, the flow of blood stopped. The text then lists the attending clans.

Other versions of the Osvāl story, including those told by the Sacciyā temple's priests as well as the *Upkeś Gacch Paṭṭāvali* (Hoernle 1890: 239), maintain that the Osvāls ultimately had to leave the town as a result of the goddess's curse. The priests have a clear interest in promoting such an idea, for its effect would be to keep meddlesome Osvāls at a distance, and these priests may well be the main transmitters of the diaspora story. By contrast, Jñānsundarjī, who wanted to promote Osian as an Osvāl center, rejects the diaspora story as baseless (ibid.: 102–03f.n.).[44]

Analysis of Jñānsundarjī's Story

Because Jñānsundarjī's text provides us with our most detailed example of a Jain origin myth, a comparison between it and other materials presented in this book is highly instructive. As a starting point, one of the most striking features of the Osvāl narrative is the way in which it uses genealogy. Juxtaposing it with the origin myth of the Dāhimā Brāhmaṇs (as described in Chapter 2), a narrative that also puts great stress on genealogy, is especially useful because of the light it sheds on certain distinctive traits of Jain constructions of group genealogy and descent.

Both accounts reach backward to a genealogical starting point—the Dāhimā Brāhmaṇs to Brahmā, the Osvāls to Parśvanāth. These two figures, deity and Tīrthaṅkar, are genealogical uncaused causes, and each is the source of a lineage. The Dāhimā narrative begins with the creator-deity Brahmā, who is the point of origination of a line of patrilineal descent (i.e., through Dadhīci to the Dāhimā caste and its constituent clans) that connects the moment of creation to the present day. Parśvanāth plays a similar role in the Osvāl story. He does not create the world, for the Jains possess no such concept,[45] but he originates a line of descent that provides the spine of the subsequent story. The crucial difference is that this line of descent is disciplic, not patrilineal as in the case of the Dāhimā Brāhmaṇs. Parśvanāth's teachings are treated as a kind of spiritual seed equivalent to the more purely physical continuity that is the basis of the Dāhimās' common descent. It was also from this seed that the Osvāl clans, which our narrative portrays as lay offshoots of a mendicant lineage, were produced.[46]

With this we are brought to a fundamental point about the nature of the social identity of Jain groups. There is a sense in which it is impossible to transmit Jain identity purely by means of physical descent. Brāhmaṇhood is different. To borrow Marriott's phrasing (1976), Brāhmaṇhood is a 'biomoral' quality that is transmitted from the very beginning of the world (as the Dāhimās understand such things) by means of physical reproduction. In contrast, no Jains come into existence at the moment of creation; indeed, because Jain teachings deny any form of creation of the world, for the Jains there can be no moment of creation. But in any case—and this brings us to the truly basic matter—Jain communities are religious–cultural, not natural, creations. That is, for Jains to exist, someone must be 'converted', a process begun by self-enlightened Tīrthaṅkars who introduce Jain teachings into the flow of time. These teachings are not transmitted by physical descent, but through the teacher–disciple tie. Membership in a mendicant lineage, conferred by initiation, is the symbolic marker of adherence to such teachings for mendicants. A Jain laity, in turn, consists of those who manifest reverence for Jain mendicants, or for a particular lineage of mendicants who transmit Jain teachings. Jain identity has a biomoral dimension, too, especially as expressed in diet. But its mode of transmission is, in the final analysis, more disciplic than patrilineal.

Thus, there is necessarily a deep social discontinuity in the Osvāl narrative. The Dāhimā Brāhmaṇs were Brāhmaṇs first and always. The Osvāls, by contrast, were warlike Rājpūts before they became nonviolent Jains. Although Jñānsundarjī does include other *varṇas* in the conversion, his writing generally strongly emphasizes the Osvāls' Rājpūt pedigree. Thus, in contrast to the Dāhimās, when the Osvāls become a caste, their transformation is truly fundamental. In a sense, they have no past—or perhaps a minimal past—outside of Jainism. Having become Jains, their significant past becomes that of Jainism itself and the mendicant lineages through which Jain teachings are socially transmitted and reproduced.

The radical nature of the change is expressed in the way the sacrificial myth model is employed. For the Dāhimā Brāhmaṇs, the sacrifice plays a ritually inclusive role. Their story is that of how a preexisting identity, that of Brāhmaṇhood, is fully realised socially when sages are given wives, property, and a social function (that of royal priests, which is to say, an institutionalised position in the sacrifice) in exchange for a fruitful sacrifice. The same theme is echoed in Māheśvarī narrative, though perhaps not at the same level of clarity. The Māheśvarīs, unlike the Dāhimā Brāhmaṇs but like the Osvāls and other Jains, must actually change their basic social personality in order to become the caste they are destined to be. But in the end, they return to the sacrifice, albeit on a new basis, which is to say that their change of identity is encompassed by the sacrificial order in which they remain. The same idea is echoed in some of the Khaṇḍelvāl Vaiśya narratives. But in the Osvāl narrative—and indeed in all the Jain narratives—the sacrifice plays the opposite role of ritual exclusion, propelling the group in question out of one social order and into another. This is why Jñānsundarjī includes Brāhmaṇs and Vaiśyas among Ratnaprabhsūri's converts. By pulling all of these groups into a single 'Mahājan Sangh' he makes the point that *varṇa* identity has been totally obliterated by separation from the sacrifice.

A main issue in the text is violence, which is true of most trading caste origin mythology, but is especially salient in Jain origin myths. Thus, Jñānsundarjī presents non-violence as the principal reason for the new Jains' break with the sacrifice. But he pairs this issue with another of equal importance, which is the need for a break with the Brāhmaṇs. After all, one can sacrifice non-violently, as we see with the Dāhimās (and also the sacrifices portrayed in the origin myths of the Māheśvarīs and Khaṇḍelvāl Vaiśyas). The Dāhimā Brāhmaṇs are, in fact, a vegetarian caste. As such, they are compelled by their own social identity to believe in the possibility of non-violent, vegetarian sacrifice, because the activity of performing sacrifices is at the core of what it means (in theory) to be a Brāhmaṇ. Osvāls, however, must break with the sacrificial—that is, Brahmanical—social order. For the Osvāls, therefore, a belief in the possibility of non-violent sacrifice is ruled out, and in Jñānsundarjī's

Figure 5.3
The view from Luṇādrī Hill.

narrative, as in the Jain materials generally, the Brāhmaṇs are portrayed as tireless advocates of blood sacrifice.

Their links with the past having been cut so completely, the Osvāls must then—in effect—exchange one set of ancestors for another. The Dāhimās venerate the sage Dadhīci as their common ancestor, and in fact he is represented by an image in a side shrine at the Dadhimatī temple. In contrast, no patrilineal ancestors from pre-conversion days are objects of worship at Osian.[47] In our Osvāl narrative, the pattern of venerating ancestral figures has been shifted to the Tīrthaṅkar (technically Pārśvanāth but generically Mahāvīr) and his spiritual successors in the Upkeś Gacch. Indeed, Ratnaprabhsūri is represented by a small image in the Mahāvīr temple and a footprint image in a shrine on Luṇādrī Hill (see Figure 5.3). As portrayed in the narrative, this is the true 'ancestor cult' of the Osvāls.[48]

An important implication of these points is that a Jain caste is actually incapable of reproducing itself fully. Of course the Osvāl caste is a social group that, at the most basic level, reproduces itself physically and socially in the normal manner. But at another level, it does not. Not all Osvāls are Jains, and, as we have suggested, 'Jainness' is a quality that is transmitted in the form of teachings and initiation, not by physical descent. These belong to the domain of mendicants, and thus the Jain component of the identity of Jain castes is in the custody of the mendicants who are its primary creators and transmitters. This suggests that even after the Osvāl caste is created, it becomes—within the world of our narrative—a sort of shadow of the mendicant lineage of which it is a lay offshoot. Indeed, without sustained contact with *some* mendicant lineage or lineages (not necessarily its mendicant lineage of origin), the caste is not capable of transmitting its essence—as *Jain* Osvāls—to the next generation.[49]

Once launched in the stream of time, the mendicant lineage produces segments, both mendicant and lay, and these moments of subcreation are the main temporal markers of the Osvāl narrative. There are three principal lay offshoots, the Śrīmāls, Porvāls and Osvāls. Using a modified idiom of segmentary descent—i.e., one in which the principles of lineage segmentation are grafted onto disciplic descent—Jñānsundarjī's account registers the fact that all three castes, though different, are similar in their social customs and adherence to Śvetāmbar Jainism. By assigning a separate creator-*ācārya* to the Osvāls, the narrative adds additional social distance to the gap between the Osvāls and the other two castes (who in any case figure only marginally in the story).

But why trace descent to Pārśvanāth in particular? As far as I am aware, all other Śvetāmbar mendicant lineages treat Mahāvīr as their apical ancestor. This being so, it seems likely that tracing disciplic descent to Pārśvanāth, who predated Mahāvīr, had the purpose of differentiating the Upkeś Gacch from other mendicant lineages in a decisive way, probably in the context of rivalry with other Gacchs for the allegiance of lay Jains. In the region corresponding to what is now Rajasthan, the Khartar Gacch was certainly a rival in this regard, which we know because of the existence of numerous Osvāl clan origin myths that trace clan descent to an ancestor converted by one or another Khartar Gacch mendicant (see Babb 1996, Ch. 4). The date assigned to the creation of the Osvāls is a crucial consideration, and this is a matter to which Jñānsundarjī gives careful attention (1929, Ch. 4: 1–40). He considers three alternatives: Vīr 70, V.S. 222, and the 10th century of the Vikram era (the latter the most realistic by the standards of modern historians).[50] As we know, he favours the Vīr 70 date, which seems to be the general Upkeś Gacch preference. This is also the date given by the

Upkeś Gacch Paṭṭāvali. This date would render implausible any claim by another Gacch to have converted the Osvāls; that is, it creates the temporal depth required for the Upkeś Gacch to lay exclusive claim to the Osvāl caste as a lay segment.

The later mutilation of the image is a puzzling aspect of the tale. The story seems to struggle with the ostensibly outrageous idea that the goddess herself is somehow embodied in Mahāvīr's image. She was the source of the milk from which the image was partly made (dropped by a cow on the spot where the image was forming below). The two flaws on the image's chest reiterate the milk/breast theme, which is further reinforced by the blood (or, in a version told to me orally by the one of the Sacciyā temple's priests, a mixture of blood and milk) that issues from the flaw or flaws when the desecration occurs. It is as if she herself were the victim of the foolish mutilation. But whatever its underlying symbolism, the episode clearly represents a rebirth or second birth of the Osvāl caste, complete with a transformative ritual (the *pūjā*) and an *ācārya* who tames the goddess.

Just why there should be a revisiting of this idea, a whiff of 'eternal return' in the midst of an origin myth, is unclear. Of course, for those who believe in the goddess's permanent curse (not, as we know, Jñānsundarjī), the mutilation-inspired curse explains the Osvāl diaspora, but this could be done without a second creation. It also seems possible that the two creations are a simple artifact of the Upkeś Gacch genealogy. Kakksūri might have been a central figure in some different Upkeś Gacch account of Osvāl creation, a story that would naturally enter the main narrative as a separate episode, and at a time corresponding to Kakksūri's position in the genealogy.

But there is another possibility. The second creation might be compelled by ritual logic. While the converted Rājpūts of Osian worked out a proper ritual relationship with the goddess at the time of their original conversion, it can be said that they had not yet established an equivalent ritual relationship with the Tīrthaṅkar. Or at least this is strongly suggested by the fact that although the Mahāvīr image was clearly in worship at the time of the mutilation, Kakksūri and the goddess nonetheless had no clue at all about what a lay ritual to quell the disturbance should actually be, until they consulted Sīmandhar Svāmī. This slight vestige of liminality in the Osvāls' status is finally resolved by the *pūjā*, a ritual performance in which they are portrayed for the first time as a bona fide caste, subdivided into exogamous named clans. The *pūjā* would then play a role similar to that of Māndhātā's sacrifice in the Dāhimā narrative. Readers will recall that Brāhmaṇ sages become an actual caste (consisting of exogamous clans) as a direct result of their participation in the rite.

As in many of the origin myths we have examined, a female figure is central to the Osvāl story, and here the ancestral goddess myth model is strongly asserted indeed. But here also—and in common with other Jain examples but in contrast to non-Jain cases—her relationship with the rite of sacrifice is negative. For the Osvāls, that is, her relationship with the rite is coloured by the assumption that Brahmanical sacrifice is always blood sacrifice. New Jains are created when sacrificers become non-sacrificers; in parallel with this, the goddess Cāmuṇḍā becomes a goddess suitable for Jains only when she no longer receives blood sacrifice.

This point is deeply linked with that most ubiquitous of themes in Jain life: diet. The conversion process begins when Jain mendicants cannot find food. This leads to the transformation of Osian's Rājpūts (with others) into Jains, which in turn makes possible a sustainable commensal relationship between a mendicant lineage and a lay community. But now the tables are turned, for the newly created Jains discover that they cannot feed Cāmuṇḍā properly (i.e., with meat). She, too, must undergo a transformation. The fact that the transformation is a change of name and diet suggests an interesting conflation of social character and substance that seems to be pervasive in these materials (on this issue, see Marriott 1976, 1990).

At precisely the point when she gives up meat and assumes a new name, she makes a momentous promise. She pledges to remove the troubles and difficulties of her devotees in Osian (by implication, the Osvāl caste) who worship the image of Mahāvīr in Osian's Mahavīr temple and who serve Ratnaprabsūri and his *santān* (his spiritual descendants, by which she means the Upkeś Gacch). In other words, at this point she enters into the paradigm of the goddess who has a protective relationship, transmitted by patrilineal descent, with the group she has helped to create. She remains a clan and/or caste goddess to her original worshippers, pledging her protection to them. But her primary relationship has shifted to Mahāvīr and the Mahāvīr temple, as evidenced by her later fury over the desecration. This part of the myth is, among other things, a charter for continuing Osvāl support for the Upkeś Gacch, the Mahāvīr temple, and of course, the Sacciyā Mātā temple at Osian.

These events seem to represent yet another reflection of the logic of rites of passage in our mythic materials. When she was a clan goddess to

Rājpūts, Cāmuṇḍā participated in their nature as a warrior community. The vegetarianisation of this community occupies the same ritual–logical niche as a rite of separation, severing them from their previous condition. This occurs precisely when they convert to Jainism on the heels of the prince's apparent restoration to life. But here, in contrast to other myths, the transition from Rājpūt to Jain occurs before the issue of the sacrifice is actually tackled. As we see, in this myth the entire question of sacrifice is left dangling until after the snakebite victim is saved and the people converted to Jainism. It is then displaced onto the goddess, where it emerges as the question of whether or not she will be given the animal sacrifice to which she is accustomed. Until Cāmuṇḍā's nature is changed, the transformation is incomplete, leaving the community in a liminal state. The myth thus shows that although it is possible to defer the issue of sacrifice, it has to be dealt with in the end if Rājpūts are to become Jains. The social identity of the newly transformed Jains is unstable and incomplete until Cāmuṇḍā's appetite for animal sacrifice is curbed. Seen against this background, the establishment of the community's new relationship with the goddess, based on vegetarian offerings, becomes the functional equivalent of a rite of incorporation.

Of course the triangular relationship between Sacciyā, the Upkeś Gacch and the Osvāl caste was a projection of the Gacch's theoreticians, and must have coincided with reality only imperfectly. And whatever this relationship once was, what remains of it today is little indeed. The Upkeś Gacch is, to all intents and purposes, extinct. The Khartar Gacch, not the Upkeś Gacch, is the mendicant lineage of greatest importance to Jaipur's image-worshipping Osvāl Jains; elsewhere, especially in Gujarat, the Tapā Gacch holds sway. Furthermore, large numbers of Osvāls have left the image worshipping tradition altogether in favour of the Sthānakvāsī and Terāpanthī sects.

Sacciyā, however, currently has a flourishing relationship with Osvāls. It is certainly not the case, and never was, that Sacciyā is a universal clan goddess for this caste. But she still functions as clan goddess for many Osvāls (and for other castes of the locality as well), and the Sacciyā temple complex has enjoyed a tremendous growth spurt in recent decades, largely as a result of donations from wealthy Osvāls. The temple has acquired a reputation for cancer-curing, and it seems possible that, if it exhibits the growth dynamic of such major temple centers as Sālāsar Bālājī, Sacciyā might someday become a goddess who altogether transcends the parochialisms of caste and locality.

Sacrifice Rejected

Our Jain narratives cannot be regarded as rigid structures in which the same elements are always configured in the same way. The recurrence of certain key elements is nevertheless quite striking: the crisis resolved by a monk's power, the evil Brāhmaṇs, the female figure, and above all, the averted sacrificial violence. These elements all cluster around the central theme, the creation of Jain castes, but not always in the same way, in the same ordering, or at the same level of prominence. In each myth, a new group is created out of an old one. It acquires a completely new identity that is then attached to a cluster of intermarrying exogamous patriclans. The central component in this new identity is Jainism, which in these materials emerges less as a matter of allegiance to Jain teachings than to Jain mendicants, or mendicant lineages, and rejection of Brāhmaṇs and the socio-religious order they represent.

The principal difference between Jain and Hindu narratives lies in the nature of the connection between the newly created group and the sacrificial order. That is, there is a fundamental difference in the way the sacrificial myth model is deployed and utilised. Having become domesticated as a caste by means of a sacrifice, the Dāhimā Brāhmaṇs become sacrificial officiants in the social order they have joined. The newly created Fire Clan Rājpūts become protectors of the sacrifice and the Brāhmaṇs who perform it; in so doing they become, in effect, protectors of the entire social order associated with the sacrifice. The Māheśvarīs and the Khaṇḍelvāl Vaiśyas present a variegated picture, but the overall trend is the same. The newly created group remains attached to the sacrificial order, but assumes a new role within it. Emblematic of this inclusion is the establishment of a relationship between the new caste and Brāhmaṇs. The Jains, however, break with this order by rejecting Brahmanical authority completely. The Osvāl narrative we have examined dramatises this break by severing Osvāl descent from their Rājpūt past and grafting it onto the disciplic genealogy of a Jain mendicant lineage, the Upkeś Gacch.

The rejection of violence is central to virtually all trader-caste origin mythology, but Jains and Hindus treat this issue somewhat differently. In the Jain narratives, three social categories emerge in relation to violence: Jains, Kṣatriyas (i.e., Rājpūts), and Brāhmaṇs. Of these, the categories Kṣatriya and Jain—those who live for violence and those who live to reject it—form an opposed pair. The Brāhmaṇs, however, are also implicated in this opposition. In this cultural milieu—seen, that is, from the Jain standpoint—violence is understood to have certain characteristic institutional expressions, and chief among these is the sacrificial relationship between Brāhmaṇs and Kṣatriyas. The Jains see this relationship as an incorrigible source of lethality. Thus, the Brāhmaṇs enter the equation as a third element, for it is in relation to them, and to the sacrifices over which they preside, that the transformation from Kṣatriya to Jain is, in the narratives we have seen, portrayed as having taken place.

Brāhmaṇs are treated differently in the Hindu-cluster myths. The Jain narratives attribute the moral fault of violence to Brāhmaṇs and the allegedly inherently violent rites over which they preside. Remove Brāhmaṇs and the sacrifice from the equation, and Rājpūts become virtuous Jains. In many of the Hindu narratives, however, the culpability seems to be assigned to the traders-to-be themselves: Kṣatriyas who spoil sacrifices and/or offend sages with violence, and Brāhmaṇs who hunt and kill deer. The Hindu narratives thus hint that there is an element of punition in the transformation to trader status. The transformation, therefore, is something of a comedown. Not so in the case of the Jains. The Jains-to-be are not punished, but rather blessed by the teachings of Jain mendicants, connection with whom is the true solvent of their former status as violent Rājpūts.

The Dāhimā narrative shows us how Kṣatriyas can turn Brāhmaṇ sages into a Brāhmaṇ caste by paying them for performing a sacrifice. The story of the Fire Clan Rājpūts (in the Darakjī version) shows us how Brāhmaṇs can turn demoniacal renegade Kṣatriyas into protective Kṣatriyas by purifying them in a sacrifice. This reflects a certain historical as well as mythohistorical reality, for Brāhmaṇs have indeed transformed brigands into Kṣatriyas and Rājpūts by performing legitimising sacrifices on their behalf. The narratives of the non-Jain traders show us how either Brāhmaṇs or Kṣatriyas (although the emphasis is clearly on the Kṣatriyas) whose relationship with the sacrificial order has gone sour (because of violence instigated by them) can be redeemed by means of transmutation into non-violent traders. These narrative lines all emphasise inclusion in the sacrificial order.

It is on this point that the Jains' narratives are in a class by themselves. Their myths do not have much to say about becoming traders, or Vaiśyas, or Baniyās. The emphasis, rather, is on their becoming *Jains* who reject the authority and ritual culture of Brāhmaṇs. This being so, and if we adopt the perspective of the sacrificial social order, it can be said that myth places the Jains in a position of symbolic externality; they become warriors who have left their former social role but who, unlike the Hindu traders, have returned to no differently defined role within the sacrificial circle. This means that there is a sense in which they remain the warriors they were before, albeit non-violent ones. And this, in turn, is deeply resonant with the fact that regal and martial themes are extremely strong in Jainism and its ritual culture (Babb 1996). Jains celebrate a spiritualised version of martial prowess. They are, as we know, followers of 'victors' or 'conquerors', but with the crucial proviso that, as Jain teachings insist, the right war is with the body and its passions, not with external enemies on worldly fields of battle. More than any other group, therefore, the Jains are the Rājpūts' reversed others. In an apparent paradox, the Jains exceed other trading groups both in the emphasis they place on Rājpūt descent, with all of its implications of martial valour, and the strength of their commitment to non-violence as a core value for the conduct of life. As an expression of social identity, Jainism thus represents the extreme and limiting case of trader identity as both dependent on, and opposed to, that of the region's Rājpūt elite.

We must now ask to what degree the images of group identity and group transformation we have seen in this and previous chapters have points of contact with the sensibilities and idioms of the late twentieth and early twenty-first centuries. The next chapter addresses this question by describing how the mythohistory of the Agravāl caste has been transmuted into a form of modern public culture.

Notes

1. For portraits of Jainism in actual practice, see Cort 2001, Laidlaw 1995, and Babb 1996. Laidlaw and Babb deal with Śvetāmbar Jains of Jaipur.
2. Many other issues divide these two great branches of the Jain world. See Dundas 2002: 45–59, Jaini 1979: 38–41.
3. On *gacchs* and their internal organisation, see Cort 1990b; 2001; 40–46. See K. C. Jain 1963: 55–69 for a survey of *gacchs* of Rajasthan.
4. On the origins of this division, see esp. Cort 2002; also Kāslīvāl 1989: 254–61. The Digambar Terāpanthīs are not to be confused with the Śvetāmbar sect of the same name. See K. C. Jain, 1963: 69–88 for a general discussion of Digambar subdivisions.
5. It is often said that Jainism is anti-caste, which is true to some extent. See Cort forthcoming for a detailed discussion of Jains and caste; a useful discussion can also be found in Laidlaw 1995: 111–16.

6. According to one author (Roy 1978: 183) the Terāpanthīs constitute about 40 per cent of Jaipur's Digambar population.
7. For details concerning Bakhatrām Śāh, see Padmadhar Pāṭhak's introduction to the 1964 edition of *Buddhi Vilas* and Lath 1981: xxviii, lix–lx. See also Cort 2002.
8. Not in all versions of the story; see Baṛjātyā (1910).
9. In other versions the king does know about and even actively participates in the sin, but as far as I am aware the Brāhmaṇs are always the motive force behind the act.
10. See Kāslīvāl 1989: 88–91.
11. The weakness of the goddess cult among Khaṇḍelvāl Jains may also be a consequence of Terāpanthī influence. The Terāpanthīs oppose goddess worship. The caste-deity status of Mahāvījī is indicated by the fact that many Bīspanthī Jains of the region have their tonsure rites performed there. My thanks to John Cort for these points.
12. On the founding of the Śvetāmbar Terāpanth, see Dundas 2002: 254–60. The sect is strongly associated with the Osvāl caste.
13. For the History of this lineage, see Vinaysāgar 1956: 241–50.
14. See, e.g., Bhaṇḍārī 1934 ('Śrīmāl Jātikā Itihās', an add-on to the final section of Vol. 2), Bhūtoṛiyā 1995, Jñānsundarjī 1929.
15. Whether he means that all of the Brāhmaṇs present were actually related to Gautam and his 500 disciples is not completely clear—to this reader at least—from the text. But Gautam was, of course, a Brāhmaṇ, and this seems to be the text's implication.
16. Other Brāhmaṇs who were vegetarianised by Gautam, according to this account, include our Dāhimā Brāhmaṇs. According to the tale, many Brāhmaṇ groups not represented at the sacrifice remained meat-eaters. Five thousand Brāhmaṇs from Sindh who attended did not accept Gautam's teachings. Rāmlājī has more to say on this subject that we need not review here.
17. Rāmlāljī (1910: 106) also says that Āsal was the originating ancestor of a 'Śrīmāl *gotra*'. How this fits with the earlier creation of the Śrīmāls with their 135 clans is unclear to me.
18. This is the story of the origin of the Osvāl caste, which we will examine later in this chapter.
19. The clan system of regulating marriage is not found among trading castes and some other castes of Gujarat. Why this is so is unclear, but Rāmlāljī is referring to this well-known feature of Gujarati social organisation. On this point, see Cort forthcoming.
20. Śankara (788–820 C.E), a Śaiva Brāhmaṇ from South India, was the founder of the *advaita vedānta* school of philosophy and an energetic defender and promoter of Hindu orthodoxy.
21. This is a probable reference to Ācārya Hemacandra Maladhārī whose writings date from the early twelfth century C. E. See Cort 1990a: 268, 282, also Winternitz 1972.
22. There is more than one acarya of this name in the Khartar Gacch. Which one is not stated.
23. The term *sat* means goodness or truth, and in this context refers to what Harlan calls an 'autogenerative moral fuel' (1992: 129). When the husband of a woman who possesses *sat* dies, it becomes manifest as a desire to become a *satī*, i.e., a woman of virtue who dies in the blaze of her husband's funeral pyre. In her superb book on *satī*, Weinberger-Thomas describes the arising of *sat* as an 'indescribable state of agitation, transport, and fervour' that culminates in the act of burning itself. The funeral pyre 'is ignited solely through the inner flame of the *sat*' (1999: 22, 23).
24. In this context, the term *yati* might refer to any Jain monk, regardless of the completeness or incompletelness of his vows.

25. Why this particular name was chosen is unfortunately not clear from the copy I was given; it is possibly an omission, or possibly included in any of several parts of the text that are unreadable in my copy.
26. The Śrīśrīmāls are considered an Osvāl clan, at least in the Jaipur area. How this fact squares with the myth I am unable to say.
27. Harlan 1992: 130–31. Harlan also reports that the Puranic account of the goddess Satī's self-inflicted death is not seen as a paradigm for satī in Rajasthan. On this same point, see Weinberger-Thomas (1999: 134–35).
28. In Udaipur, the Twenty/Ten distinction appears to be expressed as a distinction between *baṛe sājan* (high) and *chote sājan* (low).
29. Osvāl origin myths have been extensively discussed in recent scholarship; see Babb 1996 and Meister 1998.
30. I have presented other versions of the Osian myth together with the origin myths of specific Osvāl clans in Babb 1996: 137–73.
31. For details on his own sources, which were mostly Jain *paṭṭāvalis*, see Jñāsundarjī 1929, Prastāvnā, pp. 22–25.
32. John Cort has suggested to me that he was probably also the first fully initiated mendicant belonging to the Upkeś Gacch, which is most likely a lineage consisting only of *yatis* from the start.
33. On these temples see Cort 2000a, 2000b; Meister 1991: 182–91, 128; Meister 2000.
34. No dates are given for the above *ācāryas*, either here or on a succession chart provided on p. 95.
35. There are obviously significant differences between this account of the Śrīmāls' origin and that of Rāmlāljī (above).
36. It was then known (according to this narrative) as Uespaṭṭan or Upkeśpur.
37. On which see Cort 1998: 95.
38. Most accounts of the creation of Jain castes stress their Rājpūt origin, and that is definitely an emphasis in Jñānsundarjī's writing. Nonetheless, he includes Brāhmaṇs and Vaiśyas as well. His intent, I surmise, is to stress the complete elimination of the *varṇa* system and the Brahmanical/sacrificial order with which it is associated. Elsewhere in the book (Ch. 4: 34) he says that the Osvāls mostly come from 'pure Kṣatriya *varṇa*'. In the same chapter he also says that the Osvāl caste does not have any Śūdra ancestry. Also, he attributes what he calls the *vīrtā* (heroism, courage) of the Osvāls to their Rājpūt ancestry (Ch. 4: 46). But he also wants to push the line that the conversion freed the converts from the Brahmanical bondage of and *varṇa*.
39. The Minister's cow was dropping milk on the spot below which the image was being formed, and the image was discovered when a herdsman followed the cow. Similar stories are widely known in connection with other images.
40. Non-Jains, however, have sacrificed animals at (or outside) this temple until—apparently—quite recently.
41. Each Śvetāmbar Gacch has its own protector deity parallel to the protective deities of clans and lineages.
42. The assertion that the Sacciyā temple was originally a Pārśvanāth temple is not present in Hoernle's (1890) translation of the *Upkeś Gacch Paṭṭāvali*.
43. According to Jain teachings, no Tīrthaṅkars are currently present in our region of the cosmos. Sīmandhar Svāmī is a Tīrthaṅkar now teaching in a mythical region called Mahāvideh Kṣetra (see Dundas 2002: 268–70, 305 n. 75).

44. To begin with, he says, the caste was known as Upkeśvaṃś in those days, not Osvāl, and the town was called Upkeśpur; in any case, rich merchants of the Upkeśvaṃś were living in Osian until the tenth to eleventh century (V.S.). Business declined when the sea (*samudra*) receded from the city, thus driving the business community elsewhere, and a famine in the fourth century (V.S.) also caused people to move out. But nowhere, he says, is there any mention of the people all leaving suddenly.
45. The Jains do not believe in a creator god. As Jaini points out (1979: 288), Ṛṣabh, the first Tīrthaṅkar of our region and era, partially fills this role.
46. In this respect, the lay sublineage that is the Osvāl caste resembles somewhat the matrilaterally differentiated lineage segments of the Nuer as described by Evans-Pritchard in his classic monograph (1940). From this point of view, Sacciyā occupies the same structural position as a co-wife whose son's children become a new lineage segment.
47. There is a doctrinal reason for this. The Jains prohibit the *śrāddh* (the Brahmanical form of ancestor worship) because of the inconsistency between Jain rebirth doctrine, with its insistence on the instantaneous transmission of the soul between one body and the next, and the Brahmanical idea of the soul's prolonged sojourn in a liminal state between death and rebirth (see Jaini 1979: 302–04). This would seem to militate against any kind of ritual focus on the dead. But it has to be said that ritual Jainism is itself a sort of mortuary cult (Babb 1996) in which deceased mendicants are the principal objects of worship.
48. One can even speculate that a possible reason for the Jain doctrine of instantaneous rebirth is to shift focus away from other forms of worship to the veneration of deceased mendicants.
49. The Bhaṭṭāraks have played a roughly analogous role for Digambar castes such as the Khaṇḍelvāl Jains. The extent to which this is so, however, needs further investigation. See Cort 2002 for a discussion of the Bhaṭṭāraks in Digambar Jainism.
50. I use his dating terminology here. Year one of the Vikram era ended in 57 B.C.E. Year one of the Vīr system is the year of Mahāvīr's final liberation (traditionally, 527 B.C.E).

Chapter Six

Going Public

In May of 1997, the Akhil Bhāratīya Agravāl Sammelan, an organisation claiming to represent 30 million Agravāls, sponsored its sixteenth annual national meeting at the Talkatora Indoor Stadium in New Delhi. The Agravāls are the largest of India's trading castes, a rich and powerful community of great importance in modern India's economic and political life. From a national point of view, they are certainly the best known of the trading castes considered in this book.

This event was announced with much fanfare in a full-page advertisement in Delhi's major newspapers, and the advertisement itself was a culturally significant text. The version that appeared in *The Indian Express* (May 17), an English daily, contained an article entitled 'The Twenty Two Years of Awakening', which was an account of the Sammelan's efforts to 'give identity to Agrawal society'. As the context made clear, by 'identity' was meant a sense of caste membership and unity among Agravāls. The article mentioned the Sammelan's support of educational institutions and efforts to combat 'social evils' such as dowry, but it mainly emphasised its promotion of a place called Agroha 'as a religious shrine'. The importance of Agroha—located near Hisar in Haryana, about 190 km from Delhi—is that it is believed to have once been the capital city of an ancient king named Agrasen, whom Agravāls consider to be the originator of their caste.

The Agravāl origin myth will seem both familiar and unfamiliar to readers of this book. Although the story exhibits some significant variations from what we have seen before, these are variations on themes that we have encountered earlier in this book. There is, however, a significant difference between the Agravāl case and our other examples. This is the degree to which the Agravāl origin myth, or rather one version of it, has been exhibited to the surrounding society. As the example of the 1997 Sammelan meeting demonstrates, this is a case in which a caste's mythohistory has become highly visible in public spaces. As this chapter will show, the radical social externalisation of the Agravāl origin narrative has been part of the strategy of a political elite within the caste to modernise Agravāl identity, to harmonise it with general trends in Indian society, and to provide it with political punch.

This phenomenon is not only interesting in itself, but it also provides us with an opportunity to deepen our understanding of trading-caste identity in general. Variation can be the royal road to discovering essentials. This chapter will show that whatever the differences between the Agravāl myth and others considered in this book, and whatever the changes that have occurred and continue to occur in its contemporary manner of presentation, one element remains absolutely stable. This is the conjunction between social identity and ritual identity. And as in most of our other cases, the crux of the matter is the issue of violence in the sacrifice.

Agroha and Agravāls

For over 20 years Agroha has been the focus of a publicity and development effort undertaken by the Sammelan and a sister organisation, the Agrohā Vikās Trust. These organisations have published vast literature about the place and have even supported archaeological research there. They have also sponsored the installation of images of King Agrasen at various public places, promoted the use of his name for schools and other institutions, and have successfully lobbied for the issuance of a King Agrasen commemorative postage stamp. Most important, the Trust has built an enormous pilgrimage center at Agroha that embodies and glorifies basic symbols of Agravāl mythohistory.

The center looms up from the flat Haryana horizon as one approaches it on the highway. At its core is a Brobdingnagian religious complex consisting of three temples adjoining a hall large enough to seat 5,000 persons (see Figure 6.1). The temples contain images of King Agrasen and the goddesses Mahālakṣmī and Sarasvatī.[1] Behind the temple complex is a large bathing tank and a home for the elderly. Partially excavated ruins, said to be the remains of Agrasen's ancient

Figure 6.1
The temple-center at Agroha.

Figure 6.2
The ruins at Agroha with Agravāl tourists (from Udaipur and Mumbai).

capital, are a short walk away (see Figure 6.2). Also nearby are a recently renovated temple for Śīlā Mātā (a *satī* venerated by many Agravāls) and an Agravāl-sponsored medical college. The entire complex is billed as '*agrohā dhām*', the Agroha 'abode'. This is a manner of speaking usually reserved for a holy place of pilgrimage, and its use here implies that Agroha is such a sacred place. Agrasen is represented as a deity among deities, enshrined on land sanctified by the origin of the Agravāl caste.

The same symbols displayed at Agroha are also much in evidence in Jaipur. In particular, Agrasen's birthday (*agrasen jayantī*) is celebrated by local Agravāls on a truly massive scale.[2] In the same manner as the Māheśvarīs' *maheś navmi* (mentioned in Chapter Four), this occasion belongs almost entirely to the non-domestic, public domain. In essence, it is a form of outdoor theater designed to display the caste's wealth and power, and its venue is the streets, not private homes. When I saw it in 1996, the main event was a gigantic evening procession in the main business section of the walled city. The procession included three brass bands, mobile tableaus with children serving as actors, the usual marching dignitaries, and a moving temple containing an image of Agrasen. This image was worshipped at the procession's outset and from time to time as it moved through the city. The procession passed under 18 large, street-spanning arches stationed along the route, each named for one of the officially designated 18 Agravāl clans.

The tableaus presented a somewhat incongruous juxtaposition of two quite different themes. One theme was reformism. Thus, one of the tableaus portrayed the low-expense, group marriages currently being promoted by the caste's leadership, and another depicted the evils of dowry murder. The other theme was the origin of the Agravāl caste, with which the remaining two tableaus were directly concerned. One portrayed Agrasen and 18 sons, who are—according to some versions of Agravāl origin—progenitors of the 18 Agravāl clans. Eighteen young boys were dressed as princes, each carrying a shield on which was written the name of one of the clans. In the other tableau were 18 children, each sitting before a diminutive altar and performing a sacrifice, while a bearded and regal-looking Agrasen looked on from his throne (see Figure 6.3). This, as we shall see, was a depiction of a crucial juncture in the creation of the Agravāl caste as portrayed in myth. The overall message conveyed by the procession was that the Agravāls are second to none in their up-to-date responsiveness to important social issues, but that they

Figure 6.3
King Agrasen and attendant in truck-borne tableau.

are also an ancient community with a royal pedigree and deep roots in Indic religious culture.

Agravāls

Of all the castes discussed in this book, the Agravāls are the least Rajasthani. By this I mean that Rajasthan is nowhere near the actual center of this caste's geographic distribution. Indeed, the Rajasthani branch of the Agravāls is but a peninsula of the caste as a whole, which is distributed over vast areas of northern and central India. In Rajasthan, most Agravāls were originally settled in the Shekhawati region. Many of the Shekhawati Agravāls have migrated to Kolkata and other locations, but great numbers of Agravāl traders still inhabit the towns and villages of Shekhawati and other areas of the state.

Despite the Sammelan's apparent confidence in the figure of 30 million, in truth the size of the caste is unknown. Indeed, it is even difficult to find solid data on the geographic distribution of the caste and its segments. The Sammelan promotes an image of the Agravāl caste that represents its internal structure as fully rationalised and its external boundaries as clear and unambiguous. But while a full ethnography of the Agravāls does not exist, it can at least be said that this image is false. The structure of the Agravāl caste is far from fully understood, even by the caste's own elite, and its outer frontiers have never been adequately traced. There are quite likely to be subgroups and divisions within the caste about which I have never even heard.[3]

According to an official of the Agravāl Samāj Samiti, Jaipur's chief Agravāl organisation, there are about 200,000 Agravāls in Jaipur. Those Agravāls who are doing business in Jaipur appear to be mostly of Shekhawati origin. Agravāls from outside Rajasthan, probably no more than 10 per cent of the Jaipur total, tend to be in service occupations rather than business. While it is difficult to gauge these matters accurately, in general the Agravāls do not have the reputation of being at the top level of wealth among Jaipur's traders. I have occasionally heard non-Agravāl traders characterise them half-humorously as prone to the showy ostentation of the newly rich.

As a caste, the Agravāls are extremely well organised. At the Jaipur level, the caste's affairs are handled by the afore-mentioned Agravāl Samāj Samiti, which has about a dozen branches in various parts of the city. Founded in 1950, it is independent and not part of the national Sammelan/Trust. At the time of my research, however, two members of its executive board were also on the board of the Trust. It has its own publications and runs several schools. Among its most important periodic activities is the sponsorship of the annual celebration of Agrasen's and Lala Lajpat Rai's birthdays. It also manages Agravāl marriage fairs (large gatherings with the purpose of promoting and facilitating marriage arrangements) and other events. One of this organisation's main achievements in the domain of symbolic politics has been the creation of an 'Agrasen Circle' at one of Jaipur's busiest intersections. An imposing statue of King Agrasen sits serenely at the center of a traffic island surrounded by whizzing vehicles.

We shall return to details about their national organisation later.

Internal Caste Divisions

The structure of Jaipur's Agravāl community presents a complex picture that includes sectional, hierarchical, and religious divisions as well as a clan system of considerable interest.

At least two main sections of the caste are found in Jaipur: the main branch, by far the majority, and a subdivision known as the Rājvaṃśī Agravāls, the latter consisting of some 80 (possibly more) families. The mainstream Rajasthani Agravāls regard the Rājvaṃśīs as inferior, and in the past barred intermarriage with them. How effective the ban is today is hard to say. The Rājvamśīs originated in northwestern U.P. in the Meerat/Muzaffarnagar/Saharanpur region. They are latecomers to Rajasthan, having arrived only in the last 50 years or so, and have generally supported themselves in service occupations, not in business. To this day they remain somewhat cut off from the rest of the local Agravāl community.

The standard Twenty/Ten division was once very strong among the Agravāls of Jaipur and Rajasthan. An acquaintance whose father was a Twenty and whose mother was a Ten tells me that his parents' marriage, which occurred in the 1930s, caused a huge stir in local Agravāl circles. This division is much weakened today, but I am told that people are certainly still aware of which families are Twenties and Tens. The distinction is occasionally mentioned in matrimonial advertisements in newspapers, including the national English-language dailies. Campālāl Gupt refers to the existence of an even lower 'Five' stratum among the Agravāls (1996: 110–11), but this is not a category that arose in my enquiries in Rajasthan.[4]

The Agravāls are divided religiously between a Hindu majority and a Jain minority. Jain Agravāls appear to be concentrated in western U.P.; they belong to the Digambar sect, and are in fact the dominant Digambar community of Delhi. Even in Delhi, however, the Jains are a minority among Agravāls. The Jain Agravāls are quite a small minority in Jaipur and Rajasthan. One well-informed member of Jaipur's Agravāl Jain community estimates that the number of Jain Agravāls in the city is probably no more than 1,500 or so. Among the Agravāls, the Jain and Hindu subgroups have never been (as far as I am aware) actually endogamous, and intermarriage is certainly common today. However, a middle-aged Agravāl Jain from Delhi told me that intermarriage was definitely frowned upon in his parents' generation. The disapproval seems to have been less severe in Jaipur, possibly because the small size of the Jain group necessitated flexibility in marriage matters.

Relations between Khaṇḍelvāl Jains and Agravāl Jains are in fact far more distant that those between Agravāl Jains and Agravāl non-Jains, despite the fact that both Agravāl Jains and Khaṇḍelvāl Jains belong to the Digambar sect. In Jaipur, the Agravāl Jains are greatly outnumbered by the Khaṇḍelvāl Jains, and the latter are clearly dominant within the regional Digambar community. Although I personally know of one case of Khaṇḍelvāl Jain/Agravāl Jain intermarriage, it seems to be very uncommon. I have been told that the objection arises primarily from the Khaṇḍelvāl Jains, who regard the Agravāls as less purely Jain because of the high frequency of Jain-non-Jain intermarriage among them and perhaps also because of a general disdain for the Agravāl caste. For their part, many Agravāl Jains consider the Khaṇḍelvāl Jains to be rather rigid and insular. As far as I know, there is no separate organisation for Agravāl Jains in Jaipur.

Clans

The clan system of the Agravāls is basically the same as that of other trading castes, but with one very significant difference. This is the relatively small number of clans (among the Agravāls known as *gotras*) within the caste, which—depending on the source—are said to be either 17 and one half or 18 in number. The significance of these particular numbers will become clear when we get to Agravāl origin myths. Because of the invidiousness of designating one of the clans as 'half', the Sammelan currently favours a list of 18, which are the following: Garg, Goyal, Kucchal, Kansal, Bindal, Dhāraṇ, Singhal, Jindal, Mittal, Tingal, Tāyal, Bansal, Bhandal, Nāngal, Mangal, Airan, Madhukul, and Goyan (Campālāl Gupt 1996: 96–97). Many of these names will be well known to those familiar with urban North India, for they are frequently used as surnames and appear on countless shop fronts. Non-Sammelan sources give lists of clan names that differ in some respects from the official list and from each other, suggesting a degree of regional variation.

The Sammelan-approved list, however, seems likely to become the standard because of its enshrinement in Sammelan publications and at the pilgrimage center at Agroha.

Not only is the number of officially sanctioned Agravāl clans surprisingly low, but also it is far from clear that all of the official 18 actually exist. Using the list given in Sammelan and Agrohā Vikās Trust publications, I attempted a survey of Agravāl clans in Rajasthan. Initial inquiries revealed that some of the listed clans are far larger than others. In order to get a clearer picture of the situation, I did a survey of the clans of marriage candidates listed in the directory volume (Agravāl Samāj 1995) of a marriage fair sponsored by Jaipur's Agravāl Samāj Samiti in 1995. The directory listed only the father's clan for each candidate. Out of a total of 377 listings (172 girls, 205 boys), the most frequently occurring clan names were Garg (99 mentions), Goyal (80), Bansal (46), Singhal (46), Mittal (34), Mangal (29), and Jindal (11). The remaining clans were in the single digits, and Kucchal, Bindal, Tingal, Bhandal, Nāngal, Madhukul, and Goyan were not mentioned at all. In addition, five respondents listed 'none' for their clan, two girls listed 'Jain', and one girl listed 'Goenka'. The latter is actually the name of a well-known family from Shekhawati belonging to the Goyal clan, and is more properly regarded as a lineage name than a clan name. Generally similar results were obtained from an inspection of an Agravāl directory emanating from Delhi (Rāmeśvardās Gupt 1995b), with the difference that a few Goyans (or Goins) were listed and a few ostensible clan names appeared (Koṭrīvālā, Pasārī, Mudgal, Ṭibṛevāl, Singhlā) that do not appear on the official list of 18. These are almost certainly the names of local lineages that have been elevated to clan status in their own regions.

This is an extremely interesting state of affairs. One of its most curious aspects is that Agravāls themselves seem largely unaware of the discrepancy between social reality and the official list of clans. Many Jaipur respondents seemed completely surprised when I pointed it out to them. Once, while in Delhi, I raised the issue with a high official of the Agrohā Vikās Trust. When I queried him about the missing clans, he was quite taken aback, and it was clear that the fact of the missing clans was news to him. But even though he could not recall knowing anyone belonging to the missing clans, he was nevertheless adamant in his insistence that the 18 officially listed clans all exist.

The most stable feature of the official list, and indeed its foundation, is the number 18. This is, of course, a purely conventional number, and is arithmetically related to the clan totals for other trading castes considered in this book (i.e., 18 multiplied by 4 equals 72). Why the number is 18 and not some larger number, as it is among other traders, is impossible to say on the basis of any evidence that I know. The caste's traditional genealogists of all regions probably shared the same basic idea of 18 (or 17 and one half) Agravāl clans, but they obviously filled the their lists with somewhat different content, thus accounting for regional differences between lists.

How the particular names on the Sammelan list were derived is also unclear.[5] We may surmise, however, that it was done on the basis of previously existing lists. Presumably the extremely large numbers of people bearing clan labels such as Garg and Goyal ensured that these names occupied slots in most lists, so they naturally made the final official list. Some of the other labels probably belonged to smaller and more localised groups, and appeared only on local lists. In their localities of origin they were presumably well-known as exogamous clans, but they were not known at all elsewhere. Somehow some of these found their way into the official list. The result is an official list of 18 that contains some well-known clans in addition to some that, though extant somewhere, are not part of the social world of most Agravāls.

The official clan list was adopted as official by a vote of the Sammelan during its 1983 convention (Akhil Bhāratīya 1983: 17). This list of clans, with some modifications, has now become completely entrenched in the affairs of the caste, a result of the sheer weight of literary, iconographic, and ceremonial reiteration.

When the already low number of officially recognised clans is combined with the fact that some of them are nonexistent in the social world of most Agravāls, the result is likely to be significant difficulty in maintaining strict standards of exogamy. This seems to be the current situation among Agravāls. This is probably the reason for the fact that the above-mentioned marriage-fair directory designates only the father's clan for each marriage candidate, not both parents' clans, as is the usual pattern among other trading castes. I have heard that in cases where the clans of a prospective bride and groom are the same, the arrangers of Agravāl marriages sometimes count the bride's mother's father's clan as hers rather than her father's clan, thus circumventing the most basic rule of exogamy.[6]

National Organisation

As far as I am aware, the earliest all-India Agravāl association was the Akhil Bhāratīya Vaiśya Agravāl Mahāsabhā, which was founded around the turn of the century and still exists today with headquarters in Aligarh. There also currently exists an Akhil Bhāratīya Agravāl Mahāsabhā, founded in 1954 and headquartered in Delhi. There have been other organisations representing this large and important caste, but today the most important national organisation by far is the Akhil Bhāratīya Agravāl Sammelan, founded in 1975. Its inception occurred at a meeting of 1,200 delegates held in April of that year in South Extension, New Delhi.[7] This meeting called for the formation of an all-India Agravāl organisation, the Akhil Bhāratīya Agravāl Sammelan, which came into official existence that year. The Sammelan quickly gave birth to the Agrohā Vikās Trust. In December of 1975, income tax authorities informed the Sammelan that a Trust would have to be created in order for the organisation to gain exemption from taxes. The Agrohā Vikās Trust was duly formed in 1976.

From the very start, Agrohā, the supposed place of Agravāl origin, was absolutely central to this organisation's purposes and activities. This was, however, only part of a larger agenda of symbolic politics and social reform and rationalisation. A good sense of where the organisation was then going can be derived from the resolutions that were passed at the 1975 meeting. Out of a total of 22 resolutions, two were directly related to Agroha. One of these asked the governments of India and Haryana to have their archaeological departments undertake excavations at Agroha, and called for the restoration of the *janam bhūmī* (birthplace) of the Agravāls. The other proclaimed Agroha to be a *tīrthsthān* (a place of pilgrimage) and called upon all Agravāls to visit it; in addition, it called for an annual fair and religious ceremony (*agrasen mahotsav*) to be held there. The meeting also authorised a picture of Agrasen. This image, which was printed by Brijvasi and Sons (a well-known producer of framing pictures), has become ubiquitous in Sammelan/Trust publications and events. The meeting adopted an official Agravāl flag, and fixed the spelling of 'Agravāl' in both English and Hindi (the authorised Hindi spelling is given in roman characters in this book). The meeting also called on the central and state governments to declare Agrasen's birthday a public holiday, and called upon the central government to issue an Agrasen stamp.

In one of its most significant motions, the meeting also accepted an official list of the clans (the list discussed above) of the Agravāl caste, and standardised the spelling of the 18 names. In addition, the meeting passed two motions that attempted to address certain *kuritis* (improper customs) within the caste. Condemned were such practices as conspicuous expenditures and vulgar displays of material wealth at marriages, elaborate and ostentatious marriage ceremonies, hierarchical distinctions among the clans, and excessive attention to money matters in marriage negotiations, a euphemistic reference to dowry. (At the 1976 meeting at Indore, dowry was proclaimed a 'curse' [*abhiśāp*] [ibid.: 31].) The meeting encouraged the notion of *sāmuhik vivāh* (inexpensive group marriage ceremonies), and opined that prominent members of the Agravāl community should marry their sons and daughters in this fashion as a model for the rest of the community (an unrealised hope). These were standard items on the reform agendas of most twentieth-century trading-caste associations.

There was also a curious motion that advocated 'bringing Agrasen's socialism (*samājvād*) into active form in today's environment'. This motion refers to a minor mythohistory, often reiterated in Sammelan/Trust publications, that describes how newcomers were welcomed in ancient Agroha. According to the story, in the days of the city's full glory there were 100,000 houses, and when any new family came to the city, each house gave them one brick and one *mudrā* (coin). This custom enabled each newcomer to build a house and start a business, which is why there was no unemployment in ancient Agroha. The motion urges this tradition as a model of 'socialism', and makes the point that while rich Agravāls have often spent lavishly on temples and the like, they have not always been as generous to poorer members of their own caste. Rich Agravāls should therefore vindicate Agrasen's socialism by giving some portion of their wealth to their less fortunate caste brothers.

There is no question that the Sammelan and Trust have been extraordinarily successful in pursuing their goal of promoting the interests of the Agravāl caste. They have forged a highly effective national organisation for the Agravāls, which has given birth to numerous local branches. They have also succeeded in revivifying (or, perhaps more accurately, vivifying) Agroha in a spectacular fashion and bringing it and Agrasen to public attention. At their instigation, a stamp bearing Agrasen's likeness was issued in 1976; his statues have been installed in various locations (such as Agrasen Circle in Jaipur); parks and roadways have been invested with his name.

But in the long run, the most momentous of the many activities of the Sammelan and Trust may turn out to have been their sponsorship of a *rath yātrā* (chariot procession) in 1995. The use of this term connotes a royal procession in which a monarch or deity tours his dominions to receive the adulation and acclaim of loyal subjects. In actuality, the Agravāl *rath yātrā* was a media tour of India that had the purpose of spreading the word about Agroha and Agrasen in Agravāl communities. The tour's main vehicle was a truck converted into a mobile temple of Agrasen. It was accompanied by another vehicle stuffed with literature and paraphernalia having to do with Agroha, Agrasen, the Agravāl caste, and the Sammelan and Trust. This road show toured India for four years and covered about 300,000 km. It generated large and numerous donations for the development of the pilgrimage center at Agroha, and certainly aided greatly in publicising the activities of the Sammelan and the Trust. In 1997, I interviewed a number Agravāls who were small businessmen in a village just north of Sikar in Rajasthan. From what they told me, it is clear that at least in this rural area little was known about Agrasen and Agroha prior to the arrival of the *rath yātra*. But since then, they said, awareness of these matters has grown enormously, and a few Agravāls from this village have even visited Agroha.

Contemporary Agroha

It took the better part of a century for things to come together at Agroha. The first efforts to transform Agroha into a center for Agravāls occurred in the early twentieth century.[8] Efforts at restoration were begun in 1908 at the behest of a certain Svāmī Brahmānand (about whom I have no information). A well was constructed together with a temple for Agrasen and a dormitory for pilgrims. Then ensued, apparently, a long period of inactivity. A conclave of Agravāls met in 1950 and made plans to open an engineering college at Agroha. Land was obtained, but nothing came of the scheme. Matters finally began to move again in October of 1976 when the Sammelan delegated a group of important Agravāls to visit Agroha to see what could be done about developing the place. A foundation-laying ceremony occurred in September of 1976 using bricks that had been blessed by the then Chief Minister of Haryana, and construction began on a new pilgrims' dormitory in 1977. The building of Agrasen's temple began in 1979, and the inner shrine was completed in 1982. Rajiv Gandhi attended the inauguration ceremony, which is an indication of the national political clout of the Agravāl caste and the Sammelan and Trust. Construction was begun on the Mahālakṣmī temple in that same year, and the main image was consecrated in 1985. In the meantime, excavations had been started at the ruins of the ancient city.

By the time I visited Agroha in November of 1996, it had come to resemble a Disneyesque theme park. The temple complex is a huge structure consisting of a vast hall with three attached temples. Mahālakṣmī, billed as the Agravāls' caste goddess (*kul devī*), occupies an impressive shrine at the opposite end of the hall facing the entrance. To the right of the entrance is a shrine containing an image of Sarasvatī. Her inclusion, I surmise, reflects a desire to project an image of the Agravāl community as devoted to high culture and learning. To the left of the entrance is Agrasen's shrine where he sits enthroned with two guardian lions crouched at his feet. The various other displays and images in the complex evoke a strong Vaiṣṇava ambience. Outside the temple complex are the pilgrims' dormitory and a shallow pool known as the Śakti Sarover. In the center of the pool is a large and complex piece of statuary depicting the gods and demons churning the milky ocean, a well-known episode from Hindu mythology. An impressive list of donors is inscribed on a wall at one end of the pool. Close by are the alleged ruins of Agrasen's Agroha. At the time of my visit, the complex also included a rather unprepossessing 'Jurassic Park' with two or three plaster dinosaurs.

But the importance of the temple center ultimately does not derive from the glitter and ostentation, but rather from the mythohistory it represents, a narrative that traces the origin of the Agravāl caste to Agroha. The true purpose of the complex is to connect the present with that mythohistorical past, and in the process to validate the Sammelan and Trust as present-day custodians of an ancient Agravāl heritage believed to be embodied by Agroha.

The Interrupted Sacrifice

In the past there must have been many versions of the Agravāl origin myth in oral circulation, and this is probably true in some areas even to the present day. At the time of my research, however, the traditional genealogists of the Agravāls were, as far as I was able to determine, but a distant memory in the Jaipur area. Instead, the principal conduits for the transmission of lore about the Agravāl caste were the local and national Agravāl organisations. As a result of their activities, a single version of the Agravāl narrative completely dominates the scene today. And because of the centrality of this narrative to the legitimacy of the Sammelan and Trust as representative of the Agravāl community, these organisations have been absolutely relentless in the projection of their own versions of images and symbols having to do with Agrasen and Agroha. In consequence, we find that a single Agravāl origin narrative has been pushed to a level of standardisation and ubiquity that far surpasses the situation in any of our other trading castes, with the possible exception of the Māheśvarīs.

The Sammelan/Trust version of Agravāl origin has been retold many times in multiple formats. But although there is a range of literary sources for the Agrasen legend, the Sammelan/Trust retellings are mainly based on a single source. This source, which is the version that concerns us here, is a brief essay entitled 'Origin of the Agravāls' (*Agravālõ kī Utpatti*), written in 1871 by a famous Hindi author and poet named Bhāratendu Hariścandra (1850–1885).[9] The essay is frequently reprinted in Trust publications, and is a principal source for Campālāl Gupt's (1993, 1996) semi-official book on the history of Agroha and the Agravāls. Bhāratendu is a major figure in Hindi literature. Best known for his dramas and poetry, he is an author whose writings should be familiar to any well-educated person in the Hindi-speaking world. He was an Agravāl, and because of his enormous literary stature he has become something of an icon to the Agravāl community. It is understandable, therefore, that his version of the Agravāl origin narrative would have a special appeal to the caste's official organisations.

Bhāratendu is not as informative about his own sources as we would wish. He does, however, tell us that he compiled his narrative from 'tradition', from 'ancient writings', and especially from a text called 'Śrī Mahālakṣmī Vrat kī Kathā', which he claims to have found in a 'later' part of the *Bhaviṣya Purāṇa*. Investigators, including this author, have looked for the material in question in various published versions of the *Bhaviṣya Purāṇa*, but without success. This does not mean that Bhāratendu is misleading us, for this particular *Purāṇa* is a notoriously malleable document. Historian Satyaketu Vidyālankār has reproduced a copy of the 'Mahālakṣmī Vrat kī Kathā' that he found in Bhāratendu's personal library (Vidyālankār 1976: 156–95), but as best I can tell, the text contains no clue about its provenance.

The Bhāratendu Narrative

As told by Bhāratendu (and here summarised from a reprinting in Śarmā 1989: 583–87), the Agravāl story begins at the true beginning of things. That is, it starts with the well-known story of the creation (in the primordial sacrifice) of the Brāhmaṇs, Kṣatriyas, Vaiśyas, and Śūdras from the mouth, arms, thighs and feet of the Cosmic Man. God, Bhāratendu says, gave the Vaiśyas the right to four kinds of work: farming, the protection of cows, business, and banking. Just as the Brāhmaṇs are lords of Veda and sacrificial rites, and Kṣatriyas the lords of rulership and war, so Vaiśyas are the lords of wealth (*dhan*). These three are the twice-born, who are those with a right (*adhikār*) to the sacrifice (here called *ved-karm*). We may assume that the right in question is that of participation in and sponsorship of the sacrifice. Having thus established a context in universal mythohistory for a more specific account, Bhāratendu then turns to Agrasen:

> Agrasen was born in the house of King Vallabh of Pratāpnagar (location uncertain, but said to be in the 'south').[10] Vallabh, in turn, was a descendant of Dhanpāl, the first Vaiśya on earth, whom Brāhmaṇs put on the throne of Pratāpnagar.[11] Agrasen's own kingly glory was so great that even Indra (the King of the Gods) had to make friends with him, as we shall see.
>
> Now, a time came when Kumud, the King of the Nāgas (snake-deities), brought his daughter, Mādhvī, from the abode of the Nāgas to earth. Indra became enamored of her, and asked her father for her hand in marriage. Kumud gave her to Agrasen instead. (Interrupting the thread of his narrative, Bhāratendu observes at this point that Mādhvī is therefore the mother of all Agravāls, and for this reason Agravāls address snakes as 'maternal uncle' [*māmā*])[12] In any case, Indra was furious with Agrasen, and ceased sending rain to his capital, but in the end Brahmā was able to put a stop to the conflict.
>
> Agrasen then turned over his kingdom to Mādhvī and went forth on pilgrimage. When he came to the holy city of Banaras, he visited the Kapildhārā *tīrth* (pilgrimage)[13] where he performed a sacrifice for Mahādev (Śiva) and gave lots of charitable gifts. Pleased by this, Mahādev appeared on the spot and offered Agrasen a boon. Agrasen said that all he wanted was victory over Indra. Mahādev then replied that by worshipping the goddess Mahālakṣmī he would ensure that all his wishes would be granted. Having heard this, Agrasen resumed his pilgrimage. With the help of a ghost (*pret*),[14] he eventually arrived at Hardwar. In the company of Garg

> Muni (a famous Brāhmaṇ sage), he then visited all of the nearby holy spots. After his return to Hardwar, and with the assistance of Garg Muni, he then worshipped the goddess Mahālakṣmī. She was pleased, and in response she promised that he would be victorious over Indra, that his descendants (*vaṃś*) would be spared all unhappiness, and that after death he and his wife would dwell together near the North Star.
>
> Mahālakṣmī then instructed Agrasen to go to a place called Kolāpur where the *svayamvar* (a marriage in which the bride herself chooses the groom from among a group of suitors) of the daughters of Mahidhar (described as the '*avtār*' [incarnation] of Nāgrāj') was taking place.[15] Mahālakṣmī said that he should marry them and produce progeny. So he went there and married the daughters (their names and number are not mentioned in this version of the tale). He then came to the Delhi region and established his rule and spread his descendants from the north of Punjab to Agra.
>
> Now, when he heard about Mahālakṣmī's boon, Indra became fearful, and he decided that it would be wise to establish friendly relations with Agrasen. So he sent Narād as his ambassador, and presented Agrasen with an apsarā named Madhuśālinī as a peace offering. In this way, their feud came to an end.
>
> After this, Agrasen went to the banks of the river Jumna, where he performed severe austerities on behalf of Mahālakṣmī. Again she was pleased, and she bestowed the following boons: that from that day onward Agrasen's descendants would bear his name, and that she would be the protectress and clan goddess (kul devī) of his descendants, who in turn would celebrate her special festival of *divālī*.[16]

At this point in the text, Bhāratendu shifts to a description of Agrasen's kingdom. It extended, he says, from the Himalayas and rivers of Punjab in the north to the Ganges in the east and south, and the western boundary ran from Agra to the countries adjacent to Marwar (which are all areas in which Agravāls are found). The main area in which the Agravāls settled, he says, was from Punjab to Meerut and Agra. Bhāratendu also lists the names of the principal cities and places in which the Agravāls settled—Agra, Delhi, Gurgaon, and several others. These, he says, were all within the boundaries of Agrasen's kingdom. Agrasen's capital, where he built a great temple for Mahālakṣmī, was called Agranagar, which is the place now known as Agroha. Bhāratendu adds that the city of Agra was also named after Agrasen. The narrative then continues as follows:

> King Agrasen sponsored seventeen and one half sacrifices (no reason for his doing so is given in this version). The half sacrifice came about in the following manner: After Agrasen had begun the eighteenth sacrifice, he experienced great remorse for the violence perpetrated in such rites. Nobody in his lineage ate meat, he said, but nonetheless '*devī hiṃsā*' (by which is clearly meant animal sacrifice offered to the goddess) was taking place. He then vowed that animal sacrifice ('*paśu-yajña aur balidān*') would no longer take place in his lineage. Thus, the eighteenth sacrifice was never completed.

According to Bhāratendu, Agrasen had 17 queens and one subqueen (*uprānī*). Each had three sons and one daughter. To this information Bhāratendu then adds the assertion that from 'seventeen and one-half sacrifices came seventeen and one-half *gotras* (clans)' (ibid.: 1989: 586).[17] This is a somewhat confusing point because Bhāratendu has not previously indicated any connection between the sacrifices and the clans. It is clear, however, that the sacrifices had something to do with their formation, or at least this seems to be strongly implied. Bhāratendu tells us that Agrasen named his own clan, which is Garg, after Garg Muni, who was his 'helper' (*sahāyak*, presumably referring in this context to help in ritual matters). The other clans were also named 'on the basis' of the sacrifices (a point to which we shall return). King Agrasen appointed the Gauṛ Brāhmaṇs as his lineage priests (*kul purohits*), and at that time they were preceptors and priests for all Agravāls.[18]

Bhāratendu ends his account by tying up various loose ends. When Agrasen grew old, he left the throne in order to perform austerities, at which point his son, Vibhu, took over the kingdom. Jainism came to some of the Agravāls when one of Agrasen's descendants, King Divākar, was converted. Agroha was finally destroyed utterly by the invasion of Shihab-ud-din, after which the Agravāls scattered to the west (in Marwar) and to the east of their ancient kingdom.[19] Many left their religion and broke their sacred threads (markers of their belonging to one of the top three *varṇas*). The Agravāls recovered after the Mughals came to power; indeed, two Agravāls became Akbar's vizirs.

Although the Bhāratendu version of Agravāl origin became a principal source for many subsequent retellings of the Agravāl myth—especially the Sammelan/Trust version—later versions have also drawn on sources other than Bhāratendu. The issue of how the Bhāratendu version relates to others is extremely complex and it is not possible to explore all of its ramifications here. It needs to be noted, however, that there have been other narratives of Agravāl origin, although their current and future viability—given the Trust's extraordinary success in defining the public culture of the Agravāl caste—is problematical.

Comparison

We now turn to a comparison of the Agravāl origin myth with others previously presented in this book. Three main issues emerge as requiring separate discussion: the question of Vaiśya status and descent, the role of the goddess or goddesses in the creation of the caste and its subdivisions, and the role of the sacrifice in establishing the social essence of the caste.

Vaiśya Descent

The Vaiśya issue stems from the fact that the Bhāratendu version of Agravāl origin maintains that the caste's apical ancestor, Agrasen, was a Vaiśya. This, is a departure from the trend among Rajasthani traders, which is to deny Vaiśya ancestry, usually—though not always—in favour of Rājpūt ancestry. Of the trader origin myths considered in this book, the Vijayvargīya narratives have represented the only significant exception thus far. Bhāratendu's telling of the Agravāl origin myth represents a clear departure from this general pattern, and the Sammelan and Trust continue to support the Bhāratendu approach (see, for example, C. Gupt 1996: 63–66). Clearly, the Vaiśya category is more salient in these materials than in others considered earlier in the book.

It must be immediately said, however, that this view of Agravāl ancestry does not represent a consensus among Agravāls, at least not in Rajasthan. To begin with, many Rajasthani Agravāls with whom I have discussed this issue believe and insist that Agrasen was a Kṣatriya or Rājpūt. Moreover, various published narratives of Agravāl origin other than Bhāratendu's claim Kṣatriya or Rājpūt ancestry.[20] Against this background, Bhāratendu's emphasis on Vaiśya descent seems all the more curious. Was Bhāratendu himself pursuing some special agenda related to Vaiśya identity? Possibly, but I know of no actual evidence that he was. We may thus have to assume that in stressing a Vaiśya heritage for the Agravāls he was merely following the lead of one of his principal sources, the 'Mahālakṣmī Vrat Kathā', which does indeed refer to Agrasen as 'Lord of the Viś' (87–88, in Vidyālankār 1976: 157). But why this text—or any other of its sort—should assume a Vaiśya origin for the Agravāls is another question. A possible answer is that the regional milieu from which it emerged was one in which Vaiśya identity was more salient and socially more acceptable, and Kṣatriya identity perhaps less so, than in the Rajasthani cultural zone which is the primary context of this book.

But whatever the reason for Bhāratendu's stand on this issue, the question of the Trust's much later and continuing commitment to Vaiśya origin for the Agravāls is, I believe, a partially separate and more interesting matter. It might, of course, simply be a reflex of Bhāratendu's support for the idea. It seems possible, however, that it also reflects a desire to reach out socially and politically to other trading castes by using the Vaiśya *varṇa* as a unifying category. This idea seems to have been part of the mix from the inception of the Sammelan in 1975. One of its founding figures, a former member of Parliament (and person of great importance in Agravāl affairs at the time of my research in 1996–97), told me that he was originally propelled into Agravāl-related activities by his deep anger at hearing the 'business community' continually maligned in India's national Parliament. This same individual strongly believes in the importance of Vaiśya identity and its potential as a framework for organising India's trading community. He suggested to me that other trading castes—he mentioned the Osvāls, Khaṇḍelvāls (of which sort he did not say), and Māheśvarīs in particular—could well have also been descended from Agrasen. Although these views were presented to me as those of only one individual, and although they would certainly find little support among the other castes in question, I suspect they reflect the general drift of at least some recent conversation and debate within the Agravāls' political elite.

In any case, even if the Bhāratendu/Sammelan/Trust version of Agravāl identity formally asserts Vaiśya descent for the caste, the assertion seems more nominal than substantive. By this I mean that the narrative portrays Agrasen as a Kṣatriya in everything but name. He belonged to a lineage of kings, and was the founder and ruler of a kingdom. So valourous was he that he even challenged mighty Indra. He was also, as befits a Kṣatriya ruler, a sponsor of blood sacrifices until his sudden paroxysm of remorse. In other words, if Agrasen was a Vaiśya, he behaved a lot like a Kṣatriya. In fact, the Bhāratendu/Sammelan/Trust narrative is actually deeply coloured by our by-now familiar myth-historical pattern of a Kṣatriya heritage for a trading caste. Whether it arises from sensitivity about negative stereotypes of traders as physically weak or cowardly, or for some other reason, the Agravāls seem unable to accept Vaiśya ancestry without such qualifications.

This tendency is dramatically illustrated by the fact that even though the Sammelan and Trust maintain that the Agravāls are Vaiśyas, they also place great emphasis on the contention that martial valour is, and always has been, a conspicuous feature of Agravāl character. For example, the Trust has published an entire book entitled (in translation) *Legacy of Heroism: A Brief Introduction to the Valor, Sacrifice, and Devotion to Duty of Agravāl (Vaiśya) Heroes* (Bansal 1992). This book celebrates the heroism of Vaiśya kings and warriors of the past as well as modern military men from the Agravāl caste. Its tone and the spirit in which it has been published are consistent with the claim of Kṣatriya/Rājpūt pedigree so often made in the origin narratives of other trading castes. The book makes the implicit point that although they are Vaiśyas in lineage and diet, Agravāls are Kṣatriyas in their true character.

Our materials therefore suggest that a *purely* Vaiśya pedigree is very problematic to most trading castes (especially the Jain castes), with the Agravāls constituting a diagnostic case. The Vijayvargīyas represent our sole significant exception, and even this case is not a *pure* exception, as we have noted. Now we see that the Agravāls' claim of Vaiśya ancestry is, in reality, a hedged claim that overlies a deeper assumption that, appearances to the contrary notwithstanding, the Agravāls are warrior-like Kṣatriyas at heart. These facts suggest that Vaiśya identity may be fundamentally unstable, tending in the long run to decompose into identities linked to other *varṇa* categories, especially the Kṣatriya category.

The Goddess

A female figure, Mahālakṣmi, plays a key role in the creation of the Agravāl caste as portrayed in the Bhāratendu narrative, and her participation exemplifies well the ancestral goddess myth model with which by now we have become quite familiar. In this narrative, as in others, the goddess assists at the moment of creation, and then enters into a descent-transmitted protective relationship with the descendants of the apical ancestor/s of the caste. In the Bhāratendu myth, the female figure in question is the goddess Mahālakṣmī. As the goddess of wealth and prosperity, she makes good sense as a patroness goddess for the Agravāls. Currently the Sammelan and Trust are promoting this relationship, which has been given an impressive physical embodiment in the Mahālakṣmī shrine in the temple complex at Agroha.

Mahālakṣmī, however, is not the only important goddess represented at Agroha. Not far from the Agroha complex is a temple and garden complex dedicated to a goddess known as Śīlā Mātā. At the entrance to the temple stands a statue of its principal donor, Seṭh Tilakrāj Agravāl (1922–88) of Mumbai, in a devotional pose. I had heard that Śīlā Mātā is a *satī* before I visited the temple, so I was somewhat confused when the temple's main image turned out to be one of Durgā. As it turned out, Śīlā Mātā occupies a tiny basement shrine in which she is represented by a red *svastik* and seven red dots executed on the surface of one of the walls. This arrangement has the effect of universalising the identity of a purely local goddess by identifying her with pan-Hindu Durgā. But because the legitimacy of the veneration of *satīs* has become a major public issue in contemporary India, her basement location might also reflect a desire to downplay her status as a *satī* venerated by Agravāls.

Her story, as represented in a Trust-authorised narrative (Garg n.d.) put in my hands by the temple priest, runs as follows:

> Śīlā was the daughter of a rich man of Agroha named Seṭh Harbhanśāh. She was married to Dīvān Mehtāśāh of Syalkot. Attracted by her great beauty, Rājā Risālū of that place attempted to seduce her, but she resisted his advances. In his chagrin, he had a servant place his ring in her bed where her husband would find it. Her husband duly found it. Unable to account for its presence, she had to return to her father's house in shame and humiliation. Years later, a maidservant confessed to Śīlā's husband that the king had paid her to place the ring in the bed; Śīlā was, as the maidservant put it, a true *pativratā* (a wife devoted to her husband). When Mehtāśah heard this, he went crazy with remorse and began to wander about in the jungle. He finally stumbled his way to Agroha, only to die of hunger and thirst when he arrived. When she heard the news, Śīlā rushed to the scene, and when she came near her husband's body she fainted and died on the spot. The last rites of husband and wife were performed together. When the king heard of the tragedy his heart was filled with guilt and sorrow. He wanted to commit suicide, but Guru Gorakhnāth persuaded him to become a yogi instead.

It would seem that this is a sanitised *satī* narrative. Or at least this is suggested by the fact that she does indeed become *satī* in the version collected and published by Richard C. Temple in the nineteenth century

(1977 [1884]: 243–366), although at the end of this version she and her husband are restored to life by Śiva at the instigation of Guru Gorakhnāth.

Although her story (at least in the temple literature) does not utilise the in-at-the-beginning ancestral goddess myth model, Śīlā Mātā has the look of a potential caste goddess. Originally a parochial deity (we must assume a *satī*) and linked with Agravāls (for she was an Agravāl), she has been fortunate in her physical location. Her proximity to a growing pilgrimage center and the appearance of super-wealthy donors made has made it possible for her identity to evolve in the direction of greater inclusiveness. It is at least possible that she will occupy a role vis-à-vis the Agravāls analogous to that of Sacciyā for the Osvāls, and if this happens, it will be for the same reasons.

A similar process of deity evolution has been taking place in the Shekhawati region of Rajasthan. An important female deity for Shekhawati Agravāls, one whose devotees often characterise as a clan or lineage goddess, is a goddess named Rāṇī Satī whose temple is located at Jhunjhunu. As her name suggests, she is indeed a *satī*, and when I visited Rāṇī Satī's temple in 1995, pictures of Rāṇī Satī sitting amidst the flames with her husband's head on her lap were for sale in stalls outside the temple compound. She, too, is a candidate for bigger things, and in fact she and Śīlā Mātā may be individual illustrations of a general principle of continuity connecting female deities in an evolutionary sequence.

As we have already noted in connection with the 'Bharatpur version' of Śrīmāl origin (Chapter Five), *satīs* and clan goddesses are in many ways treated alike ritually. A family *satī* can therefore be said to be a clan or lineage goddess functioning at a lower level of segmentation. The clan goddess presides over clans and genealogically deep lineage segments, the *satī* over shallower lineage segments. A family *satī*, therefore, is a potential candidate for lineage or clan goddesshood within lineages or clans that ramify outward from an apical family to which she was originally attached. And it is also possible for such a *satī*-goddess to assume an even more 'generalised' form in which she becomes the patroness, not merely of a single descent group, but of an even wider constituency. Rāṇī Satī is a particularly clear example of precisely that.

Rāṇī Satī's original core constituency appears to have been the Jālān lineage of the Agravāls, to which she was an in-marrying bride. But her basic constituency has expanded greatly in recent years, and her temple is now the epicenter of a widespread and prosperous cult patronised primarily by Agravāls hailing originally from the Shekhawati region.

Locals have told me that members of many migratory merchant families return to the region only to worship her. Rāṇī Satī is perhaps too parochial ever to become a patroness-goddess for Agravāls in general, but she has obviously outgrown her local origins and has assumed the role of a caste goddess at a regional level. As Anne Hardgrove points out (2002: Ch. 6, p. 4), her veneration keeps alive the 'territorial linkage' between migrant families and their homeland and also provides a focus for community identity among diasporic Marwaris (perhaps beyond the Agravāl fold) in other parts of India and beyond.

But if the Sammelan and Trust have their way, it is Mahālakṣmī, and no other goddess, who will ultimately be the universal Agravāl caste patroness. As the goddess of wealth and prosperity, her personality fits well with the Agravāls' general caste ethos. Moreover, the Bhāratendu narrative portrays her as exemplifying the classic 'in-at-the-beginning' myth model of ancestral goddesses, and she plays this role in relation to the Agravāl caste as a whole, not in relation to a particular clan or lineage. Furthermore, the location of her shrine at the heart of the Agroha complex would seem to position her well to become ritually central to the activities of visitors and pilgrims. But the jury is still out, and it remains to be seen whether the Sammelan and Trust can engineer the affairs of the Agravāl caste to the extent of actually creating a single goddess for the entire caste.

The Sacrifice

But the sacrifice is the nub of the matter, as is true of almost all the mythohistorical material presented in this book. As projected by the Bhāratendu narrative, Agravāl identity is constructed on the foundation of a concept martial or Kṣatriya-like Vaiśyahood. The precise moment at which this identity crystallises in the narrative is when, in the last of a series of 18 sacrifices, King Agrasen gives up the ritual shedding of blood.[21] Although Bhāratendu does not tell us whether Agrasen was a vegetarian in diet, I suspect that most readers or auditors of the tale assume that he was. The issue, however, is not diet as such, but whether Agrasen and his descendants are to be—as one might say—vegetarian in social essence. Here the question of the ritual shedding of blood in the sacrifice becomes a crucial consideration. As we know, this is so because the manner of one's participation in the sacrifice is a metaphor for the manner of one's participation in the socio-religious order it represents. As non-Jains (leaving aside the special case of Agravāl Jains),

Agravāls are full members of this order. But, as in the case of all trading groups, the ritual shedding of blood is unacceptable as a manifestation or emblem of their membership in the sacrificial social order. Thus, the crux of the narrative is Agrasen's change of heart about the sacrifice. This negative stance toward violence in the sacrifice—or violence in proximity to, or in contact with, the sacrifice—is the most abiding of the themes we have seen in the culture of trading-caste identity.

We therefore see that the Bhāratendu/Sammelan/Trust narrative falls within a pattern common to most of the trading castes we have considered. In almost every instance, the ancestor/s of the caste undergo an identity transition that involves a change in the group's relation to the sacrifice, and the issue of violence is at the center of the change. The change begins with a break of some kind with the old manner of participation in the rite, but the intensity of the break varies. Among the groups considered in this study, the break is most radical in the case of the Jains, who leave the social order symbolised by the sacrifice entirely, never to return. The break is less radical for the Khaṇḍelvāl Vaiśyas and the Māheśvarīs; they depart the sacrificial order but then reenter it, albeit on a transformed basis. The Agravāls represent the most minimal break with the sacrifice, a rejection of a mere one-half sacrifice from a total of 18—i.e., 1/36 of the whole. It seems possible that this minimalism reflects a desire to stress Agrasen's kingly nature while nevertheless acknowledging the all-important rejection of sacrificial violence. In any case, so microscopic is the breach that there is apparently little scope or need for the rite-of-passage symbolisms we have noted for the other groups. But the separation occurs, symbolising a small but decisive alteration in the Agravāls' relationship to ritual violence, and thus to the sacrifice itself and the social order for which it symbolically stands.

The sacrifice is also closely associated with the creation of Agravāl clans, but on this point there is a good deal of unclarity in the materials I have been able to survey. Of those accounts that link Agravāl origin to sacrifices, one (Modi n.d.: 8) maintains that Agrasen performed the 17 and one half sacrifices because he had no sons. As a result of the rites, his 17 queens and one subqueen bore sons, who became the apical ancestors of the 17 and one half clans, each clan deriving its name from the Vedic sage who presided over the sacrifice. In other accounts, the connection between the sacrifices and the actual bearing of sons is not mentioned, and the emphasis is shifted to the link between the clans' apical ancestors and the Vedic sages who performed the sacrifices. For example, Bhāratendu links the 17 and one-half clans to 17 and one-half sacrifices. He maintains that just as Agrasen's clan was named for Garg Muni, the other clans were also named on the basis of the sacrifices (presumably also from the names of officiating sages, though this is not spelled out). In a version in which no sacrifices are mentioned at all (Rāmcandra Guptā 1926: 44–49), the clans are created when 17 sages educate and initiate Agrasen's 18 sons; the sons then become apical ancestors of 17 and one half clans, each taking its name from one of the sages. Each sage's descendants, in turn, become the family priests of members of the clan he created.[22]

The importance of the Vedic sages in all of these tales is striking and quite significant. Bringing the sages to the forefront places emphasis on the crucial fact that, whatever the transformation that created the Agravāls might have been (i.e., whether a leap from Kṣatriyahood or a smaller step from one kind of Vaiśyahood to another), the caste is firmly reintegrated into the ritual–social order over which Brāhmaṇs preside. The post-transformation Agravāls retain the status of *jajmān* (sponsors of sacrifices), but it is a *jajmān*-hood different in character from that of their eponymous ancestor, Agrasen, during the period of his life when he presided over lethal sacrifices.

Modern Spin on an Old Story

Agravāl organisations constantly reiterate this sacrificial imagery. A good example is the mobile tableau portraying the legendary 18 sacrifices (mentioned at the beginning of this chapter) that appeared on the occasion of Jaipur's 1996 celebration of Agrasen's birthday. Another example is a framing picture, distributed by the Trust and sold at the temple at Agroha, that depicts 18 sacrifices presided over by a regal-looking Agrasen. A man and his wife sit at each fire altar. Each pair is performing the rite with the assistance of two ritual officiants, and each is labelled with the name of an Agravāl clan (the names derived from the Sammelan's official list). The picture is entitled (in translation) 'King Agrasen and 18 clans'. Here are all the important elements together in a modern format: the caste's apical ancestor (Agrasen), the sacrificial rites from which the 18 separate clans emanate, clans' apical ancestors (his 18 sons), the sacrificial rite, and the Brāhmaṇ officiants. This is the moment of creation of the Agravāl caste, but—at least from the standpoint of sacrificial symbolism—it could have been the moment of creation of most of the other castes considered in this book.

However, although this scene clearly belongs to the symbolic milieu in which the origin myths of most Rajasthani trading castes have evolved, the Sammelan and Trust have made strenuous efforts to update and modernise the Bhāratendu narrative. The results of this are manifested with particular clarity in the writings of Campālāl Gupt, whose two books (1993 and a successor volume, 1996) have been published and widely distributed by the Trust.

One important recent modification is the denial of the idea that all Agravāls are actually descended from Agrasen. Author Gupt (1996: 93–95; also Badlu Ram Gupta 1975) argues that the Agravāl clans could not be descended from the sons of Agrasen because, if that were true, marriage within the Agravāl caste would be incestuous (an issue we discussed in Chapter Three in connection with the Dahimā Brāhmaṇs). The clans, Gupt argues, are actually remnants of the political organisation of Agrasen's ancient kingdom (1996: 93–95). The kingdom was divided into 18 *śreṇis* or *kuls* (by which he means leading families), and each of these sent a representative to a council where they assisted Agrasen in the governance of the kingdom. Gupt further opines that Agrasen did indeed sponsor 18 sacrifices, and a representative of each of these groups served as *yajmān* (*jajmān*). The descendants of these families became the 18 Agravāl clans, named after the particular sages who officiated at the sacrifices.[23] Agrasen loved his subjects with fatherly affection, and for this reason the idea arose that the 18 clans are actually his progeny. This is how the Agravāl caste emerged as an independent *jāti* from within the preexisting 'Vaiśya *samāj*' (Vaiśya society). Agrasen promoted the exogamy of the clans in the interest of *rakt śuddhi* (blood purity), which I take to mean avoidance of allegedly harmful inbreeding.

Gupt has also propounded a theory of the sacrifice departing dramatically from traditional ideas (ibid.: 55–56). It is, in effect, a quasi social–scientific recasting of the ancient theory of the sacrifice and group creation. In ancient times, Gupt says, kings sponsored great *aśvamedh* sacrifices (horse sacrifices). They did this as a way of asserting their fame and standing, and also as a way of fostering unity within their kingdoms. The whole kingdom would take part in such ceremonies, and this had the effect of purifying the 'mental outlook' of both ruler and subjects, leading to virtuous conduct within the kingdom. These are the reasons for Agrasen's sponsorship of his 18 sacrifices. And because the sacrifices were linked with the 18 subdivisions of his kingdom, they did indeed play a role in creating the 18 Agravāl clans.[24] In effect, Gupt replaces the ancient biometaphysical theory of how social groups emerged from the sacrifice with a rough-and-ready sociological functionalism.

These modernistic and scientistic rerenderings of Agravāl mythohistorical knowledge support an image of Agrasen, and thus the Agravāls, as enlightened and anti-obscurantist. Agrasen emerges as a social engineer who even incorporated the knowledge of genetics ('blood purity') in the organisation of his kingdom. His kingdom was a republic, run on democratic principles. Its economic system (as we saw earlier in this chapter) even incorporated a form of 'socialism'. These assertions are consistent with values embedded in the wider political culture in which the Agravāl community and its leaders must continue to find a niche for themselves. The implication is that the Agravāls take a back seat to nobody in their commitment to progressive values, an idea reinforced by the great stress given to the public display of reformist themes on such occasions (as we have seen) as Agrasen's birthday. The future will probably bring more efforts to modify the Agrasen narrative along these lines.

It is far from clear, however, that these revisions have yet achieved much currency within the Agravāl community itself, or at least among the Agravāls of Rajasthan. While I have no survey data relating to this point, my enquiries have convinced me that large numbers of those Agravāls who know or care anything about these matters believe that they are actually, not metaphorically, descended from King Agrasen. The designers of the float portraying Agrasen's 18 sons (in Jaipur's celebration of Agrasen's birthday) had obviously not gotten the new message yet, because the sons were labelled with the separate names of the 18 clans. And a framing picture that I purchased at Agroha, one that bears the imprimatur of the Trust, shows Agrasen with 18 'sons', labelled as such, along with a list of 18 derivative clans. I suspect, moreover, that few Agravāls have come to think of the sacrifice in the manner of functionalist sociologists.

But whether or not these new interpretations convince anybody, the truly important point is that the sacrificial myth model remains fundamentally unchanged. Even Campālāl Gupt, apparently forgetting himself, returns to older ritual images in the end—a testimony to their extraordinary power. As in other versions, the crux of his telling of the narrative is reached when Agrasen halts the proceedings at the eighteenth sacrifice. As always with traders, the issue is sacrificial violence. Agrasen says (in Gupt's telling) that the work of Vaiśyas is the 'protection' of creatures, not their slaughter—which is why God made the 'Vaiśya *jāti*'. It is precisely at the moment when he prohibits the further slaughter of animals that the Agravāl caste springs into existence.

The Agravāl case teaches us that the truly fundamental issue underlying the symbolism of social identity for traders is not merely violence, but sacrificial violence. Of course generic violence and sacrificial violence are related, and, as we know, a vegetarian diet and vegetarianised life-style are important markers of trading caste status. Still, as we also know, members of these castes did indeed engage in martial activities in Rajasthan, and the Agravāls have made a special point of the martial prowess of some members of the caste. Moreover, the quantum of nonviolence that marks the decisive change in Agrasen's sacrifice is truly homeopathic—as we have seen, a mere 1/36 of the total. But that small alteration is enough to make all the difference.

Precisely because of its differences from the other mythic materials we have surveyed, the Agravāl case shows us that the concept of sacrificial creative power and a negative stance toward sacrificial violence are the truly paradigmatic to trading-caste social identity. It apparently hardly matters whether the rite is rationalised as a source of progeny, prosperity, or (in a newer mode) of social cohesion. Whatever is said of it, the association between the sacrifice and creative power, especially the power to create social groups, remains a presupposition. And, as such, it appears to be beyond the reach of doubt. The social identity of trading castes is, in the final analysis, constituted by an idealised relationship between the group in question and the rite of sacrifice, a relationship from which the shedding of blood has been removed. And in the case of the Agravāls, we find that the glitzy promotional efforts of the present day are, despite the appearances of up-to-date-modernity, rooted in these same ancient symbolisms.

Notes

1. Mahālakṣmī is Viṣṇu's consort and the goddess of prosperity. Her prominent position in the temple is emblematic of the caste's aspirations. Sarasvatī is Brahmā's consort and the goddess of the arts and learning.
2. Its date is the first day of the bright fortnight of the lunar month of Āśvin (September–October).

3. For a useful survey of major Agravāl groups, see C. Gupt 1996: 111–17.
4. I have also heard oral accounts of Fives among the Osvāls. See Cort, forthcoming.
5. Interestingly, the overlap between the Sammelan/Trust list and the list given by Bhāratendu (below), the principal source of the Sammelan/Trust's favoured origin narrative, is only partial.
6. While this practice is widespread (Vatuk 1972: 94–96), I suspect it is most common among Agravāls because of the relatively small number of clans.
7. The following details are drawn from Rāmeśvardās Gupt 1995a: 29–30.
8. These details from Ṭāṇṭiyā 1996: 22–29; R. Gupt 1995a: 29–40.
9. On the relationship between Bhāratendu and the development of Hindu national identity, see Dalmia 1997; also Chandra 1992. Dalmia presents a highly informative discussion of his personal and family history (ibid.: 117–43).
10. Bharatendu does not give a date for these events. Other tellings commonly put Agrasen's birth at the end of the *dvāpar yug*, 85 years before the beginning of the *kali yug* (cf. Ṭāṇṭiyā 1996: 9).
11. I am omitting the genealogy, given by Bhāratendu, connecting Vallabh with Dhanpāl.
12. I was unable to find anyone familiar with this custom among Shekhwati Agravāls. On Agravāl veneration of snakes, see Crooke 1896, I: 17–19.
13. A very ancient and famous temple site, the fifth and last stop on the famous Pañckrośī Pilgrimage, in which devotees make a circular journey around Banaras lasting five days (Eck 1982: 353).
14. Bharatendu says nothing about the identity of the ghost and provides no explanation for the incident.
15. There thus seem to be two Nāgā kings in the story. These may be two variants of what was once the same story that arrived in Bhāratendu's tale by different routes.
16. A major annual Hindu festival falling in the lunar month of *kārtik* (October–November). The worship of Lakṣmī is a prominent feature of this festival.
17. He adds at this point the observation that some say that, when a marriage occurred within one of the *gotras*, a split resulted, yielding an extra half *gotra*, but he does not accept this.
18. From this we can surmise that one of the original agendas of this account was to cement a relationship between Gauṛ Brāhmaṇs and Agravāls. There is currently no special connection between Gauṛ Brāhmaṇs and Rajasthani Agravāls that I know of.
19. Various sources speak of various invasions scattering the Agravāls, including the invasion of Alexander the Great. In the Trust sponsored guidebook to Agroha, the Muslim invasion is said to have been the 'most ferocious' (Ṭāṇṭiyā 1996: 20).
20. For example, Rāmcandra Guptā 1926: 63–64; Cunnīlāl Agravāl 1915: 11; Bālcandjī Modī n.d. In the Cunnīlāl version, Agrasen had been cursed by Paraśurām to remain issueless; he became Vaiśya in order to undo the curse (1915: 10).
21. Not all versions of the legend refer to a sacrifice (such as Cunnīlāl 1915). Most do.
22. There were in fact only 17 sages, so that one sage had to educate and initiate (i.e., give *dīkṣā* to) two sons. One of those sons became the apical ancestor of the half *gotra*. According to the author, the system of family priests was long ago defunct (and I know of no traces of such a system). This version is quite different from others. In this telling (Rāmcandra Guptā 1926: 44–49), Agrasen and his sons were Kṣatriyas. His sons went to foreign parts, and while they were away the kingdom was destroyed. They had to disperse and give up *rājya kāj*.

23. The author, reflecting the Trust view, states flatly that there were always 18 clans, never 17 and one half.
24. At another point in the book (1996: 68–69) he proposes a somewhat different motive. At that time the Vaiśyas' rights to Vedic study and the sacrifice were being threatened. Agrasen sponsored his sacrifices in order to protect the rights of the Vaiśyas; the resulting organisation of the Agravāl caste was so sound that it lasted for centuries.

Chapter Seven

Traders Victorious

We have explored the social identity of Rajasthan's traders as expressed in myth. In the process, we have learned that those who follow the ways of trade must confront special problems of social self-definition. These problems, possibly arising in some form or another wherever business is pursued, stem ultimately from the socially ambiguous character of money itself, an ambiguity that emerges with particular clarity in societies not fully dominated by modern capitalist institutions. A comparative anthropology of the varied ways in which such problems are confronted cross-culturally has yet to be written. All that can be said with reasonable assurance is that the varied cultural milieus in which these problems are confronted are bound to affect profoundly the manner in which they are addressed. This book has focussed on how symbolisms specific to the Indic world and Rajasthan have shaped mythic constructions of the social identity of an important cluster of trading groups.

Our investigation has shown that an ancient myth model, that of the sacrifice as a source of creative power and social order, is at the heart of the origin mythology of most Rajasthani trading castes, Hindu and Jain alike. The sacrificial myth model floats loosely in the accounts of traditional genealogists, whereas it gets pinned down and codified in the recast versions promoted by caste associations in their efforts to project corporate identities for the castes they represent. But whoever the tellers and whatever the medium of the telling, the sacrificial myth model abides. The reason for this is clear. This myth model bears the seed meanings that enable myths of origin to be culturally meaningful. Our investigation has thus disclosed a thread of deep continuity uniting caste's present with Indian civilisation's past. And in the process, it has illustrated the power of mythic symbolisms to persist under the surfaces of change, and to lend to a society or civilisation a characteristic way of understanding the meaning and function of social institutions.

Violence and Non-violence

We have also learned that the trader's situation in Rajasthan is tightly intertwined with the issue of the social control of violence. How is wealth to situate itself in relation to political power—that is, in relation to those who have the means of violence at their disposal? This is probably a universal problem for those whose basic mode of existence involves holding wealth and presiding over its flow. In the particular setting of pre-independence Rajasthan, trading communities found themselves in close social proximity to the regional martial aristocracy, primarily the Rājpūts, whom they served as bankers and bureaucrats, and for whom they performed many other kinds of services essential to the exercise of political authority.[1] This relationship operated at multiple levels, from states at the top to villages at the bottom, and deeply affected the traders' position in the wider social order.

The traders wore the social colouration of non-violence. As we have insisted from the outset, however, we must use our words with care in this connection. To say that traders were seen and saw themselves as non-violent is not to say they were (or are) never violent. And to say that traders were vegetarian, which was and remains the sine qua non of trader non-violence, is definitely not to say that all traders abstained (or abstain today) from meat. Not only were there always differences in the degree to which different groups conformed to these norms, but also there have always been differences in the level of compliance of individuals. And today, it needs to be added, significant intergenerational differences are emerging. But the issue is mainly one of symbolic discourse, not of behaviour as such, and these two things are never fully congruent. The point to be stressed is that traders and non-traders alike saw (and continue to see today) non-violent, non-martial ways as highly characteristic of the traders' mode of life.

This book has also suggested that the traders' non-martial ways can be seen as adaptive in the context of their relationship with the Rājpūts in pre-independence Rajasthan. However, on this point, too, we must be careful, for in this instance, as always in social life, the relationship between causes and effects is murky. Whether trader non-violence can be considered an actual *effect* of the need to co-exist with the Rājpūts is a historical question beyond the purview of any evidence at hand and probably unanswerable in principle. But what can be said is that one *consequence* of trader non-violence was that it removed the potential for competition for political authority from the relationship between traders and Rājpūts, thus making possible a complementation of roles that has been historically fruitful for both parties. This complementation was reflected in the ritual sphere. The traders' culturally ingrained incapacity to perform animal sacrifice excluded them from the ritual culture of rule. Their inability to perform animal sacrifice was, we have suggested, of symbolic importance in light of the great significance of the buffalo sacrifice, a highly condensed expression of the Rājpūt ethos, as a state ritual in the region's former kingdoms.

Clustered around the poles of this opposition we find two antithetical cultural complexes deeply implicated in the social identities of Rājpūts and traders, both vis-à-vis each other and in relation to the social order as a whole. One, the Rājpūt complex, emphasises martial valour, relatively uninhibited affect, and redistributional generosity. The other, the trader complex, emphasises physical harmlessness, calculation, and parsimony. In mythohistorical knowledge, this opposition crystallises around the issue of violence in the sacrifice. The Rājpūts practice blood sacrifice, whereas the origin mythology of trading castes singles out the rejection of sacrificial violence as the definitive event in the transmutation of traders-to-be—usually imaged as Rājpūts—into traders. Although there are subcultural variations on this theme, it is a true constant in trader-origin mythology. We shall return to the issue of violent sacrifice shortly.

Historically these two identities were, though complementary, never equal on the regional scale of values. The traders clearly paid a price for their non-violent ways, which rendered them physically vulnerable and dependent on others for protection. And because of this and the high prestige of martial values in the region, they also paid a price in social honour. Members of other communities tended to disdain them as uncourageous and avaricious. These opinions were partly rooted in simple envy and resentment. They also reflected a more diffused uneasiness about how the traders fit in the social order, as evidenced by the fact that traders tended to be seen as social outsiders. This negative view was—as we have tried to show—reflective of the nature of the traders' engagement with local social systems, an engagement to which the socially slippery movement of cash and credit was central. We certainly do not maintain that all members of these castes were seen in this light, for we know this was not the case. Indeed, some of the trading-caste lineages that served the region's great monarchs enjoyed very high prestige. But the cultural–tidal tug was in the opposite direction, as evidenced by the negative 'Baniyā' stereotypes that still linger in the region's life.

Turning Tables

But all is not as it once was in Rajasthan. The political system and its rules have changed in fundamental ways, and the tables have turned on the old Rājpūt aristocracy. The region's once ruling elite and cultural pacesetters, the Rājpūts, have fallen on relatively hard times. It is not that they have totally lost their former high status as a class, for they have not. Nor is it the case that they are without political clout in the state, for they remain among the region's most influential communities, though of course not to the extent of pre-independence times. But when the princely states of old Rajputana were amalgamated into the modern state of Rajasthan, the world of the Rājpūts began to fall apart. Not only did the former privileges of the rulers disappear, but also the very ties that bound Rājpūt social and political structures together began to fray and disintegrate. Little is left of the old order today.

As Lloyd and Susanne Rudolph have pointed out (1984: 50–73), an important factor in the breakup of these structures was the manner in which Rājpūt interests came to be represented to the new polity. An organisation called the Kshatriya Mahasabha supposedly spoke for the Rājpūts as a community. This organisation had been founded in 1888, and was now refurbished as a modern interest group. It was, however, biased toward the interests of the great and wealthy as opposed to the lesser and poorer Rājpūts, a fact that determined the nature of its negotiations with the new state government. When the old estates (comprising roughly half the State's productive land) were broken up, the great Rājpūts were able to obtain relatively generous settlements and retain some of their influence and privileges. The lesser Rājpūts, those who served the great lords, got squeezed from two sides and were ultimately left out in the cold. They found themselves without their old positions and, typically, pushed back to their own inadequate estates. This frequently led to conflict with their peasant tenants. They were then hit with land reform, which gave agricultural land to the non-Rājpūts who had been cultivating it. As a result, a sharp class-division emerged among Rājpūts; the community's former vertical solidarity, based on feudalistic ties uniting the princes and other great Rājpūts with those in their service, was on its way out.

Over subsequent decades, the situation of the Rājpūts altered profoundly. They have certainly found viable economic niches, and some individuals have managed well, but as a class they have not flourished. As one might have expected, military service continues to be a major part of the occupational foundation of Rājpūt life to the present day. Professions related to the military such the police and private security services have also attracted significant numbers of Rājpūts. But it appears that they have not been able to find a secure economic base in agriculture, possibly for cultural reasons. Rājpūt men do not like to do this work themselves, and Rājpūt women cannot labour in the fields like the women of some other castes. Nor have they been very successful at entering business, probably because they lack the established networks of the traditional business community but possibly also for cultural reasons.

Indeed, many members of the business community favour their own variant of the cultural explanation for this, one that verges into a form of bio-cultural determinism. They regard the Rājpūts as generically unable to succeed at business by temperament. The Rājpūts, they allege, are too impulsive, too heedless, and too unable to hang onto their money to conduct business effectively. Lest these be thought to be mere trader stereotypes, I must report that I have heard Rājpūts render these same harsh judgments against themselves. To the degree that a Rājpūt culture or regional subculture actually exists—and this book has assumed that it does—these views may to some extent reflect a cultural reality. But from the standpoint of this book, the important point is that this image of Rājpūts as temperamental opposites of traders is a deeply rooted feature of regional cultures and an idea that retains its currency to the present day.

It has to be said, however, that one economic domain in which some Rājpūts have achieved real success is tourism. Indeed, the movement of Rājpūts into this industry is probably the big story of the post-independence period as far as Rājpūts are concerned. They are found at every level of the business: as hoteliers, drivers, guides, and even cooks. It can be argued—and frequently is in the region—that the Rājpūts were culturally preadapted for the tourist trade. Some Rājpūts, for example, were left with properties that lent themselves readily to conversion into picturesque hotels. Led by the 'palace hotel' phenomenon that began in the 1950s, this became something of a bandwagon for Rājpūt fort and palace owners. Not all of these ventures have been successful, but some have done extremely well. Moreover, the Rājpūt ethos emphasises such virtues as hospitality and social congeniality, and the Rājpūts' non-vegetarian ways made it easy for them to empathise with the needs of foreign guests. And finally, the presence of Rājpūts in the tourist industry (and state bureaucracy) fits well with the imagery on which the state's appeal as a tourist destination is based. This is of course the idealised Rājpūt heritage, which is relentlessly promoted by the state's tourist industry.[2]

Finally, any assessment of where the Rājpūts stand today should note that a politicised version of the Rājpūt heritage has assumed great importance in the region's post-independence politics. The political importance of the *image*, indeed, might even be said to exceed that of the Rājpūts themselves. Here I follow the argument of Rob Jenkins (1998), who has shown that the state's branch of the BJP has made extensive use of the Rājpūt ethic as a source of political mobilisation.

The BJP (Bharatiya Janata Party) is a political party, strongest in North India, vigorously promoting a Hindu nationalist ideology. At the time of this writing (2002), it is the core party in the coalition governing India. Under the leadership of Chief Minister Bhairon Singh Shekhawat (a Rājpūt), the BJP governed Rajasthan from March 1990 to December 1992.[3] It was also the core party in a coalition, also led by Shekhawat, that governed the state from December 1993 to December 1998.

Jenkins argues that the BJP electoral strategy is based on the depiction of Rajasthan as the true home of Rājpūt values. The Rājpūts, in turn, are portrayed as historical defenders of Hinduism and exemplars of a specifically Hindu form of martial valour, and the Rājpūt kingdoms are celebrated as having exemplified the highest ideals of Kṣatriya rulership. The cultic focus of this symbolism (and not just in Rajasthan) is Rāmacandra (Rāma), hero of the epic *Rāmāyaṇa* and a warrior-deity. Rāmacandra is, indeed, quite Rājpūt-like in every respect but one, a point to which we return shortly. The BJP attempts to contrast these images with a portrayal of the Congress Party as favouring a culturally deracinated 'secular' form of nationalism that erodes the distinctiveness of Rajasthan's culture and favours Hinduism's alleged enemies. The power of these images in Rajasthan draws upon regional identity and pride, and also on a cultural paradigm, to some extent shared by all the region's castes, focussed on ideals of social honour represented by the Rājpūts.[4]

This does not mean, however, that the Rajasthan BJP is dominated by Rājpūts. Nor does it mean that the state's politics are dominated by the BJP. At the time of this writing, Rajasthan has a Congress Government led by a member of the *Mālī* (Gardener) caste. But there is no question that Jenkins has described a significant component of the political culture of Rajasthan, and one that can assert itself strongly under the right conditions. For example, the disputes arising from a famous incident in 1987 in which a young Rājpūt widow of Deorala village became a *satī*, placed Rājpūt values in a dramatically critical spotlight. The result was a cause célèbre that 'galvanised the Hindu nationalist movement in Rajasthan' (ibid.: 107).

In connection with the Deorala *satī*, Jenkins stresses that the trading community became a source of financial backing for the Rājpūt defenders of the event. At least at first glance, this would seem to represent a revitalisation of what readers of this book know to be a very old pattern of complementary function between Rājpūts and their trader allies. Here are the traders of old, continuing to occupy the roles of financial enablers and behind-the-scenes advisors. And there is certainly an element of truth to this. As we shall see, however, times do indeed change, and there has also been a transformation in the relationship between traders and Rājpūts.

A possible indication of the change is the fact that Rāmacandra is the patron deity of the political symbolism Jenkins describes. Although he is certainly a martial and heroic deity, the ritual–cultural milieu focussed on him is intensely vegetarian. In consistency with this, he is never the recipient of blood sacrifice. This suggests the presence of a vegetarian militancy, a pattern more congenial to trader than Rājpūt sensibilities, with Rāmacandra emerging as an ideal deity for martial vegetarians. This is not a cultural contradiction. As we have noted earlier, even though the soldier's life has never been particularly admired or emulated by traders, there have been soldiers and military leaders belonging to these communities, and these figures have indeed been admired. And as we know, the present-day Agravāl elite celebrates Agravāl soldiers as caste heroes.

But as we also know, King Agrasen balked at animal sacrifice, which is why Agravāls came into existence. This points us back to the nub of the matter as far as the symbolism of trader identity is concerned, which is *violence in relation to the sacrifice*. It also brings us to an extremely interesting development in post-independence politics. No longer sequestered in the realm of origin mythology, the issue of sacrificial violence has burst forth into the political arena, and has done so in a way that signals a profound change in the social and political positioning of Rajasthan's traders. The sacrificial myth model remains deeply embedded in the symbolism of trader identity, but events have now supplied it with a new and totally unprecedented context.

Traders Emergent

The Rājpūts' success in tourism and the political salience of the Rājpūt ethos notwithstanding, the fact remains that post-independence Rajasthan has been much kinder to traders than Rājpūts. In general, the traders have prospered and grown in power, influence, and social honour. And if they were once seen as grubby moneylenders and subjected to sumptuary rules and the stigmas of alleged cowardice, softness, and shady dealing, the social situation and general atmosphere are now very different.

One can point to various indications of the extent of the change. One symptom, and no small matter, can be seen in dramatic changes in what many regard as Jaipur's most exclusive social club. According to knowledgeable insiders, the character of the club's membership has altered fundamentally. In the early post-independence period, this club was almost exclusively the domain of Rājpūts. Now, however, traders (in this context, the usual tag is 'Baniyās') completely dominate the club's membership. Another indication of the changed situation is what has happened to polo. More than any other sport, polo was the Rājpūts' game, the perfect athletic expression of their martial ethos. Now, however, team ownership is entirely dominated by the trading community, although Rājpūts still play on the teams. Moreover, nowadays it is rich traders, not Rājpūt chieftains, who are the winners in the contemporary tourney of conspicuous consumption, as any survey of the contemporary wedding scene would show. I know firsthand that many members of the old aristocracy resent these developments deeply, but their complaints about the presence of the Baniyās in the wrong places tend to be made behind closed doors.

This does not mean, however, that traders have become the new Rājpūts. The actual situation is more complex and more interesting than that. What we see, in fact, is new trader power and social standing, but manifested in a way that is to some extent continuous with the previous order of things. For example, although the traders as a class possess an unprecedented degree of political influence and power in the region, they tend not to attempt to translate it into overt political authority. Their main role in the state's politics seems to be that of contributing money to candidates belonging to other communities, and this often gives them leverage on particular issues. But it is a leverage that tends to be exercised unobtrusively and from behind the scenes, as was the case in pre-independence Rajasthan.

This trend is reflected in the current composition of the state's legislative assembly. On the basis of an analysis of names, I can say that out of a total of 200 MLAs (Members of the Legislative Assembly) listed in 2002, only 19 are definitely members of trading castes, with seven possible members of trading castes. Of 18 cabinet ministers, only two are clearly members of trading castes, and—to the best of my ability to judge from the names—there is no trading-caste minister among the 13 state ministers. Of course it must not be forgotten that the current political system is democratic, which means that traders are at a disadvantage in vying for high office for purely numerical reasons. But I believe that a cultural inhibition is also at work. Today, as before, traders tend to see their natural domain as that of commerce and the making of money, not power politics. Because of this, they tend to be most comfortable in their old political role of powers behind the throne, content to provide financial, organisational and intellectual support to others who do the actual ruling.

Moreover, the traders cannot be said to constitute a power bloc in Rajasthan today. Although they tend to support the Hindu nationalist BJP party, which gets most of its support from urban areas, they do not—as a class—possess an organised agenda that they are able to unite behind. There is, however, one specific cluster of issues that does indeed mobilise broad support from the trading community. This brings us to the subject of vegetarian politics.

Vegetarian Politics

As this book has shown, the rejection of violent sacrifice is an abiding theme in trading-caste origin myths. Their aversion to violence in the sacrifice is, after all, the basis of the mythohistorical mitosis that separated the traders-to-be from their (usually) Rājpūt ancestors, thus becoming a key ingredient in their conception of who they are. But recently events have taken a totally new turn. Because of their empowerment by post-independence social and political changes, traders have been able to lift their aversion to blood sacrifice out of the realm of myth and insert it into the real-life fray of state and national politics. Blood sacrifice was once a symbol of Rājpūt valour and authority. Now under political assault, it has become a symptom of Rājpūt decline and the emergence of traders as a political force. The story of how this came about illustrates another interesting development, which is the transmutation of trader social identity into a political ideology. To tell it, we must return to a subject already touched upon in previous chapters, that of the goddess and her appetites.

In Rajasthan, blood sacrifice is usually offered to a goddess. Whether or not the goddess receives animal sacrifice (as opposed to more benign offerings) is largely a reflection of the character of the group making the offering. As we have seen earlier in this book, the standard myth model portrays a goddess as assisting or participating in a lineage or caste's birth. She then becomes a protectress of the newly created group, a tie that is perpetuated by patrilineal descent. She becomes, that is, a goddess either to a specific lineage, clan or to a number of clans constituting a caste (thus becoming a 'caste' goddess). Myth-imagery portrays the character of these ancestral goddesses as reflections of the essential character of the groups over which they preside. Her character and theirs become mutually reinforcing, and she emerges as a symbol of the group's social identity.

We have already looked at various examples of this principle. In the case of the Dāhimā Brāhmaṇs, the goddess Dadhimatī is herself a Brāhmaṇ, and the Dāhimās' origin myth connects her directly with their priestly role, for she is the object of the sacrifice that converted them into a caste. The Cauhāns' Āśāpūrṇā shares their ferocity, just as Sacciyā (formerly fierce Cāmuṇḍā) comes to share the Osvāls' vegetarian ways. In general, the clan goddesses of the Rājpūts are similar to Āśāpūrṇā; they tend to be warrior goddesses with an appetite for blood sacrifice. Trader goddesses are vegetarian and pacific, at least from the standpoint of their trader worshippers.[5]

Given this cultural background, it is a highly significant fact that the sacrifice of animals in public places has been legally banned in Rajasthan since 1975. To some extent, no doubt, the banning reflected modernistic and anti-obscurantist views, but it was also, and probably mostly, a manifestation of values of deep importance to traders (and not just to traders). And it cannot be regarded as coincidental that it has dealt a heavy blow to an important element of the ritual culture of the old Rājpūt aristocracy. The law in question is the Rajasthan Animals and Birds Sacrifice (Prohibition) Act, 1975. It specifically forbids animal sacrifice in a 'temple', which is defined as a 'public' place of worship. Obviously, this creates large potential loopholes, possibly intended by the legislators, because it leaves open to debate the issue of whether particular spaces are truly public or not. But that does not mean, as we shall see, that the law is inefficacious.

The story of how the law came into existence is a complex tale, with many twists and turns. As a matter of practical politics, the Act resulted from concerted efforts of members of Rajasthan's trading community. It originated as a non-governmental bill (i.e., not introduced by the government) proposed by a Congress-party MLA who belonged to the Jāṭ caste. The Jāṭs, of course, are not a trading caste, but there is no question that the real impetus for the bill came from the traders. In the Rajasthan Legislative Assembly itself, the principal individual proponent of the bill was an MLA named Guman Mal Lodha. Still active in politics at the time of this writing, he is an Osvāl Jain who at that time was a member of the Jan Sangh Party, a Hindu nationalist party and predecessor to today's BJP. The Jan Sangh was closely associated with the trading community, as is the BJP today. In the end, the contest was extremely close. The bill passed by only one vote.

When I interviewed Lodha (in January 2000) about these events, he characterised the debate about the bill as one that was shaped almost entirely by caste rather than party differences. The Rājpūts largely opposed the legislation, which is hardly surprising considering the importance of animal sacrifice to their ritual culture. Trader support for the legislation can be understood in similar terms. The Jain and Vaiṣṇava traditions that dominate trader religion are of course opposed to bloodshed. But even more important, given the centrality of opposition to sacrificial violence to trader social identity, their support for such legislation was not merely a matter of religious conviction, but also an expression of social self-identification. But now this social identity was being expressed at a different level and in a different mode. In effect, in the process of being politicised, trader identity had been de-relativised. It was once the case that the morality or immorality of animal sacrifice was, at least to some degree, socially relative; what was wrong for traders could be right for Rājpūts. But from now on, the traders' identity-linked morality would be everyone's morality. In effect, the Act was a reenactment on a socially *universal* scale of (to take but one example) the Osvāls' socially *relative* vegetarianisation of Cāmuṇḍā into Sacciyā.

According to Lodha and others involved in the parliamentary effort on behalf of the Act, two background events created an atmosphere favourable for the push to its passage. One was the 1974 celebration of the 2,500th anniversary of the liberation of Mahāvīr. The run-up to this event generated strong anti-animal-sacrifice agitation within the Jain community specifically. The other event was further back in time, but had an equal if not greater impact on the passion of the traders' support for the Act. This was an episode of anti-cow-slaughter agitation that had taken place in November 1966 in Delhi and had culminated in eight deaths.[6] These two events had created a context especially conducive to the flourishing of what might be called 'vegetarian politics' in Rajasthan and elsewhere, and the 1975 Act can be considered a triumph of this style of politics.

Vegetarian politics is politicised non-violence. It mobilises its constituencies around such issues as cow slaughter, animal sacrifice, and the export of Indian meat. It is not, let it be said clearly, the same thing as Hindu nationalism. But it does resonate deeply with the politics of Hindu nationalist groups such as the BJP and provides such groups with valuable support. And on the other side of the coin, the strong commitment to the protection of cows (which, of course, is a cause with which vegetarian and non-vegetarian Hindus can identify) puts it at odds with Muslim communities for the obvious reason that Muslims are beef-eaters, butchers, and alleged sacrificers of bovines on Eid ul-Azha. Merely to say, however, that vegetarian politics is a political expression of anti-Muslim prejudice, as is often said, would be to oversimplify a complex political–cultural movement. Among its more interesting features is that it can be seen as a political expression of the culture of trading-caste identity that this book has explored.

The link between trading castes and vegetarian politics can be traced to cultural changes taking place in the nineteenth century. Susan Bayly (1999: 216–20) has shown that an image of 'dharmic propriety' had become critical to the social honour and credit-worthiness of newly urbanised trading families during this period. Given the centrality of non-violence to the caste cultures of these groups, such propriety tended to be manifested in the form of what she aptly calls 'ahimsa austerity'. Wealth would be conspicuously donated to temples, temple ceremonies, and shelters for the care and feeding of cows and other vegetarian creatures. The cow, especially, was a natural focus for such efforts. The cow, of course, bore a general cultural significance as an embodiment of purity, virtue, and nurturance, but Bayly also suggests that, for traders and some other groups, the cow actually became a substitute for Brāhmaṇs as an object of ritual veneration.[7] These were groups who felt snubbed by Brāhmaṇs because of their lower status, new-richness, or adherence to anti-Brāhmaṇ sects. This was the context in which militant cow protectionism took root and grew in the late nineteenth century. It was, in Bayly's words, 'the greatest of all rallying points for "communities" professing the values of the pious *ahimsa* non-blood-spiller' (ibid.: 219), who of course were preeminently the trading castes. This pattern has continued to the present day, and is a very strong subtheme in the political culture of contemporary Rajasthan.

A particularly interesting aspect of vegetarian politics is that it seems to pick a major theme from the Rājpūt culture of identity, but in a way that mirrors trader norms. I have in mind the concept of protection. As we have noted in Chapter Two, protection is central to symbolic representations of the social duty of Rājpūts (reflecting the idealised duty of the Kṣatriya *varṇa*). Loyalty to the ruler is repaid by the protection he offers in return. The ruler's ability to act in this role draws upon his most important characteristic (in the idealised image), which is martial valour manifested in normatively justifiable violence. In light of the power of this imagery in regional culture, it cannot surprise us that when traders enter the political arena they likewise reach for the ethic of protection as a legitimising ideology. They do so, however, in a manner that rids it of its symbolic connection with violence. Thus, vegetarian politics assumes the stance of protection, but the nature and object of protection depart from the Rājpūt model. According to cultural expectation, Rājpūts employ their martial prowess to protect their subjects. By analogy, vegetarian politics seizes upon the trader commitment to *ahiṃsā*, which it socially universalises and elevates to 'protective' function of the state. In this way, the now-politicised trader ethos finds (or seeks to find) modern embodiment in the laws of a republican polity. But having achieved this transformation, the new ideology confronts a contradiction, for stripping the state (in which it is now embedded, or wishes to be) of recourse to violence is a practical impossibility. Therefore, the intensity of *ahiṃsā* is lessened, its scope narrowed, and its emphasis shifted to non-human forms of life, especially the cow. In the meantime, the state maintains its monopoly on the legitimate use of violence, which it must, if only to enforce laws against such things as the slaughter of cows. This is the mindset out of which the 1975 legislation came.

Traders Victorious

It has to be said, however, that the law against animal sacrifice has not been vigorously enforced at the grass-roots level, a fact that has generated bitter complaints from some of the law's proponents. Incredibly, as of January 2000, the 1975 Act had never actually resulted in a case being brought before the Rajasthan High Court. When I asked a senior police official in the state about the law, he informed me that in his entire career as a policeman, and having served in many different locations throughout the state, he has never actually heard of an instance of enforcement of the 1975 Act. He further said that, in his opinion, the Act has had little actual effect on behaviour at the grass-roots level. Animal sacrifice to non-vegetarian deities is still common in Rajasthan.

But even if enforcement at the grass-roots level is problematic, this does not mean that the law is inefficacious or culturally unimportant. To the contrary, it has produced at least one very significant consequence. With the Act in place, it became much easier to challenge animal sacrifices in highly visible places. As a result, the law appears to have had a major impact on the public ritual culture of the region's old Rājpūt aristocracy. Indeed, I believe this was, at least to some extent, the true if unstated intent of the law. A good example of the effect is what has happened in Jaipur.

Although Jaipur State ceased to exist at the time of India's independence, the royal family continued to sponsor an annual buffalo sacrifice at the Śilā Mātā temple at Amber Fort for many years afterwards.[8] The people of the city and kingdom had always regarded it as a major state ceremony. According to legend, this goddess's aniconic image was obtained when Raja Man Singh I defeated the King of Jessore (now in Bangladesh) in 1604. The goddess took the material form of a black stone slab, which was supposedly the very same stone upon which wicked Kaṃsa dashed to death the unfortunate siblings of Lord Kṛṣṇa. The defeated King of Jessore presented the stone to Raja Man Singh in exchange for the return of his kingdom, and it was later carved into the image of Durgā Mahiṣamardini, slayer of the demon Mahiṣāsur. Śilā Mātā was never actually the lineage goddess of Jaipur's ruling family. Jamvā Mātā, a vegetarian goddess whose temple is at Ramgarh, occupied that role, and it was to her that members of the royal family went to have the tonsure rite performed and to seek post-nuptial blessings. But Śilā Mātā did occupy the role of a lineage goddess in receiving animal sacrifices offered by Jaipur's royal family. Goats were sacrificed on a daily basis during the twice-yearly *navrātrī* periods, and buffaloes on the eighth day. These occasions were considered important enough that in the days before the construction of a motorable road from Jaipur to Amber, Jaipur rulers would stay at Amber for the entire *navrātrī* period. A great crowd of observers from the city would also be present, and the actual sacrifice was done in public view at a spot directly in front of the Śilā Mātā temple.

The public buffalo sacrifice at Amber no longer takes place, and its cessation was almost certainly a direct consequence of the 1975 law. I was unable to find any written documentation of what happened, but one of the priests of the Śilā Mātā temple informed me that the old system changed at the time of Indira Gandhi's 'emergency', which took place in the years 1975–77. He further told me that the routine daily sacrifice of goats was allowed to continue thereafter, but was restricted to a location outside the walls of Amber Fort, and only vegetarian offerings were allowed inside the temple. The public buffalo sacrifice ceased entirely. Today, the royal family continues to sacrifice a buffalo on *navrātrī*, but this is done in strict seclusion in the City Palace, the King's private residence in Jaipur. No great crowds view the ceremony nowadays, and I am told that only a few of the former kingdom's top feudatory lords attend. In other words, the buffalo sacrifice to the goddess—once a public enactment of Rājpūt pride, valour, and right to rule—has now become a quasi-domestic ceremony in Jaipur.

The same retreat of animal sacrifice has occurred at less exalted levels in the region. A good case in point, one directly connected with materials presented in this book, is what has happened at Osian, the supposed place of origin of the Osvāl caste.

The goddess of Osian is Sacciyā. As we learned in Chapter Five, myth links her with the creation of the Osvāl caste, and many Osvāls venerate her as a clan or caste-patroness goddess. To the Osvāls, she is a goddess who long ago gave up the appetite for meat. This, however, is not the only view. As is often the case with important goddesses, Sacciyā also serves as lineage or clan goddess for (or at least is regularly worshipped by) many castes that have territorial links with the area, not just the Osvāls. Therefore, the Osvāls' understanding of her identity and character is only one understanding among several. The list of castes having constituent clans or lineages revering her as clan goddess includes Bhāṭī Rājpūts, Sīsodiyā Rājpūts, Māheśvarīs, Sevags (temple priests for the Jains, but not, as it happens, the Sevags who serve in the Osian temples), Jāṭs, and Nāyaks. The last-named group consists of Dalits who are required to worship Sacciyā from a position outside the main temple. Other castes could undoubtedly be added to this list.

Because some of these groups are non-vegetarian, it has never been the case that all of her worshippers have shared the notion that Sacciyā is a vegetarian goddess. And indeed, until recently many of her worshippers offered blood sacrifice during the *navrātrī* periods. Most of her non-vegetarian worshippers offered goats. However, the two Bhāṭī Rājpūt families holding estates in the village offered buffaloes in accord with the old Rājpūt tradition. The goat sacrifices were a regular feature of *navrātrī* while the buffaloes were only offered occasionally. The actual slaughter of animals was never done in the temple itself. The goats were cut at a position just down the hill from the temple, and only the heads were actually presented to the goddess in the temple. The buffaloes were sacrificed at the bottom of the hill outside what is now the main gate of the whole complex, and the buffalo heads were not taken into the temple.

These sacrifices no longer occur, or at least not in the same open manner in which they once did. Given the great practical difficulty of completely eradicating any well-established custom, and also the desire of some to deny what they do not want to see, some murkiness surrounds the entire issue of what does and does not take place at Osian on *navrātrī* these days. Although many, including both Osvāls and non-Osvāls, state that animal sacrifices have completely halted, it is certain that goats are sometimes still offered, although inconspicuously and at a distance.[9] The Rājpūts' offering of buffaloes, however, has definitely ceased. Local estimates of when this change took place range from 20 to 30 years prior to 1998 (the year of my enquiries there). This would more or less coincide with the enactment of the 1975 law. As in the macrocosm of Jaipur, we thus see the end of an old order of things in the microcosm of Osian.

It will come as no surprise that trader influence was the crucial factor in the suppression of animal sacrifice in Osian, just as it was in the state as a whole. Despite their mythohistorical connection with the town, however, it was not the Osvāls who brought it about, for the Osvāls do not have a significant residential presence in Osian. As we know, Sacciyā supposedly expelled them with a curse. There is only one local trading community of any consequence in Osian, but it is a big and important one. It consists of over 150 houses of Māheśvarīs, and village informants state that this community played the decisive role in bringing the buffalo sacrifice to a halt at the Sacciyā temple. Given the timing, it is highly probable that the 1975 Act was a key factor in their ability to do this. The cessation of buffalo sacrifices was undoubtedly not an automatic consequence of the Act. Rather, it seems likely that the Act created a political atmosphere in which the local Māheśvarīs felt encouraged to challenge the local Rājpūts, as well as a legal context in which their challenge could presumably be successful if pursued in the courts. But at an even deeper level, their ability to conceive and organise such a challenge must have reflected their sense of the declining fortunes of the Rājpūts and the traders' relative ascendancy—in this case a local ascendancy, but echoing regional and even national trends.

And so we come full circle, back again to the sacrifice and to the age-old question of its relationship with violence. Our journey has taken us from dusty villages and temple towns to the up-to-date urban world of Jaipur, from moneylending and petty shopkeeping to matters of state, and from the simplicities of ancient myth models to the complications of modern democratic politics. We have arrived at a world much changed from the older order where our excursion began, for the social position of trading communities has evolved in new directions. India's contemporary economic and political systems seem made to order for traders to flourish. They have not only done so in their old roles but also in economic and professional niches unknown to their ancestors, and they now enjoy unprecedented social honour and political clout as a class. But the political struggles over animal sacrifice remind us of the extraordinary capacity of culture to maintain thematic unity, even in the midst of the most dramatic transformations.

Notes

1. This idea may be echoed in a South Indian context by the mythohistorical motif of the Nakarattars of Tamil Nadu that portrays them as 'surrogate kings' (Rudner 1994: 190–91). This claim meshes with the their role as wielders of political authority in a variety of contexts (as was true of Rajasthani traders) and as endowers of temples.
2. On the centrality of the Rājpūt image to the state's touristic appeal, see Ramusack 1995.
3. Bhairon Singh Shekawat was also Chief Minister of Rajasthan from 1977 to 1980. At that time, the BJP did not yet exist. Shekhawat had belonged to the erstwhile Jan Sangh, a Hindu nationalist party that was a predecessor to the BJP. During this period, the Jan Sangh had become part of the Janta Party, which later disintegrated.
4. In his stress on the regional character of the BJP's mobilisation strategies in Rajasthan, I think Jenkins has perhaps overlooked the long pedigree in Indian nationalist traditions of the idealisation of the Rājpūt as a heroic resistor of foreign invaders. Jason Freitag (2001: 241–58) provides an excellent discussion of the importance of James Tod in the transmission of these ideas into nationalist historiography.
5. This qualification has to be added because some trader clan or caste goddesses might also have non-vegetarian groups among their worshippers. Sacciyā is a good example of precisely this. Certainly, however, Osvāls never offer her blood sacrifice, even if others (nowadays surreptitiously) do. This is a point to be expanded upon below. Moreover, the Bhaṇḍārī Osvāls, who trace their descent to the Cauhāns, venerate Āśāpūrṇā as a clan goddess, but to them she is a vegetarian goddess.
6. On this incident and the politics of cow slaughter, see Jaffrelot 1996: 204–08.
7. The cow is seen as an embodiment of the goddess Lakṣmī. She is also a maternal figure associated with nourishment and nurture. Eating her flesh is therefore suggestive of matricide. One author has suggested that the image of the cow has evolved into that of the mother of the 'Hindu nation', thus by reflex defining an image of Hindu manhood as the masculine protector of the female and cowlike Hindu body politic (van der Veer 1994: 86–94).
8. The following details about the goddess and ceremony are taken from Sahai, n.d.
9. A Rājpūt informant stated that goats are still offered at the main gate, but I have no independent confirmation of this.

Bibliography

Agravāl, Cunnīlāl. 1915. *Agravāl Itihās*. Kolkata: Lalit Press.

Agravāl Samāj. 1995. *Paricay Smārikā (Agravāl Yuvak Yuvatī Vaivāhik Paricay Sammelan [1995])*. Jaipur: Śrī Agravāl Samāj Samiti.

Akhil Bhāratīya. 1983. *Akhil Bhāratīya Agravāl Sammelan ke Āṭh Varṣ*. Published on the occasion of the meeting convened at Vārāṇasī, 22–23 January, 1983. New Delhi: Rāmeśvardās Gupt.

Appadurai, Arjun. 1986. 'Introduction: Commodities and the Politics of Value', in A. Appadurai (ed.), *The Social Life of Things: Commodities in Cultural Perspective*, pp. 3–63. Cambridge: Cambridge University Press.

Arya, R. P. and Arya, J. 1997. *Rajasthan Road Atlas*. Jodhpur: Indian Map Service.

Asopa, Jai Narayan. 1988. *The Brahmanas, Dadhici and Dahimas*. Jaipur: Shri Sahitya Shodha Evam Prakashan Samiti.

Babb, Lawrence A. 1996. *Absent Lord: Ascetics and Kings in a Jain Ritual Culture*. Berkeley: University of California Press.

———. 1998. 'Rejecting Violence: Sacrifice and the Social Identity of Trading Communities', *Contributions to Indian Sociology* (n.s.), 32(2): 387–407.

———. 1999. 'Mirrored Valor: On the Social Identity of Rajasthani Traders', *International Journal of Hindu Studies*, 3(1): 1–25.

———. 2000. 'Time and Temples: On Social and Metrical Antiquity', in M. Meister (ed.), *Ethnography and Personhood: Notes from the Field*, pp. 193–222. Jaipur and New Delhi: Rawat Publications.

———. 2002. 'Violence and the Construction of Trading-Caste Identity', in L. A. Babb, V. Joshi and M. Meister (eds), *Multiple Histories: Culture and Society in the Study of Rajasthan*, pp. 15–38. Jaipur and New Delhi: Rawat Publications.

———. 2003. 'Thwarted Sacrifice: On thc Origin Myths of Jain Castes', in O. Qvarnström (ed.), *Jainism and Early Buddhism: Essays in Honor of Padmanabh S. Jaini*. Freemont, California: Asian Humanities Press.

Bansal, Captain Kamal Kiśor. 1992. *Vīrtā kī Vīrāsat: Agravāl (Vaiśya) Vitrõ ke Śaurya, Tyāg evam Karttavyaparāyaṇtāū kā Sankṣipt Paricay*. Agroha: Agroha Vikas Trust.

Baṛjātyā, Rājmal. 1910. *Khaṇḍelvāl Jain—Itihās*. Mumbai: S. V. Press.

Baruā, Ṛṣi Jaiminī Kauśik. 1985. *Main Apne Mārvāṛī Samāj ko Pyār Kartā Hun*. Kolkata: Jaininī Publications.

Bateson, Gregory. 1958. *Naven: A Survey of the Problems Suggested by a Composite Picture of the Culture of a New Guinea Tribe Drawn from Three Points of View*. Second Edition. Stanford: Stanford University Press.

Bayly, C. A. 1983. *Rulers, Townsmen and Bazaars: North Indian Society in the Age of British Expansion, 1770–1870*. Cambridge: Cambridge University Press.

Bayly, Susan. 1999. *Caste, Society and Politics in India from the Eighteenth Century to the Modern Age* (The New Cambridge History of India: IV.3). Cambridge: Cambridge University Press.

Bhaṇḍārī, S. R., Bhaṇḍārī, C. R., Gupt, K. L., Sonī, B. L. and Ratnāvat, B. R. 1934. *Osvāl Jāti kā Itihās*. 2 vols. Bhānpurā (Indaur): Osvāl History Publishing House.

Bhansālī, Sohanrāj. 1982. *Osvāl Vaṃś, Anusandhān ke Alok mẽ*. Jodhpur: Kuśalam Jain Granthālaya.

Bhūtoṛiyā, Māngīlāl. 1995. *Itihās kī Amar Bel: Osvāl*. Pratham Khaṇḍ. Second Edition. Lādnūn: Priyadarśī Prakāśan.

Biardeau, Madeleine. 1994. *Hinduism: The Anthropology of a Civilization*. New Delhi: Oxford University Press.

Bihāṇī, Rāmcandra. 1983. *Māheśvarī Vaṃśotpatti*. Bikaner: Māheśvarī Sevak.

Bloch, Maurice. 1989. 'The Symbolism of Money in Imerina', in J. Parry and M. Bloch (eds), *Money and the Morality of Exchange*, pp. 165–90. Cambridge: Cambridge University Press.

Cadène, Philippe. 1997. 'The Part Played by Merchant Castes in the Contemporary Indian Economy: The Case of the Jains in a Small Town in Rajasthan', in P. Cadène and D. Vidal (eds), *Webs of Trade: Dynamics of Business Communities in Western India*, pp. 136–158. New Delhi: Manohar.

Carstairs, Morris G. 1961. *The Twice-Born: A Study of a Community of High-Caste Hindus*. Second Impression. Bloomington: Indiana University Press.

Chandra, Sudhir. 1992. *The Oppressive Present: Literature and Social Consciousness in Colonial India*. New Delhi: Oxford University Press.

Cheesman, David. 1982. '"The Omnipresent Bania:" Rural Moneylenders in Nineteenth-Century Sindh', *Modern Asian Studies*, 16(3): 445–62.

Cimino, Rosa Maria. 1983. *Life at Court in Rajasthan: Indian Miniatures from the Seventeenth to the Nineteenth Century*. Firenze: Mario Luca Giusti.

Conlon, Frank F. 1977. *A Caste in a Changing World: The Chitrapur Saraswat Brahmans, 1700–1935*. Berkeley: University of California Press.

Cort, John E. 1990a. 'Twelve Chapters from the Guidebook to Various Pilgrimage Places, the Vividhatīrthakakalpa of Jinaprabhasūri', in P. Granoff (ed.), *The Clever Adulteress and Other Stories: A Treasury of Jain Literature*, pp. 245–90. Oakville (Ontario): Mosaic Press.

———. 1990b. 'The Śvetāmbar Jain Mūrtipūjak Mendicant', *Man* (n.s.), 26: 549–69.

———. 1998. 'Who is a King? Jain Narratives of Kingship in Medieval Western India', in J. Cort (ed.), *Open Boundaries: Jain Communities and Cultures in Indian History*, pp. 85–110. Albany: SUNY Press.

———. 2000a. 'Communities, Temples, Identities: Art Histories and Social Histories in Western India', in M. Meister (ed.), *Ethnography and Personhood: Notes from the Field*, pp. 101–28. Jaipur and New Delhi: Rawat Publications.

———. 2000b. 'Patronage, Authority, Proprietary Rights, and History: Communities and Pilgrimage Temples in Western India', in M. Meister (ed.), *Ethnography and Personhood: Notes from the Field*, pp. 165–91. Jaipur and New Delhi: Rawat Publications.

———. 2001. *Jains in the World: Religious Values and Ideology in India*. New York: Oxford University Press.

———. 2002. 'A Tale of Two Cities: On the Origins of Digambar Sectarianism in North India', in L. A. Babb, V. Joshi and M. Meister (eds), *Multiple Histories: Culture and Society in the Study of Rajasthan*, pp. 39–83. Jaipur and New Delhi: Rawat Publications.

Cort, John E. Forthcoming. 'Jains, Caste, and Hierarchy in North Gujarat', *Contributions to Indian Sociology*.

Cottam Ellis, Christine M. 1991. 'The Jain Merchant Castes of Rajasthan: Some Aspects of the Management of Social Identity in a Market Town', in M. Carrithers and C. Humphrey (eds), *The Assembly of Listeners: Jains in Society*, pp. 75–107. Berkeley: Cambridge University Press.

Crooke, W. 1896. *The Tribes and Castes of the North-western Provinces and Oudh*. Vols. I–IV. Kolkata: Office of the Superintendent of Government Printing.

Dalmia, Vasudha. 1997. *The Nationalization of Hindu Traditions: Bhāratendu Hariśchandra and Nineteenth-century Banaras*. New Delhi: Oxford University Press.

Darak, Śivkaraṇ Rāmratan. 1923. *Vaiśyakulbhūṣaṇ va Itihāskalpdrum Māheśvarī-kulśuddhdarpaṇ aur Sāṛhī Bārah va Caurāsī Nyātkā Varṇan* (Fourth edition; original V. S. 1950). Mumbaī: Gangāviṣṇu Śrīkṛṣṇdās.

Datta, Nonica. 1999. *Forming an Identity: A Social History of the Jats*. New Delhi: Oxford University Press.

Devra, G. S. L. 1980. *Bureaucracy in Rajasthan (1745–1829 A.D.)*. Bikaner: Dharti Prakashan.

Dhaky, M. A. 1968. 'Some Early Jaina Temples in Western India', in *Shri Mahavir Jaina Vidyalaya Golden Jubilee Volume, Part 1*, pp. 290–347. Mumbai: Shri Mahavira Jaina Vidyalaya.

Dirks, Nicholas B. 2001. *Castes of Mind: Colonialism and the Making of Modern India*. Princeton: Princeton University Press.

Dumont, Louis. 1970. *Homo Hierarchicus: The Caste System and Its Implications* (Trans. M. Sainsbury). Chicago: University of Chicago Press.

Dundas, Paul. 2002. *The Jains*. Second Edition. London: Routledge.

Eck, Diana. 1982. *Banāras: City of Light*. New York: Knopf.

———. 1991. 'Following Rama, Worshipping Śiva', in D. L. Eck and F. Mallison (eds), *Devotion Divine: Bhakti Traditions from the Regions of India*, pp. 49–71. Groningen: Egbert Forsten, Paris: École Frančaise d'Extrême Orient.

Evans-Pritchard, E. E. 1940. *The Nuer: A Description of the Modes of Livelihood and Political Institutions of a Nilotic People*. Oxford: Oxford University Press.

Freitag, Jason Paul. 2001. 'The Power which Raised them from Ruin and Oppression: James Tod, Historiography and the Rajput Ideal', Ph.D. diss., Columbia University.

Fuller, Chris J. 1989. 'Misconceiving the Grain Heap: A Critique of the Concept of the Indian Jajmani System', in J. Parry and M. Bloch (eds), *Money and the Morality of Exchange*, pp. 33–63. Cambridge: Cambridge University Press.

Garg, Śivśankar. n.d. *Śīlā Mātā kā Jīvan Parica*. Mumbaī: Agrohā Vikās Sansthān.

Granoff, Phyllis. 1989. 'Religious Biography and Clan History among the Śvetāmbara Jains in North India', *East and West*, 39 (1–4): 195–215.

Gregory, C. A. 1997. *Savage Money: The Anthropology and Politics of Commodity Exchange*. Amsterdam: Harwood Academic Publishers.

Guha, Ranajit. 1985. 'The Career of an Anti-God in Heaven and on Earth', in A. Mitra (ed.), *The Truth Unites: Essays in Tribute to Samar Sen*, pp. 1–25. Kolkata: Subarnarekha.

Gupt, Campālāl. 1993. *Agrohā: Ek Aitihāsik Paricay*. First Edition. Agrohā: Agrohā Vikās Trust.

———. 1996. *Agrohā, Ek Aitihāsik Dharohar*. Second Edition. Agrohā: Agrohā Vikās Trust.

Gupt, Motīlāl. n.d. *Khaṇḍelvāl Jāti kā Prārambhik Itihās*. Jaipur: Śrī Khaṇḍelvāl Vaiśya Mahāsabhā.

———. (ed.). 1972. *Sundar-aṣṭak*. Jaipur: Sāhitya-Prakāśan Upsamiti, Akhil Bharatvarṣiya Khaṇḍelvāl Vaiśya Mahāsabhā.

Gupt, Rāmeśvardās (ed.). 1995a. *Agrohādhām ke Nirmāṇ kī Kahānī Citrõ kī Zabānī*. New Delhi: Agroha Vikas Trust.

———. 1995b. *Bhārat ke Agravāl Parivār*. New Delhi: Agravāl Nideśikā Samiti.

Gupta, Anand Swarup (ed.). 1981. *The Varāha-Purāṇa (with English Translation)*. Varanasi: All-India Kashiraj Trust.

Gupta, Dipankar. 2000. *Interrogating Caste: Understanding Hierarchy and Difference in Indian Society*. New Delhi: Penguin.

Gupta, Badlu Ram. 1975. *The Aggarwals: A Socio-economic Survey*. New Delhi: S. Chand and Co.

Guptā, Rāmcandra. 1926. *Agravaṃś arthāt Agravāl Jāti kā Itihās*. Sekhā (Rājya Paṭiyālā, Panjāb): Śobhārām Smārak Granthmālā Kāryālay.

Gupta, Satya Prakash. 1986. *The Agrarian System of Eastern Rajasthan (c. 1650–c. 1750)*. Delhi: Manohar.

Hardgrove, Anne Elizabeth. 1999. '*Sati* Worship and Marwari Public Identity in India', *Journal of Asian Studies*, 58(3): 723–52.

———. 2002. *Community and Public Culture: The Marwaris in Calcutta 1897–1997*. New York: Columbia University Press (Gutenberg-e).

Hardiman, David. 1987. 'The Bhils and Shahukars of Eastern Gujarat', in R. Guha (ed.), *Subaltern Studies V: Writings on South Asian History and Society*, pp. 1–54. New Delhi: Oxford University Press.

———. 1996. *Feeding the Baniya: Peasants and Usurers in Western India*. New Delhi: Oxford University Press.

Harlan, Lindsey. 1992. *Religion and Rajput Women: The Ethic of Protection in Contemporary Narratives*. Berkeley: University of California Press.

Hazra, R. C. 1975. *Studies in the Purānic Records on Hindu Rites and Customs*. Delhi: Motilal Banarasidass.

Hiltebeitel, Alf. 1999. *Rethinking India's Oral and Classical Epics: Draupadi among Rajputs, Muslims, and Dalits*. Chicago: University of Chicago Press.

Hitchcock, John T. 1959. 'The Idea of the Martial Rājpūt', in M. Singer (ed.), *Traditional India: Structure and Change*, pp. 10–17. Philadelphia: The American Folklore Society.

Hocart, A. M. 1950. *Caste: A Comparative Study*. London: Methuen and Co.

Hoernle, A. F. Rudolph. 1890. 'The Pattavali or List of Pontiffs of the Upkesa-Gachchha', *Indian Antiquary*, 19 (August): 233–42.

Hopkins, E. Washburn. 1902. *India Old and New with a Memorial Address*. New York: Charles Scribner's Sons.

Jaffrelot, Christophe. 1996. *The Hindu Nationalist Movement in India*. New York: Columbia University Press.

Jagannāthdāsjī, Śrī Mahant Mahārāj. n.d. *Śekhāvāṭī ke Prasiddh Tīrth: Lohārgal Māhātmya*. Sīkar: Rādhikā Priṇṭing Press.

Jain, Kailash Chand. 1963. *Jainism in Rajasthan*. Sholapur: Jain Saṃskṛti Sanrakṣak Sangh.

———. 1972. *Ancient Cities and Towns of Rajasthan: A Study of Culture and Civilization*. Delhi: Motilal Banarsidass.

Jaini, Padmanabh S. 1979. *The Jaina Path of Purification*. Berkeley: University of California Press.

Jenkins, Rob. 1998. 'Rajput Hindutva, Caste Politics, Regional Identity and Hindu Nationalism in Contemporary Rajasthan', in T. B. Hansen and C. Jaffrelot (eds), *The BJP and the Compulsions of Politics in India*, pp. 101–20. New Delhi: Oxford University Press.

Jñānsudarjī Mahārāj, Muni. 1929 (V.S. 1986). *Śrī Jain Jātimahoday*. Śrī Ratnaprabhākar Jñān Puṣpmālā, Puṣp Nos. 103–108. Phalodi: Śrī Ratnaprabhākar Jñān Puṣpmālā.

———. 1940. *Osvāl Jāti kī Aitihāsiktā*. Phalodi: Śrī Ratnaprabhākar Jñān Puṣpmālā.

Jones, J. Howard M. 1991. 'Jain Shopkeepers and Moneylenders: Rural Informal Credit Networks in South Rajasthan', in M. Carrithers and C. Humphrey (eds), *The Assembly of Listeners: Jains in Society*, pp. 109–38. Cambridge: Cambridge University Press.

Kane, Pandurang Vaman. 1974. *History of Dharmaśāstra (Ancient and Mediaeval Religious and Civil Law)*. Vol. II, Part I, Second Edition. Pune: Bhandarkar Oriental Research Institute.

Kapur, Nandini Sinha. 2002. *State Formation in Rajasthan: Mewar during the Seventh-Fifteenth Centuries*. New Delhi: Manohar.

Kāslīvāl, Kastūrcand. 1989. *Khaṇḍelvāl Jain Samāj kā Vṛhad Itihās*. Jaipur: Jain Itihās Prakāśan Sansthān.

Khaṇḍelvāl, M. C. 1984. 'Khaṇḍelvālõ Kī Utpatti', *Khaṇḍelvāl Mahāsabhā Patrikā*, 23 (1–2): unnumbered pages.

Khaṇḍelvāl, Ramanand. 1984. 'Khaṇḍelvālõ Kī Utpatti Kā Itihaās', *Khaṇḍelvāl Mahāsabhā Patrikā*, 23 (1–2): unnumbered pages.

Kramrisch, Stella. 1981. *The Presence of Śiva*. Princeton: Princeton University Press.

Kyāl, Bholārām. 1995 (V.S. 2052). *Śrī Lohārgal Māhātmya evam Malkhet Parikrama Paricay*. Basāvā (Jodhpur Dist.): Śrī Śyām Satsang.

Laidlaw, James. 1995. *Riches and Renunciation: Religion, Economy, and Society among the Jains*. Oxford: Oxford University Press.

Lath, Mukund. 1981. *Half a Tale: A Study in the Interrelationship between Autobiography and History. (The Ardhakathanaka translated, introduced and annotated by Mukund Lath)*. Jaipur: Rajasthan Prakrit Bharati Sansthan.

Lévi-Strauss, Claude. 1963. *Totemism* (Trans. Rodney Needham). Boston: Beacon Press.

Little, Lester K. 1971. 'Pride Goes Before Avarice: Social Change and the Vices in Latin Christendom'. *The American Historical Review*, 76(1): 16–49.

Lodrick, Deryck O. 1994. 'Rajasthan As A Region: Myth or Reality?', in K. Schomer, J. L. Erdman, D. O. Lodrick and L. I. Rudolph (eds), *The Idea of Rajasthan: Explorations in Regional Identity*, pp. 1–44. Columbia (MO): South Asia Publications.

Madan, T. N. 1987. *Non-Renunciation: Themes and Interpretations of Hindu Culture*. New Delhi: Oxford University Press.

Maḍāḍh, Iśvar Siṃh. 1987. *Rājpūt Vaṃśāvalī*. New Delhi: Cetnā Prakāśan.

Mahilā Samiti. 1994. Sanskār: Jauhrī Bāzār Digambar Jain Mahilā Samiti, Jaipur (1994 Smārikā). Jaipur: Jaipur Digambar Mahilā Samiti.

Malinowski, Bronislaw. 1954. 'Myth in Primitive Psychology', in *Magic, Science and Religion and Other Essays by Bronislaw Malinowski*, pp. 93–148. Garden City (N.Y.): Doubleday Anchor Books.

Manusmṛti. 1989. *The Laws of Manu* (Trans. Wendy Doniger and Brian K. Smith). London: Penguin.

Marriott, McKim. 1976. 'Hindu Transactions: Diversity without Dualism', in B. Kapferer (ed.), *Transaction and Meaning: Directions in the Anthropology of Exchange and Symbolic Behavior*, pp. 109–42. Philadelphia: Institute for the Study of Human Issues.

———. 1990. 'Constructing an Indian Ethnosociology', in M. Marriott (ed.), *India through Hindu Categories*, pp. 1–39. New Delhi: Sage Publications.

Mayer, Adrian C. 1960. *Caste and Kinship in Central India: A Village and its Region*. Berkeley: University of California Press.

Mehta, Lalit. 1999. *Caste, Clan and Ethnicity: A Study of Mehtas in Rajasthan*. Jaipur and New Delhi: Rawat Publications.

Meister, Michael W. 1991. Articles on 'Osian, Saciyāmātā temple' (p. 128), 'Osian, Mahāvīra temple' (pp. 182–91) and 'Goth-Manglod, Dadhimatimātā temple' (pp. 252–54), in M. W. Meister and M. A. Dhaky (eds), *Encyclopaedia of Indian Temple Architecture, North India, Period of Early Maturity, c. A.D. 700–900*, New Delhi: American Institute of India Studies.

———. 1998. 'Sweetmeats or Corpses? Community, Conversion, and Sacred Places', in J. E. Cort (ed.), *Open Boundaries: Jain Communities and Cultures in Indian History*, pp. 111–38. Albany: SUNY Press.

———. 2000. 'Ethnography, Art History, and the Life of Temples', in M. Meister (ed.), *Ethnography and Personhood: Notes from the Field*, pp. 17–45. Jaipur and New Delhi: Rawat Publications.

———. 2002. 'Light on the Lotus: Temple Decoration or Essential Form', in L. A. Babb, V. Joshi and M. Meister (eds), *Multiple Histories: Culture and Society in the Study of Rajasthan*, pp. 232–53. Jaipur and New Delhi: Rawat Publications.

Mishra, R. L. 1991. *The Haldias and Their Role in States Politics*. Jaipur: Champa Lal Ranka and Co.

Mitchiner, John E. 1982. Traditions of the Seven Rsis. Delhi: Motilal Banarsidass.

Modī, Bālcand. n.d. *Śrī Mahārāj Agrasen: Sankṣipt Jīvan Caritra*. Kolkata: Akhil Bharatvarṣiya Agravāl Mahāsabhā. Date not given, but bound with other booklets dating from the 1930s.

Nāhṭā, Agarcand and Nāhṭā, Bhanvarlāl. 1978. *Jainācārya Pratibhodit Gotra evam Jātiyā̃*. Pālītāṇā: Śrī Jinharisāgarsūri Jñān Bhaṇḍār.

Obeyesekere, Gananath. 1981. *Medusa's Hair: An Essay on Personal Symbols and Religious Experience*. Chicago: University of Chicago Press.

———. 1992. *The Apotheosis of Captain Cook: European Mythmaking in the Pacific*. Princeton: Princeton University Press.

Pandey, Gyanendra. 1990. *The Construction of Communalism in Colonial North India*. New Delhi: Oxford University Press.

Parry, Jonathan. 1989. 'On the Moral Perils of Exchange', in J. Parry and M. Bloch (eds), *Money and the Morality of Exchange*, pp. 64–93. Cambridge: Cambridge University Press.

Pāṭodiyā, Rāmkiśor. 1986. 'Khaṇḍelvāl Vaiśya Jāti kī Utpatti', in *Sambhāv: A. Bh. Khaṇḍelvāl Vaiśya Mahāsabhā 27th Adhiveśan,* Alvar (Rajasthan). (26–28 December 1986). Unnumbered pages.

Pīpalvā, Ānand Śarmā. 1997. 'Khāṇḍal Vipra: Vartmān ke Kandhõ par Ṭhaharā Tejasvī Atīt', in *Khāṇḍal Vipra Samāj (Jaypur Mahānagar) Paricay, 1996*. Jaipur: Śrī Khāṇḍal Vipra Śakha Sabhā.

Qanungo, Kalika Ranjan. 1960. *Studies in Rajput History*. Delhi: S. Chand and Co.

Rāmlāljī, Yati. 1910. *Mahājanvaṃś Muktāvalī*. Mumbaī: Nirṇaysāgar Press.

Ramusack, Barbara N. 1995. 'The Indian Princes as Fantasy: Palace Hotels, Palace Museums, and Palace on Wheels', in C. A. Breckenridge (ed.), *Consuming Modernity: Public Culture in a South Asian World*, pp. 66–89. Minneapolis: University of Minnesota Press.

Ṛg Veda. 1981. *The Rig Veda: An Anthology* (Trans. Wendy Doniger O'Flaherty). New York: Penguin.

Roy, Ashim Kumar. 1978. *History of the Jaipur City*. New Delhi: Manohar.

Rudner, David West. 1994. *Caste and Capitalism in Colonial India: The Nattukottai Chettiars*. Berkeley: University of California Press.

Rudolph, Susan, H. and Lloyd I Rudolph. 1984. *Essays on Rajputana: Reflections on History, Culture and Administration*. New Delhi: Concept Publishing Company.

Śāh, Bakhatrām. 1964. *Buddhi-Vilās*, Padmadhar Pāṭhak (ed.), Jodhpur: Rajasthan Oriental Research Institute.

Sahai, Yaduendra. n.d. 'Silla Mataji of Amber' Unpublished Manuscript.

Śankar Pujārī. 1991. *Śrī Sālāsar Bālājī kā Itihās evam Mahimā*. Sālāsar: Śrī Bālājī Mandir Samiti.

Śarmā, Hemant (ed.). 1989. *Bhāratendu Samgra*. Vārāṇasī: Hindi Pracārak Sansthān.

Simmel, Georg. 1978. *The Philosophy of Money* (Trans. T. Bottomore and D. Frisby). London: Routledge and Kegan Paul.

Singh, Munśī Hardiyāl. 1986. *The Castes of Marwar*. Second Edition with Introduction by Komal Kothari (First Edition, 1894). Jodhpur: Books Treasure.

———. 1997. *Riport Mardumśumārī Rājmārvāṛ San 1891*. Reprint of 1894 edition. Jodhpur: Śrī Jagdiś Siṃh Śodh Sansthān.

Singhi, N. K. 1991. 'Jains in a Rajasthan Town', in M. Carrithers and C. Humphrey (eds), *The Assembly of Listeners: Jains in Society*, pp. 139–61. Cambridge: Cambridge University Press.

Singh, R. B. 1964. *History of the Chāhamānas*. Varanasi: Nand Kishor and Sons.

Smith, Brian K. 1994. *Classifying the Universe: The Ancient Indian Varṇa System and the Origins of Caste*. New York: Oxford University Press.

Smith, Fredrick M. 1987. The Vedic Sacrifice in Transition: A Translation and Study of the Trikāṇḍamaṇḍana of Bhāskara Mísra. Pune: Bhaṇḍārkar Oriental Research Institute.

Somānī, Rāmballabh. 1997. 'Khaṇḍelvāl Sarāvgiyō ke Prācīn Śilālekh', in *Mahāvīr Jayantī Smārikā, 1997*. Jaipur: Rājasthān Jain Sabhā, 3/3–5.

Spykman, Nicholas J. 1925. *The Social Theory of Georg Simmel*. Chicago: University of Chicago Press.

Śrī Dadhimathī-Purāṇam. 1981. Jaipur: Śrī Dadhimatī Sāhitya Śodh evam Prakāśan Samiti.

Śrīmāl, Mangal Siṃh Jain. n.d. *Śrīmālō kā Itihās*. Handwritten ms.

Śrīmāl, Rājendra Kumār. n.d. *Śrımāl Jāti (Ek Paricay)*. Jaipur: Śrī Lābhcand Pustakālaya.

Taft, Frances and G. S. L. Devra. 1999. 'The Thikanas of Rajputana: Some Insights from Ravatsar Thikana of Bikaner', in N. K. Singhi and R. Joshi (eds), *Religion, Ritual and Royalty*, pp. 276–83. Jaipur and New Delhi: Rawat Publications.

Ṭāṇṭiyā, Harpatrāy. 1996. *Agrohā Darśan*. Agrohā: Agrohā Vikās Ṭrasṭ.

Taussig, Michael T. 1980. *The Devil and Commodity Fetishism in South America*. Chapel Hill: The University of North Carolina Press.

Temple, Richard C. 1977. *The Legends of the Panjab*. Vol. 1. Reprint of 1884 edition. New York: Arno Press.

Thapar, Romila. 1984. *From Lineage to State: Social Formations in the Mid-First Millennium B.C. in the Ganga Valley*. New Delhi: Oxford University Press.

Timberg, Thomas A. 1978. *The Marwaris: From Traders to Industrialists*. New Delhi: Vikas Publishing House.

Tod, James. 1990. *Annals and Antiquities of Rajasthan*. 3 vols. Reprint of 1829 edition. Delhi: Low Price Publications.

van Buitenen, J. A. B. (translator and editor). 1975. *The Mahāhbārata: 2. The Book of the Assembly Hall; 3. The Book of the Forest*. Chicago: University of Chicago Press.

van der Veer, Peter. 1994. *Religious Nationalism: Hindus and Muslims in India*. Berkeley: University of California Press.

van Gennep, Arnold. 1960. *The Rites of Passage* (Trans. M. B. Vizedom and G. L. Caffee). Chicago: University of Chicago Press.

Vatuk, Sylvia. 1972. *Kinship and Urbanization: White-Collar Migrants in North India*. Berkeley: University of California Press.

Vidal, Denis. 1997a. 'Rural Credit and the Fabric of Society in Colonial India: Sirohi District, Rajasthan', in P. Cadène and D. Vidal (eds), *Webs of Trade: Dynamics of Business Communities in Western India*, pp. 85–107. New Delhi: Manohar.

———. 1997b. *Violence and Truth: A Rajasthani Kingdom Confronts Colonial Authority*. New Delhi: Oxford University Press.

Vidyālankār, Dharmcandra. 1992. Jātõ Kā Nayā Itihās. New Delhi: Akhil Bharatvarṣiya Jāi Mahāsabhā.

Vidyālankār, Satyaketu. 1976. *Agravāl Jāti kā Prācīn Itihās*. Masūrī: Śrī Sarasvati Sadan.

Vijayvargīya, Āśārām. 1993. 'Vijayvargīya Vaiśya Varṇ kā Itihās', in L. Vijayvargīya, (ed.), *Vaijayantī (Vijayvargīya Niredśukā)*, pp. 9–14. Jaipur: Akhil Bhāratiya Vijayvargīya Vaiśya Mahāsabhā.

Vijayvargīya, Rāmgopāl. 1969. 'Vijayvargīya Samāj—Udbhav aur Vikās', in Omśaraṇ "Vijay", (ed.), *Smārkiā, A. Bh. Vijayvargīya Mahāsabhā kī Kāryakāriṇī ke Jaypur Adhiveśan ke Uplakṣ mẽ, 13–14 Sitambar, 1969*, pp. 7–14. Jaypur: Śrī Vijayvargīya Vaiśya Sabhā.

Vinaysāgar, Mahopādhyāy (ed.). 1956. *Khartargacch kā Itihās*. Pratham Khaṇḍ. Ajmer: Dādā Jindattsūri Aṣṭam Śatābdī Mahotsav Svāgatkāriṇī Samiti.

Vyās, Kailāśnāth and Devendrasiṃh Gahalot. 1986. *Rājasthān kī Jātiyõ kā Sāmājik evam Ārthik Jīvan*. Jodhpur: Jagdīśsiṃh Gahalot Śodh Sansthān.

Weinberger-Thomas, Catherine. 1999. *Ashes of Immortality: Widow Burning in India* (Trans. J. Mehlman and D. G. White). Chicago: University of Chicago Press.

Wilson, H. H. (Trans.). 1868. *The Viṣṇu Purāṇa: A System of Hindu Mythology and Tradition*. Volume 4. London: Trübner and Co.

Winternitz, Maurice. 1972. *A History of Indian Literature*. Vol. 2. Reprint of 1933 edition. New Delhi: Oriental Reprint Corporation.

Zelizer, Viviana A. 1994. *The Social Meaning of Money*. New York: Basic Books.

Ziegler, Norman Paul. 1973. 'Action, Power and Service in Rajasthani Culture: A Social History of the Rajputs of Middle Period Rajasthan', Ph.D. Diss., University of Chicago.

Index

About the Author

Lawrence A. Babb is currently Professor of Anthropology and Asian Studies at Amherst College, Massachusetts, where he has spent most of his career. His previous books are—*The Divine Hierarchy: Popular Hinduism in Central India* (1975), *Redemptive Encounters: Three Modern Styles in the Hindu Tradition* (1986) and *Absent Lord: Ascetics and Kings in a Jain Ritual Culture* (1996). He has also co-edited *Media and The Transformation of Religion in South Asia* (1995) [with Susan S. Wadley] and *Multiple Histories: Culture and Society in the Study of Rajasthan* (2002) [with Michael Meister and Varsha Joshi].

About the Authors